Regional Development in Europe:
Recent Initiatives and Experiences

Regional Development in Europe: Recent Initiatives and Experiences

Proceedings of the Fourth International
Conference on Science Parks
and Innovation Centres
held in Berlin, November 12-13, 1987

Edited by
Jürgen Allesch

Walter de Gruyter · Berlin · New York 1989

Editor

Jürgen Allesch
Technologie-Vermittlungs-Agentur Berlin e.V.

Library of Congress Cataloging-in-Publication Data

International Conference on Science Parks and Innovation Centres (4th : 1987 :
   Berlin, Germany)
   Regional development in Europe.
   1. Research parks--Europe--Congresses. I. Allesch, Jürgen.   II. Title.
T175.7.I58   1987   607'.114   88-33480
ISBN 0-89925-515-9 (U.S.)

Deutsche Bibliothek Cataloging in Publication Data

Regional development in Europe : recent initiatives and experiences ; proceedings
of the fourth International Conference on Science Parks and Innovation Centres held
in Berlin November 12 - 13, 1987 / ed. by Jürgen Allesch. - Berlin ; New York :
de Gruyter, 1989
   ISBN 3-11-011815-7
NE: Allesch, Jürgen [Hrsg.]; International Conference on Science Parks and
Innovation Centres <04, 1987, Berlin, West>

Copyright © 1989 by Walter de Gruyter & Co., Berlin 30. All rights reserved, including those
of translation into foreign languages. No part of this book may be reproduced in any form —
by photoprint, microfilm or any other means nor transmitted nor translated into a maschine
language without written permission from the publisher. — Printed in Germany. —
Layout: B. Busch. — Druck: W. Hildebrand, Berlin. — Bindung: D. Mikolai, Berlin.

Foreword

Regional development policy has the declared objective of promoting economic growth in all regions of a country while reducing regional disparities with regard to employment opportunities and income.

Since the mid-1970s in Western industrialized countries a reorientation has been taking place in the implementation of this policy. Strategies of financial incentives to attract business to new locations, which previously stood in the forefront, are increasingly being replaced by new innovation-oriented measures aimed at developing a region's endogenous potential. Real transfers in the form of information, advice and know-how are replacing conventional instruments.

The reason for this trend is the impact for present-day economic change. The growth potential of microelectronics and other new technologies is leading to shorter innovation cycles, which in turn lead to more rapid applications of new scientific knowledge to business practice, i.e. product and process innovation.

Regional development policy must adapt to these new conditions and gear itself toward fostering the initiation and implementation of the necessary innovation processes. Central to such a policy are measures and instruments enabling a better utilization of the region's endogenous potential, its established manufacturing and service firms. New strategies need to take account of both the strengths and weaknesses of a region and treat existing industry as an essential element. In contrast to traditional concepts of regional policy making, a major focus of attention here is on small and medium-sized enterprises, which are encouraged to implement new technologies and engage in innovation processes. Policy instruments that are human-recources centered, like educational programmes for both staff and executives or personnel transfer schemes, promise to be successful in this field.

Foreword

Another aspect of current regional development policy is the direct promotion of new innovative enterprises. Science parks and innovation centres have a decisive role to play, and also technology and innovation consulting agencies which, as mediators between science and industry, provide advice and information and are capable of dealing with the particularities of both existing and newly founded enterprises.

Recent experiences in applying these concepts of regional development policy are documented in this book. The contributions, both analytical and practical, were presented at the Fourth International Conference on Science Parks and Inovation Centres held in Berlin in November 1987.

In addition to an introduction into regional development policy in Europe, the book contains practical reports on initiatives and activities in this field. Instruments fostering endogenous development in several countries are presented with attention given to the regional particularities. Various means of supporting newly founded enterprises are assessed and methods for the support of research and development activities and for the improvement of the transfer of knowledge to small and medium-sized enterprises are discussed. Also attention is given to programmes for the promotion of industrial innovation.

Thus, a wealth of practical experience in the promotion of innovation and technology transfer is being made available to the public, which hopefully will stimulate further discussion on regional development policy. Economic change will continue to demand flexible adaptation to an altered environment, and the key to future successful regional development lies in increased efforts to implement innovation-oriented measures.

Strong regional innovation networks are required which will support a holistic approach to the promotion of innovation, taking into account the infrastructural, spatial, socio-political, financial and manpower factors pertaining to the region. In addition, future regional development policy must give considerations to interregional networks supporting innovation and new technology. There is the danger that the impact of structural changes induced by advances in technology will give rise to new and more severe forms of competition between regions and countries. This danger should be confronted by strategies of co-operative relations conducive to a positive synergy effect on the international level.

I would like to take this opportunity to thank European Business and Innovation Centre Network (EBN), the European Association for the Transfer of Technology,

Foreword

Innovation and Industrial Information (TII), and the International Association of Science Parks (Club des Technopoles), who were co-organizers of the conference. I also want to thank the Commission of the European Community, Directorate-General XVI (Regional Policy) and the Senate of Berlin for their financial aid. Special thanks go to Wolfgang Gessner, who was responsible for the organization of the conference, and to David Weissert, who took charge of the tasks involved in bringing this book to publication.

Jürgen Allesch

Contents

Welcoming Address

Wolfgang Watter   1
Albert Strub   5

1 Introduction

1.1 Technical and Market Changes and Regional Development Potential
Hans-Jürgen Ewers   9

1.2 The Science Park Phenomenon and Regional Development
Pierre Laffitte   13

2 Regional Development Policies in the International Context

2.1 European Community Regional Policy Developments
T. Joseph Mulcahy   21

2.2 Science Parks in Europe
Pierre-Yves Tesse   25

2.3 Regional Development Policy in Europe
Dirk Jan Dekker   29

2.4 Strategies of Regional Development in Europe and TII Activity in the Context of an Innovation-Oriented Regional Policy
Antonio Pedinelli   33

2.5	Regional Development Policies in the OECD Countries: Trends and Coments on Recent Developments *Jean Paul de Gaudemar*	43
2.6	Strategic Management of Endogenous Regional Development Processes *Alexander Gerybadze*	55
3	**New Experiences in Applying Endogenous Strategies for Regional Development (Working Group 1)**	
3.1	Innovation and National-Level Regional Development and Planning Policies in France *Véronique Debisshop*	71
3.2	Recent Changes in the Policy Tools for the Development of Italy's Mezzogiorno *Nino Novacco*	85
3.3	Local Initiatives for the Promotion of Innovation in the Federal Republic of Germany *Hans Heuer*	93
3.4	The Development of Regional Technology Centres in Great Britain: An Overview and Progress Report in the Context of Technology Policy in the United Kingdom *David Croome and David Hardy*	103
3.5	Industrial Technological Complexes: A Case Study of Brazil *Marilia-Rosa Millan, Jacob Frenkel and J.G. Malcher*	107
3.6	Innovation-Oriented Policy on the Regional Level as Well as in Border Areas of Southern Germany *Holger Haldenwang*	127
3.7	Regional Development and Vocational Training *Maria Pierret*	153

4 Instruments of Regional Policy for the Furthering of New Business Ventures (Working Group 2)

4.1 Conceptualization of Technology Centres and
Regional Venture Capital Funds
in Conformity with the Market Conditions
Klaus-Dieter Otto — 163

4.2 Models for the Creation of New Business Ventures
in the Vicinity of Science Parks and Universities
Harry Nicholls — 175

4.3 Four Years of Innovation and Technology Centres in the
Federal Republic of Germany:
An Evaluation
Karl Heinz Wodtke — 179

4.4 Assisting Businesses in Problem Areas
Gerhard Burian — 183

4.5 Enterprise Creation in Italy: The Role of SPI
Giovanni de Felice and Claudio Fornari — 187

4.6 Results and Requirements for Promoting Technology-Oriented
Enterprises in Infrastructurally Weak Regions:
The Example of Eastern Bavaria
Eberhard Auchter — 191

4.7 Mobilizing Higher Educational Institutions as a Source
of New Technology Based Firms
Andrew J. Gould — 201

4.8 Dutch Spin-Off Companies as a Means for Successful
International Technology Transfer:
The Case of the University of Twente
Dick van Barnefeld — 205

4.9 The Twente Centre for Innovation and Entrepreneurship:
An Example of Public-Private Partnership
for the Development of Business Opportunities
Willem E. During — 215

Contents

5 Initiatives in the Context of Regional Policies in Order to Intensify R+D Activities and Technology Transfer as well as to Improve the Qualification Structures (Working Group 3)

5.1 Are Science Parks Effective ?
Proposal for Cross-National Research
Hans-Dieter Ganter 229

5.2 Tecnopolis: Between International Tendencies and Regional Development
Umberto Bozzo 235

5.3 Technology Transfer:
Enhancing Scotland's Competitiveness
David Lightbody 239

5.4 Pilot Projects as an Instrument for Technology Transfer
Hermann Kösters 241

5.5 Promoting Research Advancement in the Lagging Regions of Italy
Stefano Boffo and Francesco Gagliardi 247

5.6 Information Technology Centres:
Instruments of Regional Policy to Promote Information Technology in the Federal Republic of Germany
Norbert Tüschen 255

5.7 Contacts and Contracts Between Universities and Small and Medium-Sized Enterprises:
Possibilities and Limitations
Pim Berculo 265

5.8 Research and Development of Projects:
A New Service Offered by BIC
Claudine Guidat de Queiroz 279

5.9 Lifelong Education and Training as Decisive Factors of Regional "Training for Innovation"
- a Programme for Berlin's Industry
Dagmar Brodde 287

Contents

6 Programmes and Concepts in Promoting Industrial Innovations in Different European Regions (Working Group 4)

6.1 Piedmont and Aosta Valley, Italy:
Technology Transfer Services for Entrepreneurs
Renzo Mosagna 297

6.2 Structural Changes in the RuhrArea:
Development Strategies in Promoting Innovations and
Technology and Knowledge Transfer
Michael Morath 305

6.3 Wales, Great Britain:
Strategies of the Welsh Development Agency
Alun Daniel 313

6.4 Regionalization in Niederösterreich (Lower Austria):
Strategic Outlines and First Experiences with a
New Instrument of Regional Policy
Richard Plitzka and Theodor Krendelsberger 317

6.5 Technology Transfer Networks in Nord/Pas-de-Calais:
Accomplishments, Limits and Questions
Martine Delpierre and Christian Mahieu 327

6.6 The Leoben Technology Transfer Centre:
A Contribution to Structural Change in the Problem Region
of Upper Styria (Austria)
Peter Paschen 337

6.7 Technology Based Economic Development in Northern Ireland
Thomas B. Copestake 343

6.8 Research as an Economic Factor:
Initiatives in the Region of Aachen, F.R.G.
Wolfgang Heidrich 353

6.9 Selected Qualifications-Oriented Measures in the Saarland:
Initial and Continuing Training for
Small and Medium-Sized Enterprises
Bernd Bach 361

Contributors 365

Welcoming Address

Wolfgang Watter

Dear Mr. Strub,

dear Senator Laffitte,

dear ladies and gentlemen at home and abroad!

May I welcome you most heartily on behalf of the Senate of Berlin in the name of the Governing Mayor, Eberhard Diepgen, and the Senator of Economy and Labour, Elmar Pieroth.

We are glad that for the fourth time now this International Conference on Science Parks and Innovation Centres is taking place in Berlin. We feel it both stimulating and challenging that the theme "Strategies of Regional Development in Europe" was chosen and that this choice has met with such a lively response from representatives of science parks and innovation centres. This reflects the great commitment of those engaged with "entrepreneurial culture". But it also speaks well for the organizers, who managed once again to assemble a challenging, inspiring and progressive programme.

The Senate of Berlin views the fact that so many of you have come to Berlin as recognition of this city that has achieved so much along the rocky road of structural change. Marketdynamics and accelerated technological progress have set new tasks for all those involved: the enterprises, individuals and policymakers. For a long time Berlin's economic development policy was criticized for not having conducted a dialogue with industry and not having set up the neccessary framework to give the city the power to set standards for structural change. For many years Berlin was behind in what was going on. But a city that claims to be a metropolis must not lag behind. It is not even enough to be on a par. A metropolis is expected to take the lead in structural change and it is with such a perspective that we made a new start in the early 1980s.

I think all those who come to Berlin often will agree that something has changed here. In all political parties it is accepted that the former Governing Mayor of Berlin and present President of the Federal Republic of Germany, Richard von Weizsäcker, has given Berliners their ancestral identity back. Elmar Pieroth has "delivered" the economic philosophy, according to which the mentality of subsidization must be restrained for the benefit of innovation and entrepreneurial daring. In this connection the state plays a part, too. It must take action, but only to the extent of constructing a framework, which has to be filled in by the entrepreneur. It is the entrepreneur who forms the economy - or does not, something which we have found to be a shortcoming for many years.

It is well known that Berlin has certain disadvantages of location because of its delicate geopolitical situation. The starting point of our considerations was that in Berlin there must also be advantages of location, which could be taken into consideration when enterprises make decisions about choosing new locations or staying at old ones. Our advantage of location, which we regard as the key to renewing the economy of Berlin, is the immense technological and scientific potential of the city. It has been here all the time, but it was buried. The universities did not always have the openness they have nowadays. It has been a long process to initiate and make technological transfer work, a transfer from science into the economy, and - this must be acknowledged - from the economy back into science. There had been inhibitions on the part of the universities as well as on the part of industry. Economic policy in Berlin had to take that into consideration. The new conceptualization takes into account all these problems and tries to solve them by means of a market economic policy. I cannot here give you a lengthy presentation of the economic policy of Berlin, but three representative transfer measures from our technology policy should serve as an illustration.

First, the innovation assistants programme should be mentioned. It enables small firms to get the newest technical know-how of qualified university graduates whose recruitment is temporarily subsidized. Although there has traditionally been a great deal of difficulty involved in the acceptance by industry of academic knowledge, we have overcome this by means of appropriate incentives. More than 660 assistants have been engaged to date in about 280 firms and 75 % of them were subsequently taken over into permanent employment. I find this to be a remarkable result.

Another example is the consideration whether the state should give venture capital to regional enterprises. This seems audacious to those who know about the workings of the public sector. But we tried and we have realized that a lot has been initiated by public venture capital, which is more and more mixed with private venture capital. This development led to the foundation of venture capital companies here so that Berlin is now, to put it modestly, one of the two centres for venture capital companies in Germany. We now have 11 such companies in Berlin, and we hope that this number will increase. The foundation of a national association of venture capital companies has been announced for December 1987; it will have its head office here in Berlin.

The last example, which is certainly known to you, is the flagship of the Berlin technology and innovation policy: the Berliner Innovations- and Gründerzentrum (Berlin Innovation Centre). The effects of this institution emanate onto the whole city. It goes without saying that not all projects can establish themselves on the market and some have to give up. But in a free-market economy this has to be accepted.

To sum up: Innovation and technology policy have been the starting point, from which we are now enlarging by means of a qualification policy, i.e. our policy of revitalizing and modernizing the economy of Berlin follows a double strategy of technological innovation and personnel qualification.

When I read the programme for this conference, I was gratified to see that these aspects of Berlin's economic policy are reflected therein. The broad range of topics to be discussed makes a comprehensive overview possible, from rather general considerations with regard to the aims and feasibility of regional economic policy, to specific regional programmes and initiatives of individual public and private institutions. This is the basis for new considerations on innovation-oriented economic policies. I noticed, too, - or perhaps I read it between the lines - that the programme is designed to be discussed frankly, to tackle sometimes controversial issues and to approach questions and problems in a new way.

I would like to mention one last thing. The problems of regional economic development can nowadays be solved less and less in regional isolation. In many cases we need interregional and international co-operation, and the first step towards this is always the international exchange of ideas. In the name of the Senate of Berlin I therefore want to emphasize our particular appreciation of your coming to Berlin from so many countries to exchange experiences, concerns, and future prospects, to comment on and to work out new proposals.

The presence of such an outstanding audience urges me again - and I do it with pleasure - to express my thanks to the organizers: the European Business and Innovation Centre Network, the European Association for the Transfer of Technologies, Innovation and Industrial Information, the Club des Technopoles - International Association of Science Parks, and our Technologie-Vermittlungs-Agentur Berlin. I also thank the Commission of European Communities, General Direction XVI, which has supported this conference and contributed substantially to its taking place here in this form.

I wish all of us here inspiring reports and, above all, discussions, for discussions nowadays are very important. Doing without discussions means doing without co-operation, too. And doing without co-operation - as can be observed often - always means doing without some good ideas. Everyone who wants to be or who must be innovative, and politicians want that too, can afford that least of all. You who are involved in tackling the problems of the new entrepreneurial culture, of innovation centres and science parks, are in any case innovative.

I thank you and look forward to today's programme.

Welcoming Address

Albert Strub

It is with pleasure that I come to Berlin to convey to all participants at this meeting best wishes and greetings on behalf of the Commission of the European Communities, since technology transfer and the stimulation of innovation within the EC are part of my tasks and responsibilities within the Community's programmes SPRINT (Strategic Programme for Innovation and Technology Transfer) and SPUR (Strategic Programme for the Utilisation of Research Results). Berlin is certainly an excellent choice for a conference dealing with strategies for regional development and with the role which innovation-stimulating measures can play in that context. Berlin is known for its innovative climate and for hosting, especially during this year, a great number of events related to this vital subject.

Though this is only a welcoming address, I should like to make a few remarks which might be debated during this conference.

Europe, depending as strongly as it does on its industrial base, must catch up and keep pace with its competitors from both the East and West. This requires changes in its industrial structures, in its working methods and in the general environment on which our innovative behaviour depends.

It is my conviction that this requires not only support for basic research and for the development of leading-edge technologies, but also corresponding efforts to facilitate the transfer of new technologies towards those who apply and transform them into modern products and services. And I am afraid that in Europe we tend to perform very well at the research level, but very often fail to transfer to our traditional industries proven technologies which are already known, but in other branches of industry.

In my second remark I should like to encourage us all to give more thought to how to maintain Europe's relatively high level of product and service quality. Our competitors are catching up, and in the future quality will no longer depend just on good work at the production stage and on systematic quality control. It will require the introduction of comprehensive quality concepts, addressing the production stage, but also the phases of design, marketing, after sales services, etc.

Thirdly and finally, we should not forget that the most efficient and reliable way of stimulation and transferring innovation still passes via human beings. Data bases, networks, and printed matter are all useful tools, but they can not replace human carriers of information. Communication between individuals, experts, planners, and advisers is the purpose of this conference. I therefore congratulate its organizers for their initiative and wish you all a fruitful meeting.

1 Introduction

1.1 Technical and Market Changes and Regional Development Potential

Hans-Jürgen Ewers

The traditional concept of regional policy has been a strategy involving direct and indirect financial investment incentives. Such a strategy requires a pool of investment projects with spatial mobility which can be made more profitable through financial aids. Setting aside the well-known critique of being biased towards standardized mass production and large firms as well as of causing "picking-up" effects, the main argument against the strategy of financial investment incentives is that, as opposed to what was the case in the 1960s, its basic requirements can no longer be taken for granted. There has been a loss of overall economic pressure for growth and, therefore, of flexible investments, too. The pool of spatially mobile investment is close to empty.

Since the beginning of the 1970s the basic conditions of industrial growth have changed considerably in Western European industrialized countries. New shortages of resources in the fields of energy, raw materials and the environment have forced an adaptation of the production structure towards manufacturing processes and products which conserve energy, raw materials and the environment. The new international division of labour between industrialized and developing countries requires a production structure characterized by few standardized, technologically complex, human-capital intensive, manufacturing processes and products.

Waves of basic innovations in the fields of microprocessors and optoelectronics (information and communication technologies), biotechnology, new materials and laser technology have brought about new possibilities of production and revolutionized the technological basis of existing industries. A fundamental consequence of this new industrial revolution is the tendency towards services in industrial production (changing the activity structure in producing industrial products). The big cities of Western Europe and North America are trend-setters in this development. They have undergone a transformation from centres of physical production and real capital to centres of technological-organizational knowledge, production of information and communication in a broad sense.

In such a situation traditional promotion strategy keyed to the mobility of investments is doomed to failure. A lack of pressure for growth leads to too little flexibility of investments. The problem is not to direct existing growth potential to suffering regions, but to create *new* growth potential in the declining or less developed areas. New ways of regional economic promotion therefore go on from the existing stock of enterprises ("endogenous potential") and try to promote the flexibility and the growth potential of this stock. They do not support old industries but favour selectively the creation of new jobs in prospective growth branches, which are adapted to the changed basic conditions, namely

1. In the field of industrial production: goods which can only be produced in face-to-face contact with the customers or with specialized research and development (R&D), because of their variety or technical complexity (luxury goods, complex capital goods)

2. In the field of services: on the one hand, all kinds of production-oriented services, especially those activities which are concerned with new technologies (development of software, plant leasing, market research, advertising, management consulting), and on the other hand, household-oriented services in the field of more sophisticated and more expensive recreational activities and social and health services

Human capital is the strategic starting point of the new regional policy. New founders as well as small and medium-sized firms are the most important addressees of the regional strategy of revitalization. The main instruments are not financial incentives for capital investment, but real transfers, especially the improvement of consulting and training services, the disposal of R & D institutions, as well as the transfer of R & D results and R & D staff.

An innovation-oriented strategy of regional development includes the following four aims:

1. Creation of an "innovation infrastructure": compensatory disposing of supply in deficient fields of small and medium-sized firms (R&D

management and organization as well as gathering and evaluation of information). To find the optimal mix of activities offered by the state for an improvement of the regional infrastructure three criteria have to be fulfilled at the same time. There must be:

- A promising field with respect to technology and/or with respect to the market prospects
- An already existing R & D local infrastructure
- Some private production activities within the regional economy, which can serve as a nucleus

2. Creation of an efficient consulting and transfer infrastructure: regional economic promotion, in the sense of a comprehensive concept, should take over the function of a moderator for technical and market changes. It should:

   - Motivate the firms of a locality to check the positioning of their products and manufacturing processes within the technical and market surroundings and analyse development bottlenecks
   - Help to articulate development problems and mediate contacts with appropriate research and consulting institutions and suppliers of innovation-relevant resources
   - Advise these contacts early with regard to prevention of difficulties
   - Assist in the application of financial aid and in getting information

3. Creation of targeted supply of qualification possibilities at all levels
4. Creation of an internal and external reputation of the region such that it is conducive to innovation

The task is to create intermediate networks which facilitate and promote innovation and structural change in the regional economy. These networks seem to be an essential precondition for a modern local economy whose products represent more creativity and less hardware.

1.2 The Science Park Phenomenon and Regional Development

Pierre Laffitte

The science park phenomenon is linked to two major factors, namely

1. A concentration of brain power, teachers, researchers, engineers, industrialists, financial experts and consultants of all kinds. In terms of institutions this means universities, "grandes écoles", research centres and innovative companies.
2. A strong interaction tying together competence and action, knowledge and know-how, research and industry. As we know, this necessary interaction does not happen spontaneously in Europe. It requires therefore, institutions and structures to provide opportunities for interaction: hotels, restaurants, cafés, conference and exhibition centres, and the organization of cultural, social and sports events.

Most of those involved in setting up science parks usually only think of providing the infrastructure and to attracting companies. In my opinion organizing contacts and interaction is even more important than the real-estate aspect. The software is more important than the hardware. Without opportunities for easy contact there would be little creativity, little innovation, no transfer of innovation and few induced economic developments.

Science parks have varied characteristics; there is no one single model. They can be the product of initiatives of educational establishments, universities and grandes écoles. In these cases technology transfer and the establishment's image are priority aims. Stanford Park, forebearer of the science parks, is of this type. The Compiègne project is similar, and Berlin's BIG is a third such example.

Other parks owe their existence to the concerns of private industrialists or real-estate agents. Their aim is to make money by creating wealth and jobs. Most of them, however, are due largely to the initiatives of local authorities, even if, as in the case of Japan, the state intervenes.

A complex typology could be drawn up: in terms of their closest linkages (parks set up by a university, parks developed as the result of a local authority's initiative) or in terms of their stage of development (early, developing, established).

Finally, a distinction can also be drawn between parks set up from scratch and those where the existing industry and skills are concentrated.

With regard to the influence of a science park on the region's economy, the stages of development are an important consideration.

New or Young Science Parks

In a first phase, the basic problems of a park are linked to creating an infrastructure (roads, water, gas and electricity networks and other equipment). At the same time, local socio-political interests have to be mobilized to help define and implement the concept: the companies and research centres have to be sought out and allured.

Most of the regional impact is connected to the physical infrastructure and involves first and foremost the construction and public works sector. It may happen that the project interests certain professions or services which then become involved; however, this involvement is often marginal, with the exception of the hotel and restaurant sectors. This can lead developers to involve hotel and restaurant chains, together with building and public works contractors in the design of the project, and even perhaps to share the financial risks in the initial development stage.

Developing Science Parks

The second phase of development makes way for interaction between the park's residents and the regional economy. Apart from an increase in interaction with the construction and public works sector and the hotel and restaurant industry, this second phase gives rise to a growth in subcontracting. It is appropriate to mention here that this subcontracting is not restricted to the immediate area. Very often incoming organizations stick to previous habits and keep up strong links with their headquarters or organizations which may be located in distant administrative-decision centres, sometimes even abroad.

The role of a management unit responsible for the science park community and interaction among tenants - which, as we have said, is vital as it promotes creativity - can and must be extended to a wider regional development promoted by the presence of a concentration of buyers of goods and services.

There are many kinds of mechanisms: symposia, conferences, visits to potential subcontractors, newspapers and other publications, etc. Just let us here point out their necessity and decisive influence on development.

Established Science Parks

It is in this phase that the economic spin-offs can be the most important. In addition to the implications for the construction and public works sector, the hotel and restaurant industry and subcontractors, there are the phenomena linked to entrepreneurial dynamism.

The major factor in the success of a science park is cultural in nature: a new optimistic and entrepreneurial state of mind has to take root. There is no sense of depression and disaster in an established science park, only one of creative dynamism; there is a sense of enterprise, "going for it" and success. The motto is "fortuna audaces juvat". I will not talk here of the complementary measures required for promoting this entrepreneurial dynamism inside the science park, as this subject deserves in-depth elaboration on "incubators", the search for entrepreneurs, support for spin-offs including specialized training courses, clubs, etc.

At the same time as firms are set up, we see the flourishing already of a wide range of service companies highly specialized in consulting and finance: management, marketing and industrial property consultants, international legal consultants, auditors, "head-hunters", public relations and advertising companies, banks and insurance companies, financial institutions, venture capitalists, etc. This range of services found in the most developed regions is generally only available in the large urban centres. It enables young firms to access the network of skills and international relations which are indispensable for the take off of innovative companies with a strong growth potential.

At this stage of the development process the park's management has the responsibility of identifying the ways and means in which all the firms in the area and all the neighbouring local authorities can take advantage of the powerful network of relations which this multitude of specialized companies represents.

many and their implementation depends largely on the interest shown by regional socio-political groupings. The more the government services, the local authorities, regions, "départements", communes or cameral organizations (chamber of commerce, chamber of handicrafts, chamber of agriculture), development agencies, employer and trade union organizations, government bodies, etc. are more or less dynamic, motivated, open and co-operative - subject to the differences between them in people, interests and policies - the more the structures to be set up and their effectiveness vary.

Can general rules or a prototype be implemented anywhere without being adapted? I would suggest just these rules:

1. A continuous effort is required, backed up by information and training.

2. A strong public relations effort is required which implies the use of the media. Public opinion must be involved, kept informed and in agreement with the project.

3. Everyone must understand and support the wish to implement the modernity and quality of life which characterize the science park.

4. It is the virtue of democracy to rely on the involvement of everyone.

The outline which I have traced here is based mostly on the efforts undertaken at Sophia Antipolis, where we may flatter ourselves as having succeeded in involving to a great extent all the socio-political interests in the Alpes Maritimes "département": higher education bodies, the university, the Mining School, the College of Commerce in particular, research units, the chamber of commerce, and local authorities with the "département" at the top of the list, and the press, with *Nice Matin* strongly supporting the project from the very beginning when it was only a vague idea and continuing untiringly to provide information and understanding.

We are now in a fully developed phase, willing also to aid regional development by adopting an active role in implementing an international network which will help create links with all science parks throughout the world. The International Association of Science Parks (IASP) acts in this way. The worldwide network which IASP offers is already very useful specially for the tenants of the parks, and we are developing the use of video-conferencing in order to help the small and medium-sized high-tech companies find international joint ventures.

But this brings us to a new exciting development scheme, in connection with the answer to the following question: How could we use the brain-power concentration of "technopoles" to promote local development in rural cities and villages? The technopole core could act like a node of a local network linking any small and medium-sized enterprise (SME) to an international network. The first steps of this local network have already been successful in the vicinity of mature science parks like Sophia Antipolis, using the brain-power concentration as a new tool of development linked with the power of modern telecommunications. To develop this idea further would, however, involve us in another subject, i.e. the link between the science park phenomenon and the revolution in intelligence, a subject which we will leave for another symposium.

2 Regional Development Policies in the International Context

2.1 European Community Regional Policy Developments

T. Joseph Mulcahy

I should like to outline briefly the background or perhaps more correctly framework within which European Community regional policy action is likely to be taken within the next five or six years.

The Single European Act recently ratified by the twelve member states of the Community and now part of the EEC Treaty, marked a further fundamental step in the evolution of the European Community and its regional development objectives.

The new Treaty recognizes past inadequacies and reemphasises the ongoing need for action to strengthen economic and social cohesion and for renewed efforts to rectify the continuing imbalances between regions. In this context the importance of research and technological development is fully endorsed.

Article 130 of the Treaty singles out the reform of the Structural Funds and concentration of their resources as important steps in the achievement of the foregoing aims, namely the reduction of disparities between regions. The Commission is required to draw up and submit a comprehensive proposal to the Council of Ministers in this respect and the Council is obliged to act on it within one year. The Commission has submitted its proposal, sometimes called the Framework Regulation, at the end of July 1987 and intensive negotiations have ensued. It is hoped that an outline agreement could emerge at the Copenhagen Summit in December 1987.

Within this framework specific regulations will be proposed by the Commission in respect of each of the Structural Funds, i.e., the European Regional Development Fund (ERDF), the European Social Fund (ESF) and the European Agricultural Guidance and Guarantee Fund, Guidance Section (EAGGF). The facilities available under the European Coal and Steel Community Treaty (ECSC), New Community Instrument (NCI) and European Investment Bank will contribute to action being taken under the Structural Fund headings.

Essential to the expeditious achievement of the aims already mentioned are adequate financial resources. A doubling of the Structural Fund budgets from 7 billion ECU in 1987 to 14 billion ECU in 1992 is envisaged which, of course, accentuates the need for approaches which use the Funds effectively and in turn will provide a basis for influencing the stronger member states to make the additional monies available.

Of the five objectives spelled out in the Commission's framework proposal, a clean priority is allocated to helping the structurally backward regions attain a status somewhere near that of their more prosperous partners, and to this end the greater part of the resources will be devoted. Linked to this objective is that of assisting the conversion of declining industrial areas.

The other three objectives which are not regionally determined and will apply throughout the Community, are

- Help for the long-term unemployed
- Placement of young people in jobs
- Assistance in the adjustment of agricultural structures and promotion of the development of rural areas

Given the foregoing factors, the strategic importance of the Regional Fund is evident, as is the incorporation of new techniques in its operations.

These techniques will involve three basic concepts: (a) complementarity, (b) partnership, and (c) programming. Complementarity means responding to member states needs supported by analyses and evidence, and focusing the resources of the Funds on responding to them. Partnership means consultations with and involvement of national, regional, local and other authorities including the business sector, to ensure simplification and openness together with a readiness to provide technical assistance where required. Programming means taking a coherent overall medium-term view of the measures to be undertaken in relation to the objectives and establishing a co-ordination system.

One of the four main tasks set out for the Regional Fund in the Framework Regulation is the exploitation of the potential within regions for internally generated development. The others involve support for productive investment, infrastructures, and physical planning.

Experience to date with Regional Fund operations clearly indicates that regions must rely to a far greater extent on indigenous resources, both human and physical, and that wider and more dynamic approaches must be introduced, particularly in relation to the small and medium-sized business sector, involving public/private partnerships or indeed wholly private initiatives. Measures envisaged in this respect include a more comprehensive and systematized stimulation of entrepreneurship and innovative business projects, European Community participation in venture and seed capital funds, and in loan-guarantee and interest-subsidy schemes. While technological development is undoubtedly necessary and will be supported, the complementary business planning and management effort required to ensure that technical ideas and development are carried through and translated into growth businesses is equally essential.

Hence the Commission's promotion of and support for its business and innovation centre model as well as the European Business and Innovation Centre Network (EBNs about which you find more in Mr. Dekker's contribution.)

The foregoing is a broad outline of the European Community's proposed Framework for regional strategies for the next five or six years in line with the theme of this conference. The Commission welcomes and supports the initiative taken by the organizers of the Conference and greatly appreciates the hard work undertaken by the organizing team.

2.2 Science Parks in Europe

Pierre Yves Tesse

Introduction: Description of the Association

The Technopole Association was formed in 1984 at the instigation of Pierre Lafitte. Today it comprises in Europe 64 science parks and "technopoles", in 11 countries. These 64 parks involve more than 2000 enterprises.

The objectives of the Association are:

1. To assist its membership in the development of science parks, including links with associated universities or other centres of higher education and research, as an aid to the transfer of technology and business skills and to encourage the formation and growth of business enterprises

2. To promote an awareness and understanding of science parks and provide information on their objectives and achievement

3. To facilitate the interchange of concepts, ideas and operational experience between those most directly involved in the management of science parks, and to act as a forum for the development of collaborative initiatives between managers of science parks

4. To exchange information relating to the planning, development and management of science parks

5. To promote additional initiatives of value to the tenants of science parks

The European division is presently working on:

1. The creation of a European Directory of science parks

2. The realization of an information system which allows interchange between the enterprises of the parks

3. The organization of the network of common projects (e.g. COMETT)

Four Remarks Regarding the Science Parks Phenomenon

Science parks are generating local dynamism. While taking the same objective as a starting point they show the wide range of approaches and the differing methods to be applied to associate them. Science parks are concerned with their local environment. They can properly operate only in the form of networks.

Generating Local Dynamism

In Europe, science parks do not result from a national policy, but often arise from a local will. This implies the participation of multiple actors, i.e. a real public/private partnership for their implementation. Moreover, it is very interesting to notice a great variety of driving forces, including universities, (Herriott Watt, Bari Technopole); researchers with local responsibilities, (ZIRST of Grenoble); individuals conveying a conviction (Sophia Antipolis); local authorities; and Chambers of Commerce and Industry (Lyons technopolys).

As a first tool it is necessary that the partners meet each other, to mobilize all the actors, for animation and cross-fertilization - so that there will be a relationship.

Diversified Approaches

Diversification to the approaches occurs according to type (incubator, science park or technopole) according to stage of development, and according to functions and objectives.

From this point of view and within this context, the Association can offer a wealth of experience and current experimentations concerning all stages and types of operations. These range from the incubator (such as in Trondheim (Norway) or Heidelberg), to the science park which is clearly identified as such (Aston Science Park in Birmingham, Herriott Watt Research Park in Edinburgh, or Plassey Technological Park in Limerick); to "technological areas" or technopoles (such as the Sophia Antipolis) involving rebuilding the city in all its functions from the science park phenomenon; to Lyons, where it is necessary to reinforce the links between the pre-existing poles.

Concern with Local and Regional Roots

We cannot and we should not set up "high-tech ghettoes". I will not embark on a definition of high technology, but as for the function of technopoles in regional development, everybody apparently agrees that they play three major roles:

1. They encourage the creation of companies in technological fields, notably by ensuring a proper transfer of skills and know-how as well as of research results. It is important to underline that since ours is a worldwide association the data network function is of utmost importance.

2. They attract companies looking for a new location close to a "tech pole", or a research pole.

3. They have the role of communicating technologically traditional activities within their own local economic environment. (As an example of the effect of the technopole on the mutation of traditional activities, consider the meeting of the French Section of the association in Lyons).

It is not a matter only of supporting, but also of inducing processes or technological products in activities regarded as traditional (e.g. from textiles to materials).

Networks on a European Scale

Finally we are convinced that such development inevitably occurs through the implementation of networks on a European scale. Hence, the majority of parks participate in operations such as COMETT with regard to technological training. Also important is the development of networks between firms, for in numerous technological fields the market is at least European.

Conclusion

The network is first of all the exchange of experiences, methods and implementation of tools analysing both successes and failures. It is important to take time into consideration. We all started from the same analyses of the success of large development poles which managed to combine training, research, entrepreneurs and financiers - but we sometimes forget how many years have been necessary to succeed. We are all impatient: Give time time.

Development is located in poles. As it is their networks are hard to be implemented on the local level. That is why the policies which will have the best chances to succeed are those where development takes place in cities dispersing information via the communications media, which are essential to an urban scientific network.

2.3 Regional Development Policy in Europe

Dirk Jan Dekker

Regional development policy has been directed historically at those geographical areas which were not following the general movement towards industrialization, accumulation of wealth and growth of employment. They have generally been called peripheral areas, regions removed from the engines of economic growth in a geographical or functional sense. Some examples of such regions are the Mezzogiorno in Italy, the Islands and Scottish Highlands in the U.K., and Bretagne in France. These were development areas 40 years ago or even longer and they still are.

Traditional regional policy has mainly been geared to such backward areas. It has concentrated on three things: building in-infrastructure, attracting foreign investment and developing growth poles. In a market economy these are instruments which public authorities can use since they may influence but should not directly control private industry. They are, however, expensive instruments which, except for infrastructure, run the risk of deflecting trade. Building infrastructure, too, can easily lead to "building cathedrals in the desert" and we all know of some such cathedrals.

Investment grants to multinationals bear a very high cost and nobody can guarantee they will stay where they were promoted. In fact they generally leave after some time when corporate policy imposes a change in production facilities. The paradox is, if the policy succeeds, no government can afford it; if it can afford it, the policy is not successful. It is a Catch-22 situation.

The intellectually most interesting instrument has been the growth pole concept. It was a whole school of regional development economics that under the leadership of Rodan Rosenstein and Francois Perroux promoted the concept. The theory held that one very large industrial impulse in an area relatively devoid of industry would lead to indirect effects that would multiply the original input. The three such examples of international repute were the automobile industry in Scotland (disappeared), the steel industry in Mezzogiorno (no multiplyer), and petrochemicals in Puerto Rico (Walter Isard, no multiplyer). None of the three reached their objectives. Today we can say with full confidence that the growth pole concept has proved to be a failure.

More recently, the decline of activities dating from the industrial revolution and most recently the decline of all activities which are easily transferable to low labour cost or low tax or otherwise attractive areas, have led the scope of regional development to be concentrated more firmly on declining areas than previously. The same instruments do not apply in these old industrial areas to the extent they do in backward areas.

Adaptation and improvement of infrastructure will be necessary but less through new construction than in the creation and improvement of services. Investment subsidies will continue to be granted but there are few large investment projects that create many jobs in one stroke and small firms are hardly stimulated by investment grants. The growth pole concept continues to survive in the form of industrial parks located close to a university in order to attract subsidiaries from multinationals.

It is clear that with the current and third industrial revolution, the emphasis for regional policy has shifted to endogenous development and the general concept of technology transfer, by which is basically meant the application of scientific knowledge in the market, both need software and not hardware.

The present emphasis on endogenous development is based on three facts:

1. In practically all metropolitan areas in Europe there now exists an infrastructure of capabilities (universities, technical schools, large firms, business services) which can be mobilized for development without spending huge amounts for investment grants or for growth poles.

2. We have rediscovered the virtues of small businesses in manufacturing, services to manufacturing, innovation and job creation and we see that contrary to the U.S.A., Europe lacks the environment of many small innovative firms that feed the large corporations, not only for subcontracting but also as windows on technology; both are necessary.

3. We are witnessing a revival of the market or entrepreneurial economy.

The question now arises of what the function of central government should be in this new economic environment. If traditional regional policy was the domain of national government, the new economic situation we are facing has considerably changed the function and possibilities of central government to promote the economic development of backward areas and the restructuring of old industrial areas. What we are facing is a shift in two directions.

Endogenous development is by definition a local affair. Central governments may wish to promote homegrown industry, but they cannot control it as they could the three instruments of traditional regional policy. They cannot provide and control software. Endogenous development is about the establishment of local entrepreneurial networks.

On the other hand, the new situation we are finding ourselves in imposes an international approach both in the field of technologies and of markets because of the globalization of economic development.

New companies have to exploit their growth potential by exporting immediately and technology is a worldwide phenomenon. Compared with the Americans, we Europeans have a big handicap. In the U.S.A. a new company which is an average success is an average success in a very large market and will be a large company by European standards. In Germany, to take our host country and which has Europe's strongest economy, an average success will go unnoticed on the world stage. Local development efforts have therefore to be linked from the very beginning into international networks in order to be successful. Such networks are in the process of being evolved and one of them is the European Business and Innovation Centre (BIC) Network of which I have the honour of being the Secretary General.

The word network is easily used by everybody but I think we should make a serious effort to understand more clearly what we mean by it in relation to BICs and knowledge based new companies. For our purposes and for the subjects we are interested in the noun means, according to the *Oxford Dictionary*, "a chain of interconnected persons or operations". It is often associated with the mysterious word "synergy", which appears to mean that when one adds up a number of things or operations the resulting total is more than the sum of its parts. This concept, which is a logical impossibility, exposes one to the dangerous attitude of grouping a number of operations together, sitting back, and expecting the mysterious synergy to appear. It is therefore to be recommended to use the word as a verb. "Networking" means, according to Roget's *Thesaurus*, nothing more mysterious than cooperation.

There are, of course, very many networks in the sense of chains of interconnected persons or operations which cooperate with each other. It is also clear that if one wants to speak about a network, the interconnecting between its members should have a purpose. Depending on the purpose, many networks are possible between European Business Network (EBN) BICs and its associated members and between the client firms of BICs.

One subset of all possible networks is the one between BICs alone in order to learn from each other and thereby avoiding each of them having to reinvent the wheel. Unless they are located very close to one another, the interesting fact is that they do not compete with each other. Cooperation for this purpose is therefore possible. Another network is the one necessary for the purpose of establishing public/private partnership at the local level for the creation of BICs and their operation but also at the European level. EBN is supported now by a great many large corporations that look beyond the national territories they originated from. This state of affairs has also been recognised by the European Commission which promotes EBN, TII, the SPRINT Programme, COMETT, BC-NET etc. - all of which are in the same family.

Among these initiatives, EBN specifically aims at the endogenous development of home-grown innovative industry and is structured accordingly by promoting public/private partnership at a European level. We believe that if we wish to be ready in 1992, when the One European Market will hopefully be a reality, we must prepare ourselves urgently. Otherwise only the large firms will reap the benefits of it; the small firms will miss a great opportunity and many regions in Europe will be left behind.

2.4 Strategies of Regional Development in Europe and TII Activity in the Context of an Innovation-Oriented Regional Policy

Antonio Pedinelli

We know that regional policies are not static but subject to continuous revision and adjustment in the light of changing circumstances and work experience. I could also add that today the state of the regions is influenced ultimately by national and international factors, rather than the impact of regional policy.

The regional "adjustment" approach has been in operation for many years and is motivated by the authorities' concern with how regional economies adapt and respond to changing circumstances: the "positive adjustment" is a strategy which aims to promote technological development.

"Adjustment" theory with its dynamic and history being based on the passage of time and events, is fundamentally concerned with disequilibrium rather than equilibrium. While economic events may be anticipated or unanticipated, from an "adjustment" viewpoint what matters are the spatial patterns of response and the process of restructuring. In a constantly and rapidly changing world, all countries face recurring and new problems of adjustment. The necessary concern of governments with economic and social conditions has always dictated the need to consider what policies for industry and employment are best suited to the circumstances of the time. On the other hand, the impact of regional policy measures, or their effectiveness in improving the position of the peripheral or disadvantaged regions, depends not only on the absolute level of benefits offered but on the relative impact on the conditions in which they operate. We can foresee that in the near future regional policy will be based on a mix of macroeconomic and microeconomic measures, which differ from those applied today. Global growth objectives and redistribution will probably be the target of regional development, taking into account two fundamental variables:

1. The endogenous or exogenous control of economic activities
2. The technological level and the ability to innovate in the respective regions

A sustained flow of technological innovations is in fact a necessary constituent factor for a more balanced development of the regions, but to be efficient it has to be integrated into a whole series of measures.

In such a context, industrial policy and technological policy, at the national level, together with regional policies, should interact in order to produce a "locomotive", or stimulatory effect on technological development.

The aim of these policies is to promote:

1. A better interface between public and private research
2. Horizontal measures in support of R&D
3. Incentives for the dissemination of certain particularly promising technologies
4. Aid of a more or less sector nature to develop new products and processes
5. Development of management skills among entrepreneurs
6. An adequate financial backing for these developments

There is, by definition, a strong element of the "picking up the winners" approach inherent in the selective incentive system of regional policy. Nonselective incentives might tend instead to attract the wrong kind of industries, which are not viable in the longer run without assistance.

A region can be characterized by a high or low grade of technological development. Technologies can be endogenous or exogenous (induced technologies). Enterprises can place their efforts on exports or on the internal market. The interaction of these parameters has a strong influence on employment which represents a basic factor of regional policy.

High technologies, generally related to new products, are sometimes given as typical examples of an innovation-oriented regional policy, because new products are easily identifiable and are likely to increase competitiveness and employment, while less-developed technologies (frequently associated with mass production) may consist of process innovations which could reduce employment. In my opinion, the high-tech flag can crown a national technological policy, but it would be risky to consider high-tech as a determining factor of an innovation-oriented regional policy. Regional policies should give preference to endogenous development, although such an approach will impose certain constraints and require a lot of imagination. Regional policy-makers should never forget that overall productivity growth is the result of a sequence of innovation improvements, which become important on account of their cumulative effect.

A large part of the technological change in an advanced industrial economy is not even apparent. Often it does not require a sophisticated scientific knowledge, but a thorough knowledge of production techniques. Technological innovation is a continuous, never-ending process and sometimes subsequent improvements are more important than the original innovation. I will give you four examples: the steam locomotive in 1830, the automobile in 1905, the airplane during the First World War, and the computer in 1950.

The economic impact of a technology is closely related to its diffusion and the mechanisms through which new technologies are integrated into the economic system can be analysed in terms of dissemination, selection and induced innovation. Empirical research has confirmed that the innovation process is geographically concentrated and that the diffusion of new technologies requires a considerable time lapse.

This reminds me of Kaldor's theory of the self-perpetuating growth of core regions in the developed countries and the persistent depression of peripheral regions in the same countries. However, the assumption upon which Kaldor's model was based now appears to be somewhat out-of-date in light of recent trends in the spatial organization of production and consumption.

Strong local external economies continue to play an important role where they involve a large supply of highly skilled workers and an environment in which innovations diffuse rapidly, as well as the availability of specialized services and other inputs, close to the location of brain-trust establishments and venture capital institutions. On the other hand, peripheral and depressed regions suffer from "functional deficits", which penalize SMEs (small and medium-sized enterprises). Highly skilled labour is scarce, the flow of technical, economic and market information inadequate, and local consultants are hard to find. A "functional deficit" constitutes a bottleneck factor for less-developed and peripheral EC regions, which, therefore, have little chance of competing in the innovation race against the dynamism of highly industrialized regions where the growth rate of activity has a positive feedback.

These considerations remind me also of what Myrdal called "cumulative and circular causation". A similar remark can be made with respect to the quantitative/qualitative supply of specialized services, which could compensate to a certain extent for the "functional deficit" and the lag in innovation and adaptive capacity prevailing in depressed areas.

A large number of studies have examined the role of the diffusion and availability of technological information in explaining the lag between invention and its regional application. Among the factors which influence the speed of the flow of information are: the proportion of nonproduction workers to total employment, the type of sectoral specialization, access to transportation and communication networks, population potential, the size of urban centres and the levels of education. A variable which is closely connected to all these factors is the availability of service activities. In fact, these activities deal explicitly with the collection and elaboration of information and may be defined not only as factors in the diffusion of information but also as indicators of the level of the available information.

An insight into the problem of the diffusion of innovation may be gleaned from studies which deal with the problems of the location of service activities. In particular, many studies stress the roles of the market potential in various areas, of the high and ever-increasing economies of scale in the production of services, of the agglomeration of economies among the various service activities, both private and public, of transportation and communication networks, of the availability of qualified labour and also of the residential quality of the urban areas.

Functional deficiencies at the enterprise / regional level, however, could be compensated for by establishing a system of services specialized in the supply of the required functions. We can only hope that the situation will change gradually in this direction as a consequence of structural evolution and of the implementation of prospective rather than corrective regional policies. Should such strategies prevail, the technological policy of a country could become a determining factor of regional development, but a precondition is that governments become aware of the importance of technological and innovation policies, and of the correlation with regional innovation-oriented policies.

We know that a technological policy aims more at the creation of new technology-based industrial activities than at structural changes. Such a policy should ensure that all technological options are taken into consideration and that scientific research results are translated into industrial innovation, mainly through an interaction between industrial and public scientific research institutions. This is an area still characterized by bottlenecks and gaps which efficient methodologies and adequate instruments could at least reduce, if not overcome.

Finally, a technological policy should ensure that the technological trajectories followed by competing manufacturers correspond to the "best practice" trajectories in the international context.

The present economic and technological scenarios and the spatial characteristics of the innovation process make it imperative for regional policies to aim at:

1. Facilitating structural changes, which are more intrasectoral and innovationoriented

2. Creating an environmental, cultural and psychological climate favourable to innovation and suitable to better preparing at least some of the assisted areas for the new qualitative competition by developing their endogenous potential

This is a strategy appropriate to an innovation-oriented regional policy, for which it is important that newcomers, generally SMEs, are helped to take advantage of a new technology, by obtaining the necessary information and having access to qualified technological and management services.

We can assume that the innovative potential and the "adjustment" capacity of a region are larger than the aggregate innovative potential and the adjustment capacity of the global production system. This "added value" is represented by particular forms of interaction between research activities and the elaboration of information and communication systems, which characterize the economic development of a region.

We could envisage a "binary" system of economic policy that would build a bridge between demand and supply-oriented interventions. Regional authorities should be mainly engaged in supply-oriented policies, while central authorities would be primarily responsible for a demand-oriented strategy. A demand-oriented policy is by its very nature aggregate and therefore comes under central government. A supply-oriented policy is not aggregate, on the other hand, and can therefore be best out by local authorities.

Supply-oriented policies are, e.g. those related to the use of land, the environment, professional training, the services sector, etc. They combine horizontally and are interfaced with the policy which we may call "functional", because it relates to manifold functions: management, R&D, engineering, financial and marketing assistance, technical and organizational counselling, etc. The aim of such policies is to develop the endogenous potential and transform local resources into strategic factors of competitiveness and productivity.

An innovation-oriented regional policy should above all aim to promote the innovative and adaptive capability and the market potential, while national technological and innovation policies should take on a spatial dimension.

In a regional system where SMEs represent the prevailing endogenous potential for innovation, public intervention should be focused on the establishment, particularly in peripheral and non-urban areas, of a network of services for industry formed preferably by private or semipublic consulting firms, specialized in technology transfer and innovation, patents, management, engineering, etc.

A necessary support to SMEs is also represented in the form of the availability of scientific, technical and economic information (ISTE) brokers. A strategy based on the supply of appropriate ISTE information, however, will not prove effective if SMEs are not able to acquire, select and elaborate on the information offered and to introduce innovative technological inputs in their production processes and in their marketing policies. This is why an innovation-oriented regional policy should:

1. Devise methodologies and actions appropriate to persuade SMEs that information inputs are necessary, if they want to remain competitive

2. Promote the adoption of incentives, not necessarily of a financial nature, which will facilitate access to the market for consulting services, for which SMEs represent their potential market

My opinion is that incentives of this kind will prove more beneficial to the development of endogenous potential than the traditional nonselective financial incentives. The goal of an innovation-oriented regional policy is the global improvement of the "quality" of local enterprises as regards their behaviour, management style, innovative capacity and adaptability, etc.

I would now like to tell you something about TII, the European Association for the Transfer of Technology, Innovation and Industrial Information, and the role that TII can play in the context of innovation-oriented regional policies. In this connection I would like to make four preliminary remarks:

1. The activity of the majority of TII members has a regional dimension.
2. TII can contribute to creating access to one country's regions from other European regions, through cooperation between regional development bodies and specialized agencies, which are members of TII possessing a thorough knowledge of local problems and of SMEs and which can therefore play a strategic role locally and at the regional transnational level.
3. TII members have access to the "knowledge stock" in Europe and internationally and can therefore serve as catalyzers in the exchange of ISTE information.
4. TII can contribute its innovation-oriented regional policies through a network, which is currently being established, of national relational focal points and regional talent pools.

TII's aim is to contribute to the technological development of SMEs by helping them to gain access to the European market and improve their potential (and thus helping them to enter the international market) and take advantage of all the most up-to-date technological developments at the Community level.

TII's activities can be summarized by combining, at the European level, three key words: technology, innovation and information.

As for the Association, our target is to galvanize, if you permit me to use the expression, our members - who are professional innovation advisers, whether working in public, semipublic or private organizations, or for that matter independently "to meet and work together" which is basically the way innovation comes about and to provide them with the facilities they need, especially in terms of access to information.

When our European network of consultants and experts in innovation, technology transfer and scientific, technical and economic information (ISTE) is in full operation, we will also enhance our role vis-à-vis SMEs by helping them to establish their own international networks, to explore opportunities for joint ventures and to develop competitive products and services.

TII exists because on 23 November 1983 the EC Council of Ministers approved a three-year plan, the Plan for the Transnational Development of the Supporting a three-year plan, the Plan for the Transnational Development of the Supporting Infrastructure for Innovation and Technology Transfer. This plan with its rather awkward name has been replaced by a two-year interim plan called SPRING (Strategic Programme for Innovation and Technology Transfer). The plan's basic aim was "to promote rapid penetration of the Community's economies by new technologies as they become available, having regard especially to small and medium-sized undertakings". The Association's strategic aims are:

1. Develop a TII culture and diffuse it to SMEs

2. Develop products / services of real interest for our members

3. Develop the market for TII members

4. Create the above-mentioned supporting transnational infrastructure or network in order to increase TII potential, facilitate members' access to TII projects/services and improve their added value

This strategy has been consolidated in our 1987/89 business plan which is now being updated. TII's three-year programme is based on a package of co-ordinated, realistic actions, of high-quality information products, studies and services for which there is a demand and therefore a market. Our wealth is the know-how of our members; our basic aim is to contribute to its development and promotion.

In order to make things happen, we have focused our attention on the human and financial resources needed, on the methodological aspects and the necessary operational instruments, primarily in the following fields:

1. The marking of industrial information with added value and the management of ISTE services

2. The analysis of SMEs information sources and inhouse information management

3. The marketing of university / industry transfer points and of links with science parks

4. Professional up-grading by organizing seminars, principally on the following topics: technology auditing; marketing of "added value" industrial information; marketing of technologies developed by universities and research institutions; and patents

These seminars are organized under the COMETT programme of the EC.

TII's wealth lies also in the variety of its 245 members. Our computerized data bank offers the opportunity of selecting members according to various criteria, such as available services and fields of specialization, geographic area and so on. At the same time we have to expand what I call "TII's pool of expertise" (or if you prefer, its talent pool). Indeed, an information transfer service (ISTE) is nothing other than an SME which markets multidisciplinary, scientific, economic and technical information.

Remember there is a tremendous stock of knowledge within the Community. Our members have handled a lot of technological "dossiers", which could be made available under different degrees of confidentiality. Of course, the exchange of specialized information is a "must" for TII. What is needed is well-prepared, and above all, useful information. I need hardly emphasize to this audience that quality comes first.

TII is also concerned with the definition of joint university/SME research projects; financial, technical and management assistance to new enterprises, and the establishment of a network of university transfer points. Moreover, part of TII's strategy should be to encourage academics to undertake transnational consultant work for SMEs. TII is certainly in a privileged position to fill this role, in as much as many universities and university transfer points are already members. According to an estimate carried out by TII, there are at present in Europe 5000 consultants specialised in technological development, mainly of SMEs, where more than 30000 would be required to provide the necessary support to SMEs and improve their innovation and adaptive capacity.

Allow me to close by saying that the expertise of the Association's members and TII's strategy, which aims to promote and up-grade this new profession, so essential for the long-term development of industrial competitiveness in Europe, can play a prominent role in the context of innovation-oriented regional policies. There are other important components of regional development innovative strategies which could have been dealt with, e.g. the role of the EC Commission, but they will have to wait for another occasion.

2.5 Regional Development Policies in the OECD Countries: Trends and Comments on Recent Developments

Jean-Paul de Gaudemar

The aim of this paper is to lay out certain findings and make a number of statements with respect to the major trends which are to be seen in the current developments in regional policy in the OECD countries. It consists in particular of presenting:

1. The work produced by the ad hoc OECD working party, chaired by the author, in particular the report entitled "Recent Developments in Regional Policy in the Countries of the OECD" released for publication in April 1987
2. The conclusions of the meeting of ministers responsible for regional policy in the countries of the OECD, held at Nice- Sophia-Antipolis on 25 September 1987, and prepared by the same working party

Development of the Concerns and Aims of Regional Policies

The early 1980s represented a turning point: few of the traditional principles of regional development and planning policies were actually abandoned, but new objectives were developed. In most countries, one can speak of a new ranking of regional policy objectives, rather than of a conflict over priorities.

Reducing Troubled Employment Areas

The sharp increase in unemployment linked to the economic recession hit first and sometimes hardest in the most-developed regions. The less-developed regions were also affected by high levels of unemployment, due to their weak industrial fabric and also to existing structural unemployment. In the mid-1980s the highest unemployment levels are to be found in the areas with a concentration of traditional industries undergoing diversification, and in the poorest regions. In addition to structural unemployment, which has been the target of regional policies in the past, we now encounter unemployment caused by structural adjustment in the most-developed regions.

The fight against unemployment, which remains an integral aim of regional policy, coincides only in part with its original aims. The measures adopted, such as job creation and training programmes and tax concessions to encourage economic activity, have more general implications than strictly regional. The fight against extreme situations of underemployment is enshrined in most countries in general national policies with occasional regional sections. The latter are targeted basically at pockets of unemployment of particular concern. Many countries have adopted specific action measures in these areas, which are mostly urban, by designating them as diversification areas or free enterprise zones.

Reducing Economic Disparity Between Regions

The aim of reducing economic disparity between regions has traditionally been the preoccupation of regional policies in developed countries. This concern is still a central element of regional policy, but it has tended to be relegated to second position, particularly in industrialized countries. Three reasons can be given, which seem to have played a vital role over the past few years:

1. Regional gaps in income, of which we were aware in past decades, have been considerably narrowed, due to the combined effects of implicit and explicit transfers linked to national budgets, the voluntary or natural process of decentralization of industrial activity and, more recently, a slowing down of the increase in income of the most-developed regions. The debate as to whether voluntary regional policy measures contribute to narrowing these disparities has not really been decisive, particularly in those countries where the regions were fairly equal in terms of infrastructure. Some countries, like the United States, where explicit policies have seldom been carried out, have experienced long-term results which are comparable to those of countries which have implemented these policies.

2. The huge strains on nation budgets encourage, as far as is politically possible, policies which aim to reduce the load of direct intervention and

the expenditure on infrastructure which is in direct competition with public spending on social measures or aid for industrial diversification.

3. Regulation of development in the most advanced regions is used less and less. The growing restrictions of supply-side economics and the need to consolidate national growth make it difficult, particularly at a time of decentralization and the regionalisation of government, to apply measures aimed at helping the less-developed areas by obstructing the development of the most dynamic regions. Most countries which had legislation to approve or forbid the introduction of new activities in the most prosperous areas either abandoned it or let it fall into disuse.

If the problems of the underprivileged areas are no longer given the same priority today as during the growth years, they nonetheless still exist. Many of the OECD countries are still faced with large areas which are relatively underdeveloped. The meeting of ministers responsible for regional policy in the countries of the OECD, which was held in September 1987, in Nice, marked nevertheless a change of direction.

While emphasizing the importance of decentralization, several ministers expressed their concern about the risks implied by the latter of increasing inequalities between regions, as well as the dangers which fierce competition might involve for the weaker regions. The concern to prevent these inequalities from possibly getting worse, which would hardly be tolerable politically, is linked to that of long-term economic development. The "desertification" of rural areas and the congestion of some urban areas, for example, have an economic price for society as a whole. Preventing or reducing these phenomena, i.e. utilizing the whole of the country, requires a strengthening of the overall efficiency of economies.

These considerations lead quite naturally to the conviction of the need for a national policy in regional matters. The need to continue or strengthen these policies (strengthening by Japan, Canada and Sweden) was raised by several ministers or high-ranking civil servants (but not by all). The political objective to reduce disparities still exists therefore, but formulated in a new way, whereby today it aims to create, at a reasonable price, lasting conditions for economic development based on available resources and factors of production.

Developing the Regions' Attractiveness for Firms

The political objectives of reducing regional disparities aim nowadays at creating the conditions for economic development which is both exogenous and endogenous, i.e. which is able to attract and create economic activity. On the one hand, it is a question of promoting the creation of conditions for development in keeping with the interregional and international division of production. The growing segmentation of production processes, the change in restrictions on location, the emergence of a new type of "foot-loose" firm and the recent tendency for design activities to move out of built-up urban areas into those with a better environment, all offer certain lesser developed regions new development opportunities based on the attractiveness of their natural "endowment" and not, as in the past, on their status as a poor region. These conditions for development imply in particular a transformation in the locational environment for companies, both the physical and human environment.

On the other hand, the aim of endogenous development, as formulated by most member countries, seeks to give peripheral regions the means to exploit their own "endowment". This development model is based directly on the observation that some regions have developed spontaneously thanks to the diversified nature of their economies, the cohesion of their cultural and social fabric and as a result have been better able to adapt to recent economic trends. The aim of regional policy in many countries is to encourage the creation of an economic, social and cultural fabric in the peripheral regions. Policies undertaken in these regions are based on the creation of a differentiated structure of small and medium-sized enterprises, based on the existing urban structure and utilizing local physical and human resources. This endogenous regional development strategy is indeed founded on the observation of a real type of development in certain regions of member countries. However, this approach may rather have been imposed during a period of recession due to an insufficient contribution of exogenous factors to regional development. Most members states are aware of the inadequacies of depending on endogenous factors only in solving regional problems.

Development Fostered by Technological Innovation

Nowadays it appears that technology is the decisive factor for growth and prosperity in the industrialized countries. The new wave of interest in technological innovation is related to a number of observations. The high technology industries have played an important role in the upsurge of growth in the most-developed countries. Production in the high technology industries is increasing much more quickly than production in the manufacturing sector as a whole, with higher gains in productivity. Whereas the active industrial population in most countries has decreased, employment in the high technology industries has expanded rapidly in the United States and even more so in Japan.

The development of these new technologies has also had an effect on "normal" industry with the introduction of more productive manufacturing processes. It also has an influence on the service sector. The latter has tended to expand in all countries at the expense of the industrial sector. In some households and firms high technology industrial goods can substitute for certain tertiary sector jobs. The brake which we can currently observe on growth in the service sector is related to this mechanism and may suggest a new allocation of value added with renewed emphasis on industrial production.

The priority of promoting high technology activities is supported in all countries of the OECD in their regional policy aims. A clear distinction can be made between two approaches in the relationship between technology and regional development.

1. The first tends to regard the spatial dimension as an important factor in the innovative process. The region is therefore considered as a factor of national growth. This approach is reflected in the promotion of technology complexes, "high-tech" zones and science parks on the model of those which have grown up spontaneously in the most-developed countries and have contributed substantially to their prosperity. The main aim in this case is not so much to reduce disparities between the regions as to contribute to economic growth in general. In fact, the areas which are rich in technological innovation are the most densely populated, the best equipped and most favoured regions. Certain countries, such as the United States for reasons of scale or Japan due to its particular economic and social situation, have opted to spread technology complexes throughout the regions. In most other countries the major concentrations of technology have been developed in the richest areas. The few restrictions attached to locating some high-tech firms offer development opportunities to certain more disadvantaged regions which possess a natural, cultural or climatic heritage which is particularly attractive. However, such regions are an exception among the less-developed areas of member countries.

2. The second approach aims to help develop the disadvantaged regions through innovation. Introducing new technologies into traditional manufacturing processes of goods and services, transport and communication helps utilize better and open up the economic, social and cultural fabric of these regions. This objective which will be found in future in most regional policies of member countries, is linked to that of endogenous regional development.

Development Fostered by Cooperation Concertation Between National and Local Governments

It is generally agreed that local potential is better utilized by a systematic working in concert of the central government and local authorities. The more the various regional and local levels play an active role in regional development, the more central government has to intervene. It has to prevent *competition* and one-upmanship, to which the lower levels of government might be inclined and which could change the balance between private and public sector as preferred by national government and which could even create distortions in international trade and aggravate interregional disparities. Central government must therefore make the effort to give at worst an equal chance to all the regions and at best preference to the less-developed areas in order to let them catch up.

To this end, national government makes an effort to harmonize policies. It also makes use of special instruments to which some ministers referred at the Nice meeting and which are becoming increasingly commonplace, even though remaining unfamiliar - namely block grants. In all countries, central government is increasingly transferring considerable resources to local government. The criteria for granting these transfers are often complex and not always obvious. However, one can detect a trend to take account of regional policy criteria, i.e. to give (all other things being equal) to the poorer regions.

Development of Regional Policy Instruments

Regional policy instruments in the OECD countries can be regarded as having developed from four different points of view:

1. A change in emphasis of public aid - away from direct aid to more general aid

2. A policy deliberately oriented towards transforming the environment of firms, particularly in the field of technological development

3. Increased cooperation between the public and private sectors

4. Increased cooperation between the central government and local authorities

Change in Emphasis of Public Aid

Over the past years we have been witness to the development of an apparently contradictory mechanism: at the same time as regional policy aims have widened, the means at their disposal have been cut. In most member countries the funds allocated to incentives and direct regional aid tended to be reduced. This observation nevertheless needs qualification:

1. It is becoming increasingly difficult to distinguish and therefore account for amounts which are strictly allotted to regional economic development as opposed to amounts allocated to general economic development.

2. A simple assessment of funds allocated as regional aid is less and less reliable for the purpose of evaluating the real financial input allocated to these incentives. In fact, there is a development in the form of this kind of aid: it is therefore necessary to take into account the new types of aid, such as taking a public share in firms' capital, the use of venture capital, and especially fiscal expenditure, which is becoming more and more widespread and which is generally seldom assessed.

3. It must be noted that the decrease in public funds allotted by central government to regional aid has in many countries been in part taken over by local government.

4. Finally, regional policy is not only a financial policy, but it also involves politico-administrative organization, regulations, industrial services and management. A decrease in funds allocated to direct measures does not necessarily correspond to a reduction in the intensity of regional policies.

Nevertheless, one can observe in many countries a drop in spending on regional aid since the beginning of the 1980s, following an upward trend at the end of the 1970s. This observation is particularly relevant in Denmark and the United Kingdom, where budgetary cuts have been highest. It should, however, be said in the case of the United Kingdom that while spending on regional aid was cut back at the beginning of the 1980s, urban policy spending increased over the same period at such a rate that overall spending on regional and urban policy increased during these years. This change in budgetary emphasis is also true of countries such as France, Germany, Ireland and Belgium. Few member countries have maintained or increased spending levels on regional aid, with the exception of Italy, which has preserved the broad lines of its traditional regional policy in the face of a recent deterioration in the economic situation of the southern regions.

Policy Deliberately Oriented Towards Transforming the Environment of Firms, Particularly the Technological Environment

The purpose of aid policy is in each case to promote economic activity. The member countries, especially the most advanced, agree on the premise of economic development based on restructuring the industrial fabric, improving productivity (which sees investment as a priority) and reducing the burdens on companies. In parallel to this aim to develop economic activity, most member countries have to introduce measures to solve their acute problems of unemployment. These aims are covered by national regulations and social policies. They also appear in regional policies in the form of incentives, over limited periods of time, in the worst-hit areas and by a more qualitative targeting in terms of firm size and economic sectors.

A new approach to extending aid involves making it available to sectors, other than the industrial sector. The services sector, and more particularly those private services to firms, and the commercial sector are now assisted in the same way as industrial activity. These are developments which have been recently observed in countries such as France, Norway, Sweden, Great Britain and Austria.

Still more striking in recent years is the targeting of aid towards technological innovation. Denmark, which has made substantial cuts in budgets for regional aid, has explicitly transferred savings thus made to general measures to promote technological innovation. This approach takes three main forms in OECD countries: it is noticeable (a) in the redeployment of existing instruments, (b) in the introduction of new tools to disseminate new technologies, and (c) in aid towards the establishment of technology development "poles".

In most countries, existing instruments for assisting actively are now modulated according to the type of product and production process introduced. This approach often involves extra incentives (such as in Belgium in assisted zones) granted to innovating sectors as against more conventional sectors.

New aids have been introduced with a view to promoting high-technology activity. Such aids are direct, as in Germany, where the recruitment of highly qualified employees and the acquisition of patents or the launching of investments may be assisted, or in Austria and Italy, where high-technology activities qualify for major aids for location in conversion zones. Promotional measures are implemented in countries like Ireland, Sweden and Norway to disseminate information and knowledge of new technologies. The dissemination and training role of universities, which in most countries are spread evenly throughout the regions, is also stimulated. Telecommunications networks, as in the United States, France and Germany, are developed in order to open up peripheral regions. Japan has developed a major database which may be consulted by firms (Technomart). In France it has been noted that the use of these new networks has developed considerably in the less-developed regions, unlike the case of the telephone in the past. These new services to firms are often offered to all the enterprises in the country, wherever they are located. However, they have a special role in the development of the least-advanced regions, as unlike much of the infrastructure and many of the services in the past, they do not have spatially segregative effects.

Most countries have recently begun to promote science parks. Such projects are aimed at generating new innovations, the regional fabric being considered a decisive factor in national growth. The innovative aspect of such projects does not stem so much from their originality as their multiplication in most countries (cf. in particular the April 1987 OECD report on science parks and high technology complexes in relation to regional development).

The geographical or regional orientation of this high-tech zone development policy varies substantially from country to country. Japan seems to have made it the main vehicle of its policy to reduce regional disparities with the substantially state-aided institution of 19 science parks. The science parks are spread throughout the territory, including outlying areas. The incentives involve a continuing package of direct aid covering infrastructure and investments, services to firms as well as attention involving the environment, quality of life and accommodation. The government provides an impetus for this policy, but the definitive aid planning of such zones is largely the task of regional institutions. Other countries, be they small and highly urbanized like Belgium or vast and sparsely populated like Australia, have opted for the most highly urbanized areas. The Belgian "T" zones are depressed urban areas equipped by the government with a view to getting economic activity started up again. For ten years high-technology enterprises setting up in these areas benefit from major tax incentives. Similarly, free enterprise zones set up in the United States to combat underdevelopment in the poorest urban areas have switched to economic activities using or developing advanced technologies. Australia is pursuing a policy to concentrate such activities around its main cities.

In most countries two trends are apparent: first, major technological innovation "poles" are encouraged in the most-developed areas, those with the best urban, scientific and cultural infrastructures; second, hundreds of technological complexes are distributed in regions throughout the OECD countries. The great dispersion of these high-tech zones, in particular in the least-favoured areas, is aimed less at earth-shaking innovations than at disseminating innovation and adapting sectors of economic activity in those regions. Some of them, which have special advantages, in particular in terms of the quality of their environment or their climate, are assisted in strategies to attract research and development activities.

Greater Cooperation Between the Public and Private Sectors

This subject was the centre of discussions at the Nice meeting. It allowed the ministers to give numerous examples of the involvement of the private and / or quasiprivate sector in the design, the formulation and the implementation of regional policies. In particular, science parks in Japan, vocational training in the Federal Republic of Germany, flexible centres of services to industry in the United States, "conversion" companies in France, development in Finland, venture capital companies in Belgium and innovation centres in the Netherlands were quoted as examples of projects involving the private and public sectors closely.

The close involvement of private or semiprivate agents in the activity of public agents seems in this area to be a condition or guarantee of effectiveness. This may be explained partly by the fact that, in the last analysis, what is involved is changing the behaviour of the private agents, who are the real factors in local and regional development.

This distinction between public sector and private sector is, moreover, often slight. Some of the institutions most active in regional development, like the Chambers of Commerce or mixed economy companies, seem both public and private. Other institutions, like many associations, have private law status and are geared to public utility. Very large companies sometimes act (e.g. as regards vocational training or technology transfer) like public bodies because they are or feel themselves responsible for the future of their region, or because they are concerned about their public image. At the same time, a growing number of public bodies behave towards management and efficiency in a way similar to that of the private sector.

Greater Cooperation Between Central Governments and Regional and Local Authorities

Another development which is very clear in most countries, relates to the political decentralization or deconcentration measures adopted. This development aims to bring decision-makers and aid recipients closer together so as to improve efficiency. The regions thus have the means of expressing their choices and their specific guidelines. In the OECD countries much aid is now allocated by regional bodies. In countries like France, Finland and Sweden, most decisions relating to regional development projects were entrusted in recent years to regional bodies. In Greece, 35% of decisions on infrastructures were transferred from the central government to the regional prefectures.

In Nice all the ministers also stressed the need for central or federal governments to cooperate closely with the other levels of government in the field of regional policy. This is obvious in federal countries, since responsibility for regional policy falls on the federal states. But this need is also felt keenly in unitary states. Decentralization is seen as the response to a political request for participation, and as the condition for effective intervention in the field.

Regional policy must, therefore, be the result of the combined action of two, three or four levels of government, plus, in the EC, the Community level. The problem is to harmonize, coordinate and organise the action of these various levels of government. There is no simple, easy solution.

Three approaches were mentioned by the ministers, namely concerted, effort, cooperation and contractualization. Concerted, effort consists in the various agents concerned informing each other of their analyses and intentions. To this end many countries set up committees and commissions and organize discussion and coordination meetings. Cooperation entails two or more levels of government jointly financing certain projects or actions; this induces or compels them to agree on common objectives and procedures. Contractualization is a wider, formalized version of cooperation; two or more levels of government sign a contract under which each undertakes to carry out or finance, generally over a period of several years, specified projects. The contractual procedure is still not very widespread explicitly, but is tending to develop in the OECD countries. It takes the form of planning contracts between central government and the regions in countries like France, the Netherlands and Canada. The EC develops integrated programmes coordinating and concentrating local, regional, national and Community resources for regional development programmes in Ireland and in the Mediterranean regions. In reality, even if such programmes are not called integrated programmes, they are nevertheless developing in most countries: the major decentralized and deconcentrated movement clearly indicates that development strategies are the subject of overall negotiations between the various levels of government and are aimed at improving the consistency of intervention in a homogeneous structural programme on a national and regional scale.

As a general conclusion, one may state that there is thus a *dual* shift in regional policies:

- On the one hand, towards policies of structural adjustment to technological change
- On the other hand, towards policies in which central governments see themselves less and less as the sole agents and are increasingly keen to involve the other regional development agents, subnational governments and the private sector

Reference

OECD, Recent Developments in Regional Policy in the Countries of the OECD, 1987

2.6 Strategic Management of Endogenous Regional Development

Alexander Gerybadze

Introduction

As regional development tends to emphasize more and more endogenous change by mobilizing existing strengths within a region, two principal questions arise:

1. How can we find out in an unambiguous way, what our real strengths and weaknesses are compared to other regions?
2. How can we jointly agree on the direction and the targets of future development within a multi-constituency regional context?

The problem to be solved is not much different from strategic management within large private companies. We shall thus outline below, how strategic management concepts and tools, originally developed for business firms, were adapted and applied to solve regional development problems. Then a case study of strategic management of a major municipal development project is described. Finally, an outline is presented of key criteria that should be fulfilled for the successful implementation of the strategic management of endogenous regional development.

New Concepts for the Strategic Management of Regional Development

Strategic management of regional development emerged as an interdisciplinary concept and was based on consulting experience gained from numerous cases involving private companies, public institutions, and regional development agencies. It required communication, interaction, and cross-fertilization of researchers and consultants, who originally had to work separately either on regional development projects or for private company strategies. New concepts were developed by bridging "business people" and the "regional planners". (1)

Previous work for strategic management projects completed successfully for many large companies in Western Europe, in the U.S.A. and Japan, led to the consideration of applying similar tools to regional development problems. Some of these cases for private firms were at least as complicated and difficult as many economic development projects; in some situations, strategies had to be developed for several hundred business units within one company, each pursuing its own objectives, and all of them involved in a politically complex atmosphere. Similarities between private company development and regional development abound, although many people remained doubtful whether strategic management tools developed for business firms could ever be successfully applied for economic development purposes.

Criticism was expressed by people who pointed out that regional development is an "organic", historical process, very difficult to anticipate or even to plan. Any attempt to design strategies and to apply strategic management tools, according to their view, would be a hopeless exercise. In spite of this criticism, a number of cases in which strategic management tools were successfully applied showed the feasibility of these new concepts and resulted in a gradual improvement of appropriate methods.

Effective management and implementation of regional development strategies requires an integrated approach, for which four different levels of expertise have to be pursued (as depicted in Fig. 1):

1. Strategic management has to be applied and adapted to the specific requirements of regional development strategies. This means that strategies of separate independent groups, problems of multi-constituency as well as the pursuit of "hidden agendas" have to be taken into consideration.

2. Regional development planning has to be effectively applied. Strategic management of regional development is different from earlier attempts of

---

(1) This was attained within Arthur D. Little by supporting the mobility of people who had an interest in working on "both sides", as well as through an effective project organization involving joint work of both management consultants and regional developers.

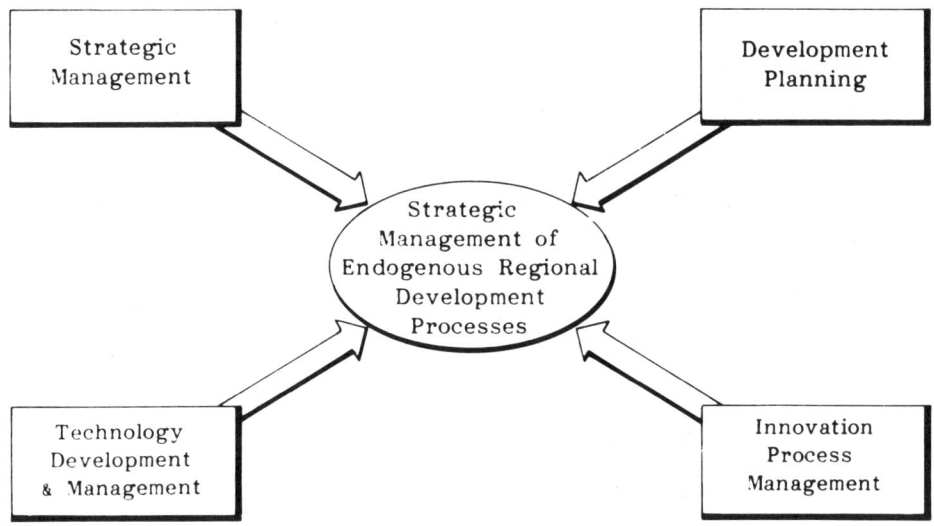

Figure 1: Strategic management of regional development requires a merging of four different approaches

regional policy in so far as planning is not pursued at a conceptual, "green-table type" level. Instead, regional strategies are regarded as a residuum of the strategies and actions of the major decision-makers involved. It is thus much more action-oriented than former approaches to regional planning.

3. As a result, process guidance and innovation process management and innovation management play an increasing role and often take up at least 50% of the whole effort. It is not so much the design of strategies which is important, but much more the role of "catalysts", mediators, and "change agents".

4. One of the major driving forces for many regions is the requirement to adapt to technological change. Technology can often become a nucleus or a common denominator, through which independent actors within a region are induced to develop some joint activity. Effective management of technology is becoming an ever more important ingredient of strategic management at the regional level.

The integration of these four levels of expertise requires effective project management which can only be realized through a series of tightly controlled work-steps. A typical project of strategic management of regional development will involve the following steps:

1. Segmentation of major activity areas and identification of what we call strategic policy units (SPUs) (2)

2. Evaluation of the attractiveness and strategic fit of specific activities for a region

3. Development of generic strategies and a strategic plan for the region

4. Translation of the strategic plan into an operational development plan

5. Creation of a temporary project organization responsible for the early phase of implementing the regional development plan

6. Involvement of larger and more formalized institutions, including continuous management and organization reflecting the size of investments and the degree of support needed (3)

This sequence of work-steps is illustrated in Fig.2. The first three phases up to the development of a strategic regional plan define the major long-term directions to be pursued at the regional level. At the same time, a process of joint decision-making and opinionformation is implemented. The typical time-frame for these first three phases lies between four and six months, depending on the complexity of the issues involved, and on the degree of heterogeneity within the region. Setting up the operational plan and starting an early project organization will take another four to twelve months. Finally, an effective management organization is created, which assumes control of the future regional development activities.

Arthur D. Little International has managed a considerable number of projects involving the strategic management of regional development, including:

1. Projects for major cities: Cologne MediaPark; Berlin Service Centre; New York Teleport

---

(2) This concept is related to the term strategic business unit (SBU) used for private company strategy development. Strategic policy or business units require a subdivision into activity units for which effective and non-conflicting strategies can be designated.

(3) Many projects pursued on a regional level have resulted in the establishment of large development organizations (e.g. the Irish Development Agency, the Welsh Development Agency, among others). In the long run, organizational change and adaptability of such an institution will become a key issue, and will have to be attained through strategic management at the institutional level.

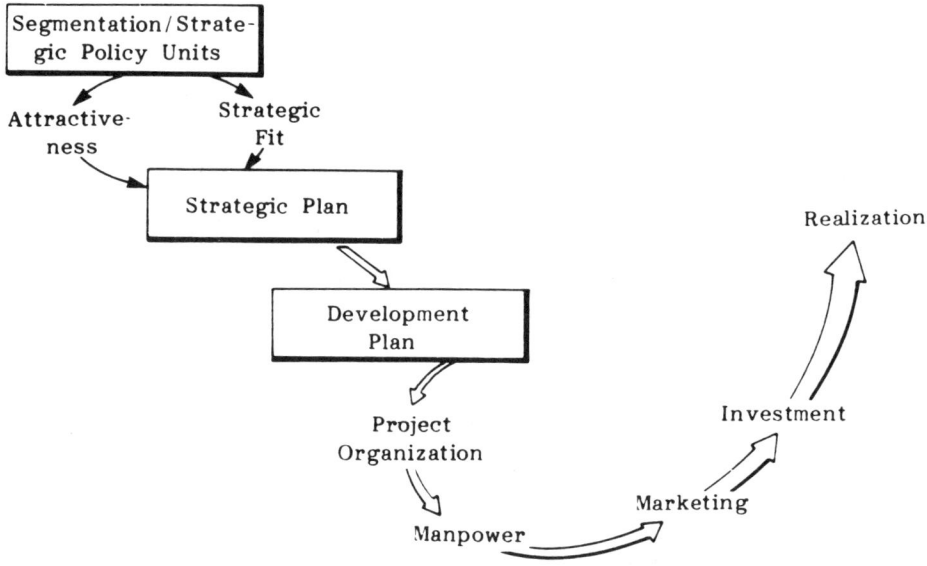

Figure 2: Major steps of a typical project for the strategic management of regional development

2. Development strategies for major states: microelectronics strategy for North Rhine-Westphalia; strategies for the Irish, Scottish and Welsh Development Agencies; electronics strategy for the Basque government

3. Large infrastructure projects with strong regional implications: Eurotunnel project; long-range plan for the Austrian Railways; investment models for the German high-speed rail systems

For illustrative purposes, the project for the Cologne MediaPark has been selected as a case study, and will be described in the following section.

Case Study: Strategic Management of the Cologne MediaPark

In 1985, the Municipality of Cologne was considering a major urban development project involving an area of more than 200 000 square meters within the city which was formerly used as a railway yard. Original project ideas were influenced by recent developments in real estate spurred by advances in information technology. A number of cities in different countries were developing projects like Teleports, Infomarts, Shared Tenant Services, Smart Buildings, Information Centres, and

Technology Parks. As the media and other information technology-based services were regarded as a key sector for the future strategy of Cologne, the development of an appropriate infrastructure project supporting these services was considered essential. Arthur D. Little International was invited to develop a feasibility study and a strategy for a MediaPark connected to a Teleport, involving:

1. An assessment of the growth potential of Cologne's media industry
2. An analysis of the demand and user profile for a new MediaPark
3. Recommendations for the design, development, and management of the project
4. A strategy for project implementation involving the participation of a number of interest groups and investors

The study required a segmentation into nine different business or policy units within the media, which had quite different characteristics and development opportunities, and for which separate strategies had to be developed. Each of these nine segments was evaluated in terms of

1. Its attractiveness for future development
2. Its rating vis-à-vis the relative strength of Cologne as a location ("strategic fit")

Even though seven segments were to display a high or medium attractiveness, Cologne did not seem to have particular strengths for all of them. The city had a leadership position only in public broadcasting and was moderately strong in information and documentation services, publishing, audio and video software, and film production (see Fig.3).

The major question arose whether or not the establishment of a MediaPark could in itself strengthen the position of Cologne as a location for the media. This proved to be the case for several segments. For private broadcasting, information and documentation, advertising, audio and video software and film production, the MediaPark could have a strong inducement effect and could lead to considerable improvements for early innovators participating in the new project (see Fig. 4).

A strategic plan for the Cologne MediaPark thus had to focus on those target groups, which expressed strongest support and which were expected to gain from the project. For each of these supporting groups, strategies had to be developed accordingly (see Table 1). At the same time, responses or recommendations of other

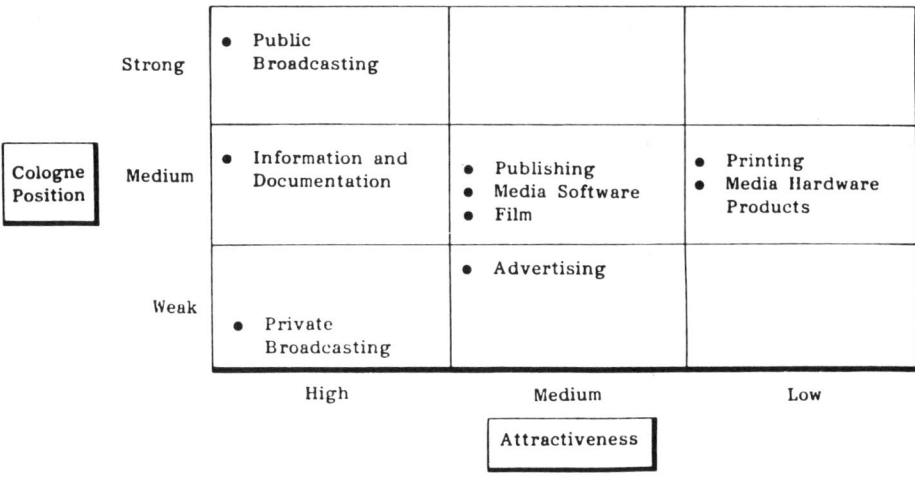

Figure 3: Assessment of Cologne as location for the media

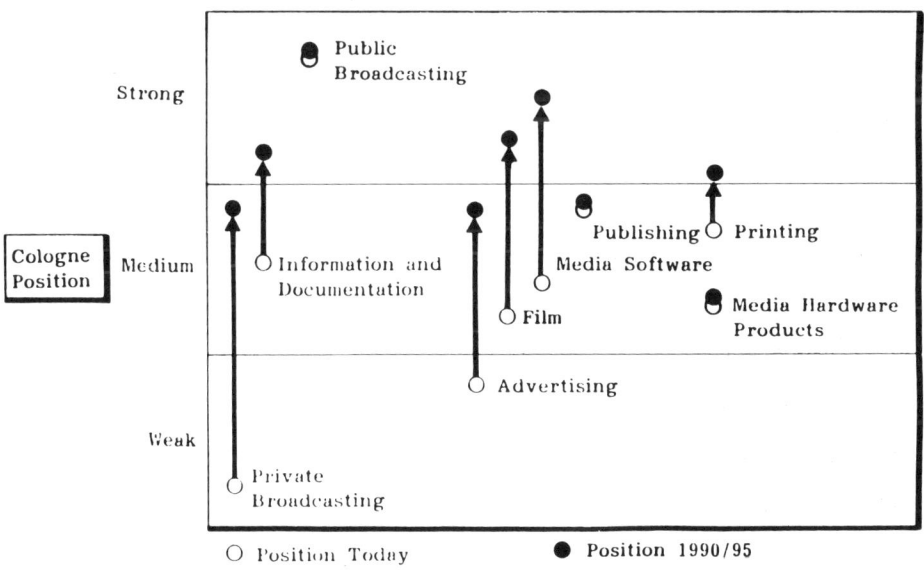

Figure 4: Potential Impact of MediaPark on Colognes position in the media

groups with only a moderate interest or which were indifferent, had to be taken into consideration. Through a series of interviews with selected key decision-makers in each of these segments, and a questionnaire sent out to practically all media firms in Cologne, information was gathered on particular requirements for technical

Table 1: Requirements and strategies for business segments with a *very strong* interest in MediaPark

Segment	Expressed Interest	Type of Support	Typical Firms
Private Broadcasting	Very High Depend on Legislation	Potential Location in Media Park, use of Facilities	Still very small end fragile companies
Advertising	High	Location in Media Park, use of Facilities	Medium-sized agencies and suppliers
Film	Very High	Location in Media Park, use of Facilities	Small, highly specialized innovative producers
Media Software	High	Location in Media Park, use of Facilities	Small, highly specialized innovative producers
Printing	High	Investment, use of facilities	Medium-sized innovativ printing houses

facilities and buildings. Responses were evaluated and led to the formulation of six project concepts:

1. MediaAcademy
2. MediaProduction Facility
3. MediaService Centre
4. Media Open Air Entertainment
5. MediaShopping
6. Media Entertainment Hall

As an example, advertising companies found it most important to establish a MediaAcademy to attract creative talent to Cologne, a service centre with most advanced technical equipment as well as an entertainment hall, where large new product presentations could be organized. As can be seen in Table 2, four institutions were considered to be very important for almost every segment analyzed: the

Table 2: User demand for specific project concepts

	Broad-casting	Publi-shing	Printing	Information & Documen-tation	Adver-tising	Consumer Electronics	Audio & Video Software	Film production
MediaAcademy	•••	•		••	•••	••	••	••
MediaProduction	•••	•			••	•	•	•••
MediaService centrum	•	•	••	••	•••	•	••	•
Media Open Air Entertainment	•				•		•	•
MediaShopping					•	••	••	
Entertainment Hall	•••				•••		••	•••

••• Very High Demand   •• Medium to High   • Average

MediaAcademy, a comprehensive service centre, a media production facility as well as an entertainment hall. These four institutions would form the core of the master plan for the MediaPark, as illustrated in Fig.5.

In order to specify in detail how these project concepts were to be further enhanced

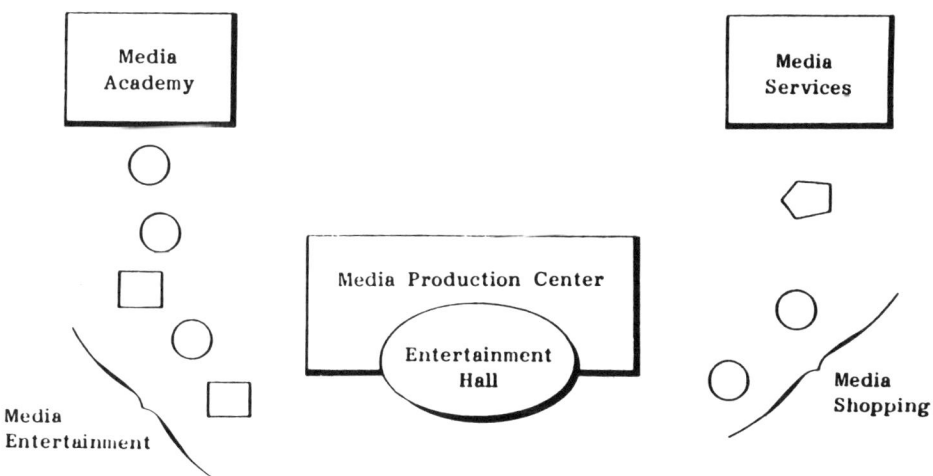

Figure 5: First master plan for the MediaPark

and promoted, three task forces were established. People who had expressed their interest and support during the first phase of interviews, and who represented the right mix of companies, were invited to participate in regular, task-oriented workshops. The key people from each task force formed a MediaPark Committee, a loose assembly of promoters of the whole project for which a specific target was set. It was supported by a task-oriented project team, established within the municipality. These informal and project-type organizations had a strong influence on the later formation of a MediaPark Development Organization (see Figs. 6 and 7).

Success of the project was dependent on formulation of an appropriate strategy and a development plan which was supported by the key decision-makers. It required the

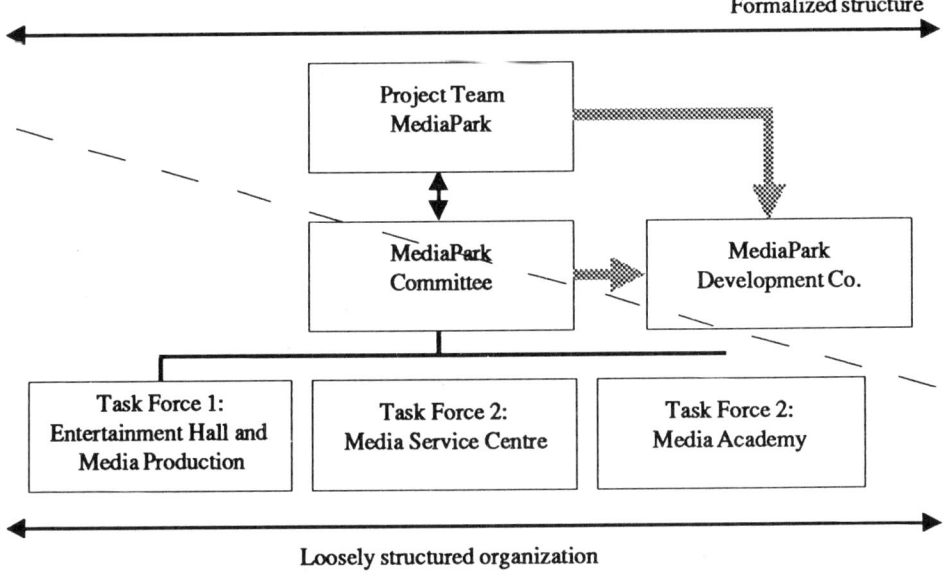

Figure 6:   Organizational structure for the MediaPark

formation of a loose organizational structure in the beginning and a more formalized planning approach in the later stages. The project is in its implementation stage today and will be realized in 1990.

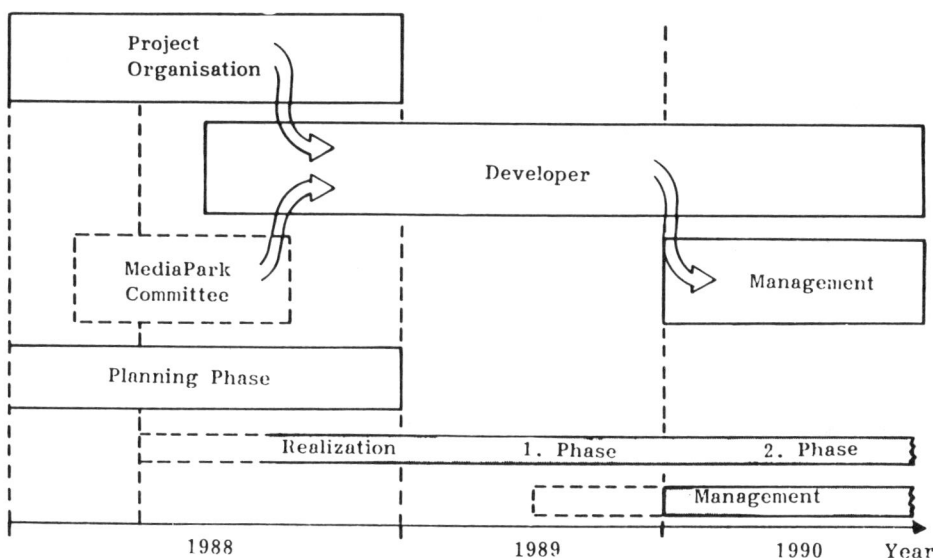

Figure 7:   Project realization and time schedule

Conclusions and Recommendations

Strategic management of endogenous regional development can work effectively if the right approach is chosen and if certain preconditions are fulfilled. A strategic policy unit (SPU), for which it is possible to find a coherent strategy and a joint solution, has to be carefully selected. The targets and objectives have to be specific and attractive enough. Objectives and strategies have to be discovered and developed interactively, and communicated to the participants.

Four factors determine whether or not strategic management of endogenous regional change will become effective:

1. Direction. Clear targets must be set and agreed upon by the different participating groups.

2. Dedication. Key individuals with perseverance and the ability to convince others play a very important role. Individual roles as champions, promoters, and gatekeepers must be clearly defined.

3. Development resources. These must be mobilized to the critical level. Very important is the presence of advanced research and educational facilities, as well as the availability of creative talent and appropriate land.

4. Financing. Major regional development projects and strategies must be funded. The existence of innovative financial institutions, and the availability of financial support programmes often play a cricital, even though not necessarily the most important role.

In the Cologne case, most of these critical success factors were fulfilled. Two clear and interrelated targets were pursued: to develop the city's strength in the media and to develop a project which would improve Cologne's locational advantage. Several key decisions-makers in the municipality had the conviction to pursue the project in spite of sometimes severe difficulties. Development resources were available; an unutilized, however, potentially attractive piece of land simply had to be redeveloped. Public funds (at the city and state level) were mobilized to get the project going.

Strategic management and a co-ordinated process to foster innovation and economic development at the regional level will become more important than financial incentives. In contrast to earlier approaches to regional development policy, which concentrated on the provision of subsidies, the emerging pattern of policy will be much more tightly knit with the ongoing activities of decision-makers in industry, research facilities, and in public or semipublic institutions. The key role of the co-ordinator or mediator of a (sometimes self-organized) development process will become more and more emphasized, while government financial support will be focused on providing seed money or back-up support (see Figs. 8 and 9).

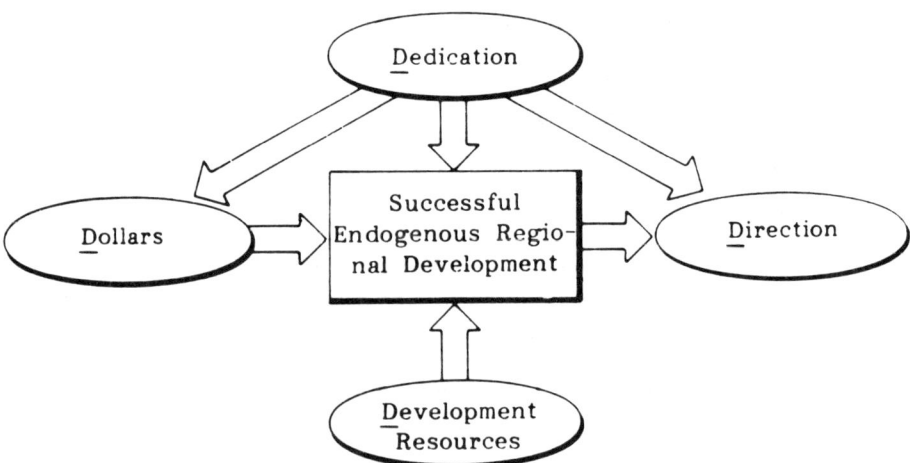

Figure 8: Strategic Success Factors - The 4-D-Modell

Strategic Management

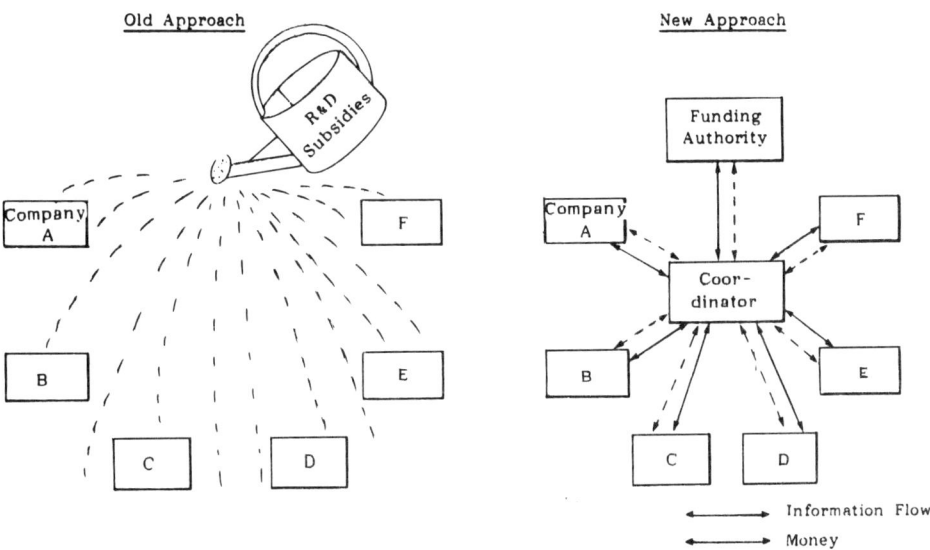

Figure 9:   Old and New Approaches of Regional Policy

3 New Experiences in Applying Endogenous Strategies for Regional Development
(Working Group 1)

3.1 Innovation and National-Level Regional Development and Planning Policies in France

Véronique Debisshop

Introduction

The following is a brief outline of regional development and planning policy in France. National regional development and planning policy began in 1963 with the creation of DATAR (Délégation à l'Aménagement du Territoire et à l'Action Régionale). This was justified by the realization, expressed as a cry of alarm in a book by Jean-Francois Gravier, *Paris et le désert français* (Paris and the French desert) published in 1947, of the incoherence and negative consequences of an economic system which was severely imbalanced spatially and too heavily centred on the capital.

DATAR has traditionally had two principal roles:

1. A regional planning role, i.e. to ensure an equitable spatial distribution of economic activity and population and to correct imbalances between regions

2. A regional development role, i.e. to propose pilot projects and to support regional development measures taken by local actors

The methods and resources used by DATAR are:

1. Interministerial co-ordination in the form of the CIAT (Comité Interministériel d'Aménagement du Territoire), which sets broad policy directions

2. Regulatory instruments, notably the special permit (agrément) required to start or expand an economic activity in the Paris region (above a certain threshold)

3. Financial incentives, namely regional development grants (Prime d'Aménagement du Territoire) for firms which set up in priority areas and the resources of two special funds, FIAT (Fonds Interministériel d'Aménagement du Territoire) and FIDAR (Fonds Interministériel de Développement et d'Aménagement Rural) through which development projects can be assisted

Regional Problems

Although there have been considerable changes since 1947, major regional imbalances justifying public intervention still exist, including:

1. Continuing imbalance between Paris and provincial France, even though the problems are now fewer than they were and there are today several other metropolitan areas of international stature. Thus, for example, in the scientific research sector, which is representative of trends, 50% of employment is located in Paris and 30% in seven or eight cities in south and southeast France.

2. Specific problem regions. These are both rural, where the population density is at a critical threshold level, as well as monostructured industrial regions, struck by the obsolescence of traditional industries undergoing structural change.

3. Subregional imbalances. The map of French problem regions cannot be simply drawn as consisting of opposing large blocs of problem and non-problem regions but rather more as a leopard skin, with areas of underdevelopment and areas of relative well-being bordering on one another. The development of France's metropolitan areas often takes the form of re-concentrating urban functions in the major city of the region, to the disadvantage of the surrounding areas.

Regional Policy Approaches

The approaches adopted in regional development and planning policy have consequently had to take account of the changing situation and in particular to adapt to two notable trends of recent years:

1. The growing importance of "grey matter" in economic development and the role of "nonmaterial investment" (e.g. training, research, culture) as opposed to "material investment" of the more traditional kind (e.g. plant and equipment, communications infrastructure)

2. The institutional changes produced by decentralization (enacted by the laws of 1982) which have changed the balance of decision-making between the subnational and national governments by giving greater responsibilities to the former. In particular, the 22 regions and the overseas territories (DOM-TOM) have been given regional planning and development functions.

The result of this trend, together with the growing role of the Commission of the European Communities in regional policy, has been that national government no longer has a monopoly responsibility for regional planning and development, but is now required to co-operate with other local and European partners.

In order to organize relations between the national and subnational governments, an interesting experiment was launched in 1984 within the framework of the IXth Plan (1984-1988). This is the system of "decentralized contractual planning" (planification contractuelle décentralisée). In parallel with the general medium-term orientation plan for national government policies, each region defined its own economic development plan. The priorities which each identified gave rise to the negotiation of "planning contracts" (contrate de plan) between the national government and each region, both partners making a financial contribution to the objectives to be achieved.

Planning Contracts

These can cover all aspects of the economics and social welfare of a region, including roads, urban development, training programmes or technical and scientific initiatives to assist firms, rural development, tourism, and cultural or social programmes.

Planning contracts have been a success. They have made possible effective working and co-ordination of the initiatives of the national and subnational governments, by organizing interaction between the partners in relation to specific contractual objectives. They have allowed the regions to experiment in the exercise of their new regional planning and development functions, and to set long-term priorities. They have also made it possible for them to make their voices heard at the national level.

At the same time, this system of planning contracts has encouraged national government ministries, often having a narrow policy sphere, to take positions on regional development objectives and thus to break down the barriers between them and to work in a multidisciplinary way.

A recently undertaken evaluation of the planning contracts experiment, which is due to end next year, has concluded that the exercise has been very successful. It has been decided to renew it for a further five-year period (1989 - 1993).

Innovation Policy in France

An innovation policy in France came relatively late and gradually as a distinct policy, i.e. as something separate from science and technology policy. It emerged at the beginning of the 1970s.

In 1969 ANVAR (Agence National pour la Valorisation de la Recherche) was set up, with the initial objective of encouraging the market application of results of public sector research. In 1978 ANVAR was restructured and given the objective of supporting innovation as such, and came to manage a series of schemes of assistance to firms which were subsequently gradually introduced. ANVAR was also regionalized at this time.

This delay in the development of an innovation policy is largely due to a cultural problem. France has historically been a country marked by administrative practices and professional habits ill disposed to innovation. One factor is the traditional separation between industry and research, between universities and "grandes écoles". Another is the administrative centralization which led to a concentration of science and technology policy on sectoral programmes launched from Paris and undertaken by public institutions and firms.

A veritable "cultural revolution" is now underway in our country to enable it to adapt to the technological challenge and the needs of innovation.

The necessity has gradually become clear of bringing together centres of knowledge (universities, research institutions) and centres of production (firms) which in the past have been two quite distinct worlds, even distrustful of one another. Industry has been motivated by its need to modernize and to diversify its products and processes in order to be able to meet international competition. The world of research has been motivated by its need to justify its economic and social usefulness and to mobilize new resources by commercializing its results.

The growing economic role of the subnational governments, in particular of the regions, has allowed them to play a role in this rapprochement between research and industry and to integrate it into a regional perspective. Regional authorities are increasingly centering their development policies (or redevelopment policies where the objective is industrial reconversion) on strategies related to "grey matter". Thus, every region included in its planning contract the priority of support for research, training and technology transfer.

The region appears the optimum level at which to organize the bringing together of research and industry and of the related interface structures, which are difficult if not impossible to organize nationally. At the same time, the regions are of sufficient size to have the critical mass necessary for a significant effort.

In 1982 a law was passed which consolidated this trend by giving the regions the responsibility for setting up "regional technology networks", as most of the main initiatives were termed. The definition given by the Ministry of Research is as follows:

> The concept of technology networks is not to be limited to the encouragement of technology transfer at the local level. It is a concentration, in a given area of technology, of resources with the objective of achieving national and even international stature, and capable also, at the regional level, of ensuring synergy with the economic fabric of the locality, both up- and downstream of specific projects.

The approach adopted by the regions in setting up such networks was essentially pragmatic to begin with. It was generally to use the existing scientific resources in the areas to respond to the technology needs of local industries, in particular SMEs (small and medium-sized enterprises).

Technology Supply

From this general kind of beginning, various approaches have been developed which can be classified in relation to a typology of technology supply. This typology corresponds to the heterogeneity of the world of research, which is no less varied than the world of industry. Thus, the term "industry-research relations" covers a variety of practices according to the partners involved. Three types can be identified by reference to three categories of technology supply.

Type One

This covers the "raw" supply of technology by research laboratories (research centres, universities, etc.) and is generally only directly accessible by large firms or SMEs specialized in product or process development, i.e. "innovative" SMEs. The reason is that only these firms have staff coming from the same scientific "milieu" as the researchers (engineering graduates of the "grandes écoles" for the most part) and thus able to communicate with them. Also, these firms are able to integrate such technology directly, either because they have R & D facilities to ensure the industrial application phase (large firms) or because they are involved in upstream activities in the technology development process (innovative SMEs).

Relations between research and industry come about spontaneously in this case without the need for an intermediary between the scientific and industrial partners. Both sides are known to one another through scientific congresses and publications or through personal networks ("old-boy" networks, for example). Geographic proximity, although not necessary, can favour this sort of contact.

Type Two

For other firms, "ordinary SMEs", direct access to the first type of technology supply is culturally difficult. They therefore need to make use of the services of intermediaries able to serve as a bridge between research and industry. Such intermediaries are industrial research associations, university institutes of technology (IUTs) and technical colleges (lycées techniques), which offer more applied kinds of technology. There firms find contacts (technicians) speaking a more accessible language and offering technical assistance directly relevant to their need to modernize processes (automation) or products (conception, design, quality). The technologies thus made available are not necessarily the result of the most advanced research, they are simply new for the firms which use them.

Relations between research and industry are mediated here by a specialized intermediary. They are rarely spontaneous because the firms are by definition poorly integrated in technology information networks. Their needs are badly expressed, if expressed at all.

Thus, research-industry relations depend on the level of technical culture in the receiving industrial sector. They often imply some prior activity of "animation" promoting firms' awareness of the need to modernize. Professional organizations and chambers of commerce often have a very important role to play here.

Geographic proximity is a necessary condition, making it easier for the firm to benefit and permitting the emergence of relations of confidence between the partners.

Type Three
This category covers technology transfers within industry itself, between large firms and innovative SMEs or other firms. Transfers of this kind are often made within subcontracting arrangements, the buyer giving his partners access to his technology in order to ensure that he receives goods of required quality.

Technology Networks

The regional technology networks can similarly be classified according to their objectives.

Type one
Some technology networks have been set up to structure the first kind of technology supply. They take the form of a functional grouping of research centres in a particular area of technology, maintaining close relations with the firms ensuring the industrial application of the results of their research. These networks are aimed at diffusing technologies in the regional economy, but in some cases have a wider regional impact. They are to be found especially in the major metropolitan scientific centres: Toulouse, Lyons, Montpellier, Rennes, Lille, Nancy, Bordeaux. The areas of technology may be spontaneous and informal, resulting from the principal economic activity of the region (e.g. electronics in Grenoble, aerospace in Toulouse) or organized institutionally (e.g. Composite Materials Institute in Bordeaux, the VERSEAU institutions (water technology), GRIDAMET and PRIAM in the food-processing industry in Montpellier, Groupement Régional des

Transports in Lille, etc.). Smaller towns may have a strong specialization in a specific area (e.g. Microwave Research Centres in Limoges, GIP Temps-fréquence in Besançon).

Type Two: CRITT

Other networks organize the second kind of technology supply and make it available to firms. They are necessarily regional, sometimes local, and termed CRITT - Centres Régionaux d'Innovation et de Transfert de Technologies. They, too, centre on a grouping of research centres, but in addition there is a "relay" organization to ensure contact with firms and the translation of research results into innovative products and processes which can be used by the firms. Conversely, they mediate technology demand by helping firms to formulate their needs. If local technology supply is inadequate in relation to local firms' needs, the CRITT itself may have its own scientific resources (personnel and equipment) and may be a supplier of technology. Mechanisms of this sort exist:

1. In the major towns and cities with a scientific infrastructure, where a CRITT is often charged with diffusing technologies throughout the region. Examples include the CRITT CT-BIO in Marseilles, CRITT ADEMAT and CRITT GBF (materials) in Lyons, the regional technology "poles" in Dijon and Poitiers, CRITT ADRIANT in Nantes, and the CRITT for glucides in Amiens.

2. As regional networks with subregional centres. Examples include the process technology transfer networks in Nord/Pas de Calais (Lille, Douai, Valenciennes) and in Britanny (Rennes, Brest, Lannion, Lorient), the CASIMIR technology "pole" in the Auvergne (Clermont, Ferrand, Montluçon, Moulins, Thiers, Le Puy, Aurillac).

3. In the secondary centres. Here the basis may be a new university or engineering school well connected to the local economy (e.g. the universities in Pau, Valenciennes, Mulhouse, Saint-Etienne, ENIT in Tarbes, ENSAM in Cluny, the Mining Schools in Alès and Saint-Etienne), or a university institute of technology (IUTs e.g. the CRITT for process technology in Bourges, the welding "pole" in Creusot, the CRITT MICROCOR in Lonwy), or a technical college (e.g. the CRITT for surface treatment in Charleville-Mézières).

4. In industrially specialized regions. Here the centre is on an industrial research institute (e.g. CETIH in Cholet, LECARIM in Mazamet, CEPROMAG in Décazeville, the Plastics Institute in Alençon, CERCHAR in Creil, or the CNET in Lannion).

Type Three

Still other networks serve to structure the third kind of technology supply. Large firms have set up technology transfer networks in the regions where they are established. Some of these have joined together in a network called CREATI (Centres Régionaux d'Appui Technique et d'Innovation aux PMI-PME) which was established some years ago by Elf-Aquitaine's CETRA. Some notable examples (see CREATI directory) are CETRA in Paux and CETRALP in Rhône-Alpes (Elf-Aquitaine), APIONAL in Cadarache (CIA: Centre d'Ionisation des Aliments), CETREP in Pont-à-Mousson (Saint-Gobain), CERCHAR in Creil and the Centre de Pirolyse in Mariennau (CdF).

Evaluation of Technology Networks

A recent study of technology networks showed the technological vitality of most French regions. Although the country's scientific potential is very unequally distributed, a certain dynamism has developed almost everywhere which can provide the basis for a truly decentralized development of new technologies. The CRITT network covers the whole of the country, and the individual CRITTs serve as support centres for innovation policies (by mobilizing skills and resources, even where these are weak). The study also showed the value of organization in a network, which makes it possible both to mobilize technology supply wherever it is available and to diffuse innovations throughout the economic fabric to a region in order to modernize it. Regional technology development agencies are in the process of being established in most regions for the purpose of managing these networks. Also underlined was the need to diversify experience in order to complete the overall structure. After a first, experimental, phase which was the creation of technology networks on the basis of a more or less uniform model inspired by the Ministry of Research, it has appeared useful to find models better adapted to specific local circumstances:

1. The CRITTs appear well suited to regions with a fully fledged technology structure capable of being activated, i.e. an industrial fabric and specialized scientific skills in particular areas of technology, such as electronics,

biotechnology, materials, etc. The prime role of the CRITT is the diffusion of innovations and new technologies to the firms in the regions, to help them to modernize. They seem to be most efficient at a regional level, being the minimum level to justify such specialization and the maximum level to permit easy contact between research and industry. At the same time, it is increasingly clear that it is useful for the CRITT to link up in national and even European networks.

2. Mechanisms specifically aimed at the creation of new firms have also been established. These "incubators" may be centred on a CRITT, which can supply the new entrepreneur with technical assistance.

3. In particularly depressed regions (rural regions and those undergoing structural change) it is the very process of innovation which has to be set in train. A policy of technological development here requires a prior initiative to raise awareness and lift the level of "technical culture" in firms. Various solutions have been tried, such as technology advisors to undertake this "educational" function or the establishment of local multidisciplinary transfer centres. Initiatives of this sort are usually taken at the level of local labour markets.

4. Encouraging firms to innovate raises demand for qualified personnel to implement new technologies. Thus, the CRITTs often need to expand their services to include ongoing training. Specific initiatives have been launched for the training of engineers by supporting in-house research in firms (financial assistance through CIFRE contracts) and for hiring technicians.

Technopoles

The development of technopoles is underway in France, just as in other industrialized countries.

The early French technopoles date from the 1970s: Sophia Antipolis, ZIRST Meylan (Grenoble), Nancy Brabois. There has been spectacular development in the 1980s, with 40 technopoles now in operation or in the planning stage. Fifteen are located in major cities, the others in medium-sized towns and cities.

There is no strict definition of a technopole in France. Technopoles are not set up under some public policy, but are the result of local initiatives. Any subnational government, but also any other public (e.g. university) or private organization (e.g.

firm) can set up a technopole. There is, as a consequence, a great variety of initiatives which go under the name of "technopole".

Most of the French technopoles are the result of initiatives by local authorities, charged with real-estate development (on land belonging to them). They may link up with a private company (association, groupement d'intérêt économique) to manage and develop the technopole. This entity then is the technopole. Examples of this latter type include Rennes-Atalante in Rennes, Nancy-Brabois-Innovation in Nancy, Montpellier-Languedoc-Roussillon-Technopole in Montpellier.

Another characteristic of technopoles is that they are centred in the first instance on existing activities and so are built close to towns and cities (there are no more major "green field" operations like SophiAntipolis, built as a new town; there may have been a case for such operations in the 1970s, but this is no longer so, given the urban hierarchy now existing in France).

They feature a site of high quality in terms of natural setting and architecture on which to house firms. Plots of land are sold, temporary rented premises may also be available. In size they vary from a few score to several hundred acres. Common services may be offered, such as meeting rooms, business services (accounting, printing), presence of public agencies (ANVAR, DRIR), and a "business incubator" (see below). A selection procedure ensures that only firms are allowed to come onto the site which use high technologies, and certain technopoles are specialized in particular technologies - such as electronics or biotechnologies, e.g. Lyons. A management function is required for organizing meetings between firms on the technopole (breakfasts in Nancy and Sophia Antipolis), a newsletter, and marketing of the technopole.

French technopoles aim at cross-fertilization, i.e. bringing together on the same site high-technology activities of public research centres, firms, universities, etc. with the aims of encouraging synergy between the different activities through daily contact ("cafeteria effect"). This synergy can give rise to new ideas and technical innovations and so to new economic activities (new products or processes), and thereby to new jobs.

Thus, the chances of success for a technopole project depend on the quality of the upstream scientific potential which can be activated on the site and the existence of an "animation" function to ensure that this scientific potential has an effect on its environment and stimulates technology transfers.

Since the prime objective of a technopole is the creation of new firms by the activation of local scientific potential (endogenous development) most technopoles have one or more "incubators" specially designed to house new firms and help them in their early years. The services offered by such incubators (which again vary greatly) include flexible rented premises, central telephone switchboard, legal advice, technical assistance with the making of applications (contact with banks, etc.), development of the firms' products or processes (in conjunction with local laboratories), and training (management, etc.).

In French, the word "technopole" can take masculine or feminine gender, and has a different meaning in each case. In the masculine form, a technopole is a real-estate operation to accommodate high-technology firms, having on-site or close-by local research institutes with which the firms interact. In this sense, technopoles provide a link that was missing in the technology networks which I described earlier, by organizing the first kind of technology supply for its recipients, high-technology firms, but on a spatial rather than functional basis. In the feminine form, the technopole is the overall town or city of high technological potential. These tend to be the major technopoles (in the masculine sense). This brings us back to the issue of regional development and planning and will serve as my conclusion.

Conclusion: Importance of Technopoles

A technopole in the feminine sense is no longer a real-estate operation but an overall policy, typically of a major municipality, aimed at changing the traditional spatial balance of economic activity in France and at challenging the dominant position of Paris. Such a policy seeks to encourage a reinforcement of the focal role of such large cities in material and nonmaterial networks of wealth and knowledge. This sometimes has adverse effects on regional balance in the immediate areas surrounding the technopole: the subregional imbalances to which I referred earlier. The idea of a hierarchy of urban centres is not new. What is new is that today innovation and technological development are what shape the hierarchy.

Technology policy is thus the means whereby towns and cities, by assuming a role of "animator", establish themselves as actors in the regional development process on a level with the regions. Initiatives of this sort are justified in terms of needing to "make a mark" in a context of increased global international competition: the regional capital needs to concentrate resources, even establish a position of regional hegemony, to play its role of promoter, of locomotive, as is sometimes said, in relation to the regional economy. When technopoles try to influence their environment, it is often from a hierarchical vantage point around the centre.

Technopoles, therefore, are more than an urban development project. They are a major element in regional planning and development. In the present situation, regional planning and development policy expects two things of technopoles:

1. That they be regional centres of strength, capable of improving the overall technological growth of France and of placing the country and Europe at the highest levels of international competitiveness

2. That they be motors of regional development, capable of bringing benefits to the whole of the regional economy and of increasing the impact of new technologies, i.e. of fulfilling the same task as the technology networks which I described earlier

Reference

Jean-Francoise Gravier, Paris et le désert francaise, Paris 1947

3.2 Recent Changes in the Policy Tools for the Development of Italy's Mezzogiorno

Nino Novacco

The Past

The "Mezzogiorno" is an extensive area occupying the southern part of the peninsula and the islands of Italy, accounting for approximately 40% of both the country's surface area and population. It includes seven entire political-administrative regions and parts of two others (the ones nearest to the "frontier" with the north-central zone).

Larger than Belgium, Holland and Luxemburg put together, with about 20 million inhabitants, i.e. double the population of Greece or Portugal, it forms a macroregion of Italy and of Europe, characterized by persisting overall economic backwardness. However, there are many who today claim that, since the Mezzogiorno no longer has the same features of global underdevelopment as it once did, it no longer requires a comprehensive, common policy, for the application of regionally diversified measures and incentives. The EEC itself, somewhat mechanically and based on an idealized model of abstract "competition", is urging the Italian government to exclude a number of southern areas (those which in the past few years have made relatively quicker quantitative progress) from the benefits still reserved by law for the whole of southern Italy.

The relative backwardness of the Mezzogiorno, with its income, employment, productivity and welfare gaps, but even more the diverging development opportunities of southern areas with respect to the centre-north, have always been typical elements of Italy's society and economy, which has understandably been regarded as a classic example of "dualism", albeit within a single nation that has constitutionally been unified since 1861. In this situation, the necessity of special legislation, capable of fostering the specific development of southern areas has existed in Italy since the beginning of the century.

There were scattered, partial and occasional initiatives of the past. However, it was not until 1950 that the Italian parliament and government defined the strategic aims of a policy of wide-ranging, long-term "extraordinary action" (special measures) in the Mezzogiorno. This policy has certainly undergone no few changes in these ensuing 30 years (from infrastructures to industrialization), and witnessed moments and phases of uncertainty and of marked alteration (concentration / diffusion, agriculture/industry/tourism, and the like), while remaining characterized by its national-central nature and its "special" features.

The trait characterizing the policy of special measures that started in 1950 is the fact that, using significant yet not exceptional resources, equal to about 2% of Italy's GNP, it has provided a co-ordinated complex of specific and functional instruments:

1. The Cassa per il Mezzogiorno (Fund for the South) was first and foremost initially established to carry out land reclamation and improvement and to create physical infrastructures. However, it immediately became a unitary centre of planning, designing, long-term financing and the co-ordinated creation also of major infrastructures and networks of public works. In time, the Fund was assigned decision-making powers in financing industry and tourism, but unfortunately this financing was split up into minor works of local scope.

2. Tax facilities have become progressively more comprehensive and considerable, but all operate in the context of a financial administration not systematically efficient.

3. Labour cost incentives, re-established the advantage to employers of providing jobs, especially after the abolition of the wage differentials between north and south (a rather "egalitarian" operation, demanded by the trade unions, which did not consider the gaps in productivity, which have continued).

4. Credit facilities were set up for the creation of new production capital, mainly in the form of capital grants and "soft loans" to industry and for the promotion of productive activities, also through special medium-term credit institutions for southern Italy (ISVEIMER for the mainland, IRFIS for Sicily and CIS for Sardinia).

5. A series of specialized agencies were created for promotion and technical assistance (IASM), training managerial and supervisory personnel (FORMEZ), agriculture (FINAM), sharing in risk capital for industry (FIME) and tourism (INSUD), industrial areas (Consortiums for Industrial development areas), marketing (ITALTRADE) and leasing (FIME LEASING).

6. The legislation provided for reserves - although these have been little respected and in any case not systematically so - in favour of the Mezzogiorno, for "public supply and processing contracts" (as support for existing activities, on the demand side) and for "investments" (at least 40% of the national total) by the national government and by public administrations.

An important role in the industrialization policy for the Mezzogiorno has been played by state shareholding companies. In relation to legal obligations these involve at least 60% of investments in the south. They have offered important incentives for the establishment of large plants in the Mezzogiorno in various sectors, such as the iron and steel, chemical and petrochemical, and shipbuilding industries (though the latter was subsequently stricken by crisis). The public sector (and in some respects also the private sector) had shown an interest, but were put off by the location in the south and due to the weak "input-output effect" of this type of plant many even deemed such undertakings to be isolated "cathedrals in the desert".

The results, even after the special measures and within the framework of the advantages determined thereby, achieved in the Mezzogiorno between 1950 and 1980 (in actual practice, between 1960, when the Mezzogiorno policy directly undertook development action, and 1974-1975, when the national and international crisis broke out) were appreciable but insufficient. Large-scale, positive structural changes - in the relative weight of the macrosectors, in the social and class composition, in the material and cultural prerequisites of development - but also the persistence of old problems and imbalances and the emergence of new ones, characterize the comparison between the 1950s and the 1980s.

1. The Mezzogiorno in 1950 was still a traditional agricultural society. In these more than 30 years it has turned into a society admittedly not yet fully industrialized, but now characterized by an urban pattern and by the spread of places and processes of advanced modernization.

2. The growth of income and investment in the south went on at least until the mid-1970s at higher rates than at any other time in the history of modern Italy; however, income increased at high rates also in the north.

3. The north-south gaps in community facilities and in public and private consumption diminished greatly, in general, and the trends in the productivity gaps were likewise improving, only in the latter years being subject to contrary pressures.

4. Within the Mezzogiorno itself there was a lively differentiation in growth from one area to another, according to geographical lines and sociological patterns - including new ones compared with the past - but without any change in the area's overall pattern and its position with respect to the north and to Europe.

5. The southern labour market - no longer characterized by the unemployment of farm labourers and the rural underemployment of the 1950s - is today moving between dramas (a very high rate of unemployment, especially for the young) and paradoxes (increase in employment, parallel to the increase in unemployment, due to the new labour demand especially among young women), while for years now there have been significant waves of immigrant labour arriving from abroad, with employment also in the south in the least-skilled jobs.

6. The different demographic prognostications for the centre-north and the Mezzogiorno until after 2000 indicate that the young job-seekers in Italy will, for many years to come, still originate mostly from the Mezzogiorno.

The positive but insufficient results achieved in the south are partly the effect of limitations and mistakes in the policies applied, but perhaps even more of the frequent contradictions between the direct measures carried out in the south and "national" policies; the effects of the latter have often ended up off-setting the full scope of achievements expected by the former as a result of action carried out most laboriously and at great cost.

In connection with the crisis that occurred in the mid-1970s and in relation to the blocking of productive investments that stemmed therefrom, especially in the Mezzogiorno, towards the end of the decade a lively debate started in Italy as to the future of policy vis-à-vis southern Italy. There has been strong criticism and self-criticism, and contrasting thoughts, on the shortcomings of the previous policies and on the new conditions shaping up - including consolidation of the EEC, the birth and organization in Italy of the autonomous regions; and the exceptionally quick spread of largely innovative technologies - all conditions that have to be taken into account in the future in pursuing the imperative further development of the Mezzogiorno.

Under these conditions, when Law 183 of 1976 expired in 1980, parliament and the government were not prepared to define new guidelines. Thus for over five years, between 1980 and March 1986, there was a very damaging lack of management with respect to southern development, rendered even more serious by the circumstance that in those years the productive machinery of central-north Italy was for its part capable of responding to a powerful series of stimuli from the market (in terms of innovation and of increased productivity and efficiency) which accelerated the pace of growth and led to fresh north-south gaps, after a period of some 15 years when these had been significantly declining.

The Future

It was in this climate that in March 1986 the Italian parliament approved a new law on the Mezzogiorno (Law 64). The philosophy behind this Law appears much in keeping with the theme of this conference. Within the scope of a strong shifting of emphasis from centre to periphery and from state to local agents, including private ones, it laid down, in a climate of both political and ideological pressures, a largely endogenous development strategy. This policy seems to want to take less account than was the case in the past of the possible contribution to development of the Mezzogiorno by external action, deeming it inadequate in being without structural links to the local resources and markets. These orientations are asserted in a context of declared attention to the quality of development, and in an atmosphere of confidence-plus-wager for a hypothesis of self-centred development of local and minor activities.

Over a time horizon of nine years, the Law envisages three-year-plans and annual programmes of initiatives proposed mainly "from below", that is, from the interests stemming from the periphery of the industrial and manufacturing system.

In parallel with these sharp changes in the philosophy and in the aims of measures for south Italy, Law 64/1986 contemplates organizational guidelines and instruments that are largely new. With the old Cassa per il Mezzogiorno eliminated, the Law provides for two bodies at the operational level: (a) The Department for the Mezzogiorno is responsible for assessments of consistency and economic worthiness of the initiatives included in the draft proposals submitted by the regions and local agents and which are to be incorporated into the plans and programmes. (b) The Agency for the Mezzogiorno is required (subject to the completion of the works still in progress according to earlier regulations) to deal only with financing the initiatives to be implemented, and with the programmes proposed by the system of specialized agencies. The whole policy is under the political authority of a Minister for the Mezzogiorno, heading the structure for promotion and co-ordination, in close liaison with the Prime Minister and with the main inter-ministerial committees for economic and industrial policy.

The system outlined in the Law is in fact characterized by the disappearance of an authoritarian-type of structure and the necessarily local approach to the programmes to be implemented. It follows, instead, the logic of "development banks", with more emphasis perhaps on their function as financing banks. This tends to upgrade the initial role of promotion/mediation of the national, political authority and its subsequent role as co-ordinator of the set of projects and initiatives, as well as of the agents required to implement these - a role which becomes decisive in its technical and above all its political complexity.

This Law stems from the confidence placed in the determination and capabilities of the southern regions and local agencies. It is no mere chance that its success has officially been termed a "challenge" with respect to the previous guidelines and methods. For this reason the Law (whose innovations especially in the technical merit of the mechanisms of financing are relatively modest) is significant in offering new complementary and substitute institutional support instruments in the service of the co-ordination functions, which have become so essential. These include:

1. "Programme agreements" promoted by the Ministry for the Mezzogiorno among the public administrations concerned in different ways with the implementation of comprehensive works, i.e. works which, being carried out at the regional level, touch on the competences and powers of a number of juridically autonomous actors

2. "Programme contracts", between the Minister and the major firms concerned with the implementation of their most outstanding investment programmes, so as to guarantee that projects assessed as being of particular interest to the Mezzogiorno will be entitled to the maximum incentives

and facilities

With this philosophy in mind, other factors to be stressed, with reference both to the Law, the first three-year plan and the first annual programme include:

1. Priority attention is to be given to all initiatives connected with R&D and with technological innovation, within a logic favouring intangible investments, as opposed to the old practices that had ended up giving privilege to "bricks" over "brains".

2. Attention is to be given to the development of new youth entrepreneurship, involving conspicuous resources and incentives, with the dual objective of encouraging small firms which have a recognizable and established local demand and of finding a solution to the problems of young people - who in this phase of their lives are seeking not only a job, but also an identity.

3. Measures and incentives are to be earmarked for better facilities in the Mezzogiorno in terms of services useful for the area and its industry. The criticism made of the old incentives for small and medium-sized firms, all mostly monetary, has been translated into a philosophy favouring real incentives - finding that upgrading the services useful for production (from public services and public utilities to private consulting and support services in the various phases of the firm's life) is the best way to be attractive to companies outside, and to assure existing ones or those setting up in the Mezzogiorno conditions of efficient and competitive economic returns.

The new philosophy of "real incentives" proposes, on the one hand, to increase the number and upgrade the quality of the southern networks of public utilities (e.g. water, energy, natural gas, railways, motorways, ports), with special attention to both traditional and new telecommunications and connecting systems, and, on the other hand, to make incentives available to both supply and demand, so as to cause the services for companies to grow. This approach is intended no longer to favour only the creation of industrial areas and buildings with basic facilities, but to support the emergence and the work of functional service centres, in which the smaller firms can find their own particular answers to their production and management requirements.

It is always hard to express a judgment on what the results of new guidelines, not yet tried and tested, might be. In this case the judgment must necessarily be a cautious one, because the change of guidelines and methods comes, with reference to the Mezzogiorno, in a period characterized - and assuredly not only in Italy, by the emergence of new trends, which make the prospect of the "development" of backward areas more arduous.

Suffice it to think of the consequences of the estrangement - in the industrialized Western world - that has come about between economic development and the employment of manpower, a pair of phenomena which until little more than a decade ago we assumed to be closely linked, and about which we spoke, almost automatically, in terms of "elasticity". Or consider the trend whereby for years now we have not seen the establishment of new plants of large unit size, for on the contrary there have been signals of structural crisis precisely in those sectors (iron and steel, chemicals, textiles, shipbuilding) requiring such large plants. Or consider the situation of sectors in which there has been a decrease of manpower, as a consequence of the ongoing process of production rationalization and of making production more competitive. This certainly does not make the creation of new physical capacities probable in areas that may be different from those where the industry was traditionally concentrated. This makes it inconceivable for such a large area as the Mezzogiorno and at the moment when Europe seems headed for the prospect (in 1992) of its birth as an actual, competitive single market - to have either a wholly agricultural or a wholly tertiary solution, or to wholly base itself on tourism almost jumping entirely the phase of the development of a manufacturing industry.

With reference to the 1986 Law on the Mezzogiorno, there are signs of difficulties and delays, which are simply the result of the necessarily slow start-up period for new mechanisms, not all of them as yet defined. If, however, a concluding remark is permitted for a "meridionalista" (student of the south), such as I would consider myself, I would like to declare my interest and confidence in some of the new guidelines as laid down by the Law - especially those linked the real incentives and to services for firms - but at the same time a profound concern about the outcome of the envisaged "polycentric programming". In Italy there are no precedents giving good grounds for hope, especially in the context of a Law that aims at a strongly redefined role of the state, and which has raised the hopes and claims of a plurality of new local agents. These peripheral subjects are in fact without any forerunners. Thus, confidence and hope in the development of the Mezzogiorno are combined with doubts and fears as to the adequacy of the new strategies and policy tools brought into being for that aim, which is not just accommodating a "local" need but one of the whole Italian state and, following this line, of the whole European Economic Community.

3.3 Local Initiatives for the Promotion of Innovation in the Federal Republic of Germany

Hans Heuer

Ten Basic Theses

1. Not only enterprises, but also towns and communities are subject to the rules of competition.
2. Towns with old industries based on traditional skills and decision-making structures are in danger of collapsing economically.
3. The new information and communication technologies are making new demands on locations, enterprises and employees.
4. The existence of a technology-oriented infrastructure has not yet become a guarantee for an innovative behaviour of the economy.
5. The importance of the locational factor "human capital" will increase further. Traditional occupations will be devalued, as new qualifications are required.
6. The problems of structural change cannot be solved by defensive strategies. The aim therefore must be the promotion of structural change.
7. Structural renewal at the local level has to occur from within.
8. In a time of increasing intercommunal competition, the reputation and the marketing of location, again, become important fields of local government policies. It is up to the towns to present themselves with a distinctive image.
9. The juxtaposition of cultural policy, urban development and economic policy offers the communities new economic opportunities.

10. New economic stimuli are expected especially from measures promoting innovation. This is being recognized more and more by the local actors, as well, and translated into initiatives.

Some Examples of Local Initiatives for the Promotion of Innovation

In recent years, in many muncipalities of the Federal Republic of Germany new initiatives and projects have been developed which essentially go beyond the traditional fields of activity in the promotion of local economic development. All these initiatives aim at strengthening the capacity of innovation and competition of the local economy and promoting local structural change. Most of the measures taken can be roughly classified into six categories:

1. Technology institutions
2. Transfer of information, technology and employees
3. Initial and continuing training
4. New promotion of the setting up of new business enterprises
5. New forms of financing
6. New forms of co-operation within the region

In what follows, eight examples from six muncipalities of the Federal Republic of Germany are presented.

Technologiezentrum Dortmund (Technology Centre Dortmund)

Since the Berliner Innovations- und Gründerzentrum (BIG); (Berlin centre for innovation and setting-up) opened late in 1983, a wave of establishing technology centres has swept the Federal Republic of Germany. Technology-oriented young firms and founders of new businesses have moved into the centre of interest. In the meantime, there are now 50 to 60 such technology centres throughout the Federal Republic of Germany.

Similar to the BIG in Berlin and the Technologiefabrik Karlsruhe (technology factory), the Technologiezentrum Dortmund (TZD; Technology Centre Dortmund) is one of the particularly successful centres. It differs from most of the other centres above all in its having fewer occupational newcomers, basing itself on existing firms and research institutions for the industries in the Dortmund region, which are spatially concentrated close to the University of Dortmund and the Fraunhofer-Institut für Transporttechnik und Warendistribution (institute for transportation and goods distribution). From the beginning it restricted itself to selected technologies, which are represented at the local research institutions and enterprises, namely systems of material flow, logistics, material technology, cutting manufacturing processes, quality control, operating systems and computer science.

The TZD conforms to the legal structure of a GmbH (Gesellschaft mit beschränkter Haftung, i.e. private limited company) and is managed by the city of Dortmund, the Industrie- und Handelskammer (chamber of industry and commerce), the Gesellschaft für Prozeßautomation (Society for process automation), and six credit institutes. Although the usual market rate of cost-covering rent was demanded - and this is also an important difference to most of the others centres - the TZD was already fully rented at its opening. Late in September 1987, 34 firms with a total of 206 employees were accommodated. Directly adjoining the TZD the Technologiepark Dortmund (technology park Dortmund) is being constructed.

MediaPark Köln (Cologne)

The project MediaPark Köln is an attempt to convert a railway station in the inner city, with excellent transportation facilities, into a media park. The Teleport concept, developed in the United States, was taken as its model. On the 20-hectare site a centre for information and communication technology, media production and media service, initial and continuing training, and research and development, as well as facilities for the application of new technologies in the arts is to come into existence. In addition to this, residential flats, shopping and services, as well as several recreational possibilities are to be located in the park-like environment.

Cologne is an important centre for media and communication, employing 20,000 people in these fields. Five broadcasting corporations with more than 800 employees are settled there. The arts and culture are also represented to an above average extent in Cologne. These strengths can be expanded upon by the Media-Park, thus enhancing the qualities of location, which are increasingly being demanded by modern firms in this, the "information age".

In preparing the project, the city of Cologne set up a special task force and requested four expert opinions on telecommunication enterprises, media economics, initial and continuing education as well as the arts and culture. Several workshops were held with interested enterprises and institutions and competitions took place to look for a concept for the future use of the site. Extensive initial canvassing of enterprises was undertaken and meanwhile the site was bought from the Deutschen Bundesbahn (German federal railways).

The realization of the concept and the marketing of the site is to be taken over by an Entwicklungsgesellschaft MediaPark (development company) in the form of a private limited company). Partners of this not yet founded limited company are expected to have an equal share with the city of Cologne as well as private investors and users.

To date the MediaPark Köln is, both in terms of concept and size, a still unparalleled project in the Federal Republic. The preparations are nearly completed and it will be possible to begin on realization of the project in the near future. In comparison, some other undertakings, like the Zentrum für Kunst und Medientechnologie (centre for arts and media technology) or the project to transform the harbourfront in Hamburg, following the model of the London docklands, are no further than the first conceptual considerations and/or political statements of intent.

Technologierunde Köln (Technology Round Cologne)

The Technologierunde Köln is a round of talks that was started at the suggestion of the mayor of Cologne in March 1984. It aims at discussing possible initiatives for strengthening the economic efficiency of the resident firms and for improving the attractiveness of the city of Cologne. The participants in this round of talks include about 70 persons from industry, the universities, credit institutes and insurance companies, consulting enterprises, chambers of commerce and business associations, trade unions, politics and administration. For the purpose of outlining, deepening and continuing the consultations, six working groups have been established to date which will deal with different innovation - and technology-oriented subjects.

As a result of the consultations in the working groups, the Gründer- und Innovationszentrum Köln and the Informationstechnikzentrum Köln were founded. The concept of a research and development centre for applied computer science meanwhile is included in the project MediaPark Köln. First considerations on the foundation of a company for the promotion of renewable energies have been developed further into a conception for a Zentrum für Energie- und Umweltsystemtechnik (ZEUS; Centre for energy and environmental systems engineering). The so-called Köln Promotion, i.e. the marketing of the region as the "economic centre west" has been prepared in one of those working groups.

Übungswerkstatt für Datentechnik in Norden
(Training Workshop for InformationTechnology)

The town of Norden is situated in Ostfriesland, a rural, depressed region, in which especially during the wintertime the unemployment rates reach 25 to 30%. On the initiative of the adult education centre in Norden, the Gemeinnützige Ausbildungsgesellschaft mbH (GAG; non-profit training company) was founded in 1983. The aim of the company is mainly to reduce the high youth unemployment by project-linked working and learning and to make a contribution to the structural improvement of Ostfriesland by appropriate measures of continuing training.

The GAG operates a workshop for information technology with training possibilities in the fields of office communication, commercial EDP applications, micro-electronics, production engineering, computer aided design (CAD), and software development. The training workshop, which already makes use of excellent technical equipment, is to be expanded to become a regional information technology centre in Ostfriesland. This project is centred on the concept for regional information technology centres, as developed by the Gesellschaft für Mathematik und Datenverarbeitung (GMD) in St. Augustin (near Bonn). With the help of these centres, small and medium-sized firms in particular, will have access to information processing technical know-how. Through presentation of the information technology, independently of the manufacturer, basic information, training and consultation are given. Employees of enterprises, public authorities, as well as students and private persons are trained in how to use the new technology. The firms are assisted in their choice of appropriate hardware and software suitable for telecommunications applications.

At present special centres for information technology called "tele houses" in several cities of the Federal Republic are being built with support of the GMD. The aim is to establish as large as possible a network of regional centres for information technology. In Stuttgart, Cologne, Trier, Bremen, St. Augustin and Norden those centres are already in operation. The opening of further centres in Siegen, Nordhorn, Karlsruhe and Kassel is anticipated.

Program for Personnel Transfer: "Innovationsassistant"
The best technology transfer is personnel transfer. Therefore, in Berlin the pro-

gramme for personnel transfer was developed in 1982. The aim is to procure university graduates of the engineering and economics fields as qualified specialists and managers in small and medium-sized enterprises. When engaging an "innovation assistant", the Senate of Berlin grants a subsidy of 40% of the labour costs but not more than 24,000 DM for one year. With this measure the recruitment risk of small enterprises is reduced.

Within the scope of the programme about 500 university and college graduates have been placed in firms in Berlin up till now. About four-fifths of all assistants went into firms with less than 50 employees. First evaluation studies say that above all young, technology-oriented enterprises and firms which already employ more than the average amount of graduates have been reached. The high acceptance of the programme conceals the fact that the target group aimed at most, i.e. the traditional small and medium-sized manufacturing firms in Berlin, have up to now been reached insufficiently. Nevertheless, the programme is acknowledged as having produced positive structural and employment results.

To date about 75% of the innovation assistants employed have been taken over into permanent employment by their firms after the first (subsidized) year. Numerous firms have meanwhile engaged several innovation assistants. The project as a whole is such a success and conceptionally so convincing that other states of the Federal Republic have also decided to promote a comparable programme. Meanwhile, the "Innovationsassistent" programme for personnel transfer has been extended by some new variations, e.g. "Mittelstandsassistent" (assistant for medium-sized firms), "Innovationspraktikum" (innovation traineeship), and "Praktiker-Transfer" (transfer of practical experts).

Gesellschaft für Neue Berufe in Berlin (Society for New Occupations)

Late in 1984 the enterprises Siemens and Nixdorf as well as the software and systems company PSI founded - upon the suggestion and with the support of the Senate of Berlin - a Gesellschaft für Neue Berufe (GNB; society for new occupations). The GNB qualifies graduates of secondary schools, colleges and universities as well as unemployed academics for future-oriented occupational fields. For example, a new occupation named "systems architect" is to be created.

Courses in three fields lasting 12 months (three semesters) are being offered: telecommunications, marketing/distribution and knowledge engineering. After a preparatory training to impart basic knowledge of data processing, the first semester creates the common basis for all systems architects. In the second term a specialization in the above fields takes place. The third semester, finally, is dedicated to a practical phase of several months within well-known enterprises in Berlin.

According to the concept of the GNB, the telecommunications systems architect will be responsible for the efficient structuring of network systems. The marketing/distribution systems architect will work in the marketing of technology-oriented enterprises and act as a consultant for users.

So far, experience shows that the placement rate of those leaving the GNB courses is extremely high, with about one-third of the participants being taken over by the shareholder firms of the GNB. Acceptance on the part of medium-sized businesses, for which the programme was primarily intended, seems, however, to be still relatively weak. Meanwhile other cities in the Federal Republic have also founded organizations with similar aims.

Wagnisfinanzierungsfonds der Sparkasse Siegen (Venture Capital Fund of the Siegen Savings Bank)

In 1983 a shareholding company for the promotion of innovation in the Siegerland was started by the Siegen Savings Bank. It was the first venture capital fund of a savings bank in the Federal Republic of Germany. For the promotion of new technologies and innovative products, the fund makes venture capital available to medium-sized enterprises, which have set up their business in the district of Siegen-Wittgenstein or relocated their business there. The partnership either takes the form of a silent holding or of a takeover of shares.

The multitude of inquiries has led to eight partnerships in the last four years. One of these has been sold in the meantime. At present, among the seven partnerships four have GmbH (private limited company) shares and three silent holdings. Two of the enterprises have been founded recently and five are young firms. Only two of them come from the district of Siegen, the rest relocated there - among other reasons because of the assistance. Besides its importance in terms of structural policy the fund has thus proved to be a successful canvassing instrument for regional economic policy.

Due to the very fact that it was the first venture capital fund of a savings bank in the Federal Republic of Germany, the shareholders undoubtedly carried out a rather reserved and prudent business policy, so that no failure has thus far been recorded. The success of the "Siegerlandfonds" and its public relations effect which extends beyond the region, has meanwhile caused other savings banks of the Federal Republic, though not very many, to develop similar activities. Certainly the success of the innovation fund, founded in 1982 in Berlin, played a role, too. It was the first venture capital fund initiated by a city-state, which has encouraged the foundation of numerous private venture capital companies. Today there are about 40 venture capital companies in the Federal Republic, no less than 12 of them in Berlin, with an investment capital of more than 1,000 million DM.

Technologie-Region Karlsruhe

On the initiative of the city of Karlsruhe the towns of Bretten, Bruchsal, Bühl, Ettlingen, Gaggenau, Karlsruhe and Rastatt founded as of 1 April, 1987 a non-trading partnership, named Technologie-Region Karlsruhe. The purpose of the company is the joint marketing of the economic region of Karlsruhe. Essential elements of the common presentation of the industrial location of Karlsruhe are:

1. The general promotion of the location by means of working out a homogeneous appearance (corporate design), carefully directed public relations work and target-group oriented advertising

2. Canvassing at home and abroad in close co-operation with the member communities and the regional development company of Baden-Württemberg

3. Close co-operation with other institutions promoting economic development and technology

4. Promotion of an economically and innovatively conducive atmosphere by lectures, panel discussions, regional exhibitions and congresses, information exchange fairs for entrepreneurs, study trips and competitions

The technology region Karlsruhe is financed by subsidies and apportioned costs to the members (1 DM per inhabitant). It has meanwhile been expanded to the city of Baden-Baden and the (rural) districts (Landkreise) of Karlsruhe und Rastatt. The Chamber of Industry and Commerce "Mittlerer Oberrhein" in Karlsruhe has temporarily taken over the management of the company. Apart from that a small circle of advisers exists comprised only of the chief officers of the various authorities.

The first big marketing activity of the company was a full-page advertisement in the *Frankfurter Allgemeine Zeitung* of 10 October, 1987 with the headline "Where the Future Holds the Highest Rates of Increase". The probationary period of this new form of co-operation is not yet over. It remains to be seen not only whether consensus can be reached on the marketing of the region, but also whether the local siting of the canvassed enterprises can be agreed upon.

Summary

The examples of innovation presented above show that the economic policy landscape in the Federal Republic of Germany has seen considerable activity since the beginning of the 1980s. With a lot of imagination and creativity, the local level tries to influence positively the technological and economic development of each city. This often happens through imitation of successful projects of other cities. In this context it is sometimes overlooked that such examples are not simply to be copied, but that successful practical realization requires specific local preconditions. One of the most important preconditions is the willingness for co-operation between those representing politics, the economy and science, as well as the creation of a cooperative atmosphere in an urban region. People with ideas can be found everywhere. One must only make sure that these ideas can be articulated, developed and tested.

What is necessary on the local level is a new philosophy of "public-private partnerships". Co-operation between local enterprises, the economy and science and all the relevant social groups, will lead to new insights into problems, new ideas and new measures. In addition, co-operation in partnerships in the regional context is required more than ever. In the long run those regions will be ahead which succeed in developing a sense of regionality, a "corporate identity", and in finding mechanisms of forming a consensus, which will lead to multiple local co-operative efforts and have a stimulating effect on the innovative behaviour of people.

3.4 The Development of Regional Technology Centres in Great Britain:

An Overview and Progress Report in the Context of Technology Policy in the United Kingdom

David Croome and David Hardy

In this paper we will summarize the main features of the UK government's policy on technology and innovation, show how this is reflected in the policies and objectives of the Department of Trade and Industry, and describe the Regional Technology Centre initiative as an example of how government policy is being realized.

Our presentation is offered for informal discussion as the personal view of the authors and does not represent any agreed official position. It is largely descriptive with the intention of stimulating wider interest and debate. In particular the authors will be grateful to learn of similar initiatives in other countries so that the developments of UK Regional Technology Centres (RTCs) can continue to be informed by the success (and failures) of schemes elsewhere.

The present British government, re-elected in 1987, is pledged to "continuc to pursue policies of sound financial management, the conquest of inflation, the promotion of enterprise and the growth of employment" (*Conservative Manifesto:* 9). Within this overall policy, the government is committed to "support research and development programmes, firmly directed towards areas of high national priority...drawing on the full range of advice from the academic community and from business" (*Manifesto 41*).

Several important strands run throughout government policy towards industry and these are central to the policies of the Department of Trade and Industry in "promoting enterprise". The Secretary of State, Lord Young, has recently summarized these policies as seeking to:

1. Produce a more competitive market
2. Secure a more efficient market by improving information to business about new methods and operations
3. Create a wider market
4. Increase confidence in the working of markets

These policy imperatives mean that government support for technology and innovation operates primarily where it is seen as necessary to support the market because private market decisions may not be optimum for long-term expansion of national wealth. In particular, the Department concentrates its support to overcome market reluctance to undertake long-run and / or high-risk technological developments. It supports innovation which assists the regional economic balance and, increasingly the economic structure of "inner cities".

To achieve these objectives, the Secretary of State has emphasized that the Department will encourage the transfer of technologies and co-operative research. The emphasis is on enterprise, market solutions, improving information, and the transfer of technological knowledge between industry and the Higher Education Division. The Division takes the lead for the Department in supporting the knowledge infrastructure in which business and technology can thrive. The main activities of the Division support extended awareness of technology in all parts of educational sectors and across industry. This includes the promotion of Design and Quality Schemes and a number of business advisory services.

Technology policy also recognizes the government's role in ensuring effective flows of information. The "public goods" nature of much information, the prime importance of the public sector in the provision of education and training and the high capital costs of co-ordination and disseminating information all contribute to this concern. The RTCs are one way in which the government will support the improvement of information flows. They can be best seen as an extension of the spectrum of technology transfer initiatives with which central and local governments have been involved. This spectrum includes joint industry / higher education research, science parks, industrial liaison officers in colleges, etc.

The initiative for the formation of the RTCs came from the Secretary of State for Education and Science who announced in November 1986 that they "will help regenerate British industry through the transfer of new technologies, materials and processes from the laboratory into commercial exploitation and support this with the research and training expertise of higher education". This concern was prompted by the government view that industry does not take sufficient advantage of the resources of higher education, and that more co-ordination of technology transfer is required between educational institutions and between industry and education. This has been claimed as both cause and effect of what some commentators have seen as the UK's poor performance in investment and technology relative to its competitors.

As the initiative developed, there has been increased emphasis on the regional technology centre as a co-ordination agency for the provision of training support for industry in managing the process of technical change. There will be about 12 RTCs in Scotland, Wales and England, forming a national network. The network, with its participating centres, involves at least three types of collaboration:

1. Between educational institutions in a region, with universities, polytechnics and other colleges combining to promote their resources and services for industry
2. Between the educational providers and the local industries they serve, with firms involved in setting the objectives of the RTC, providing some of the start-up resources and influencing its activities
3. Between the government departments sponsoring the initiatives including Trade and Industry, Education and Science and the Manpower Services Commission

Each RTC will have its own activity plan, but common features are that the RTC will act to:

1. Collect information about new technologies available to and required by local industry
2. Disseminate this knowledge to users in industry, commerce and education
3. Provide advice and consultancy
4. Co-ordinate and provide training and retraining appropriate to the management and operation of the new technologies introduced to industry

The RTC will co-ordinate and facilitate rather than directly provide its own courses, usually acting in an agency role. It will build from the already substantial industrial links of individual academic institutions and, in some cases, it will take over from an existing but more limited regional technology transfer agency. It will be closely involved with relevant European initiatives.

The government has provided £700,000 in start-up funds. However, to qualify for this, RTCs have had to show similar contributions from industry and education and thus total first-year funding is over £1.3 million. In keeping with the government's general policy on support for industry it is expected that the RTCs will be self-funding in three years on their share of extra income generated for their members from the extension of consultancy and training work.

It is too early to assess the operations of the RTCs. Nine have now been established and the national network is taking shape. Most RTCs are concentrating on building their information-base and marketing their activities. It will be interesting to discover if the economies of scale from co-ordination of regional technology activities will provide sufficient incentive for industry and colleges to continue to support their RTC after government funding is withdrawn. The signs are that this support will be given.

Reference

Conservative Party 1987 Election Manifesto "The Next Moves Foreward", London 1987

3.5 Industrial-Technological Complexes: A Case Study of Brazil

Marilia-Rosa Millan, Jacob Frenkel and J.G. Malcher

Introduction

The incentive to create industrial-technological complexes, regarded as environments in which the university, the research centre and the manufacturing sector are all present and working together, can be identified as one means to technological advancement in a recently industrialized country such as Brazil.

Some examples were selected and studied, employing as a methodology on-site visits and interviews with the main responsible personnel involved in the various processes. The principle projects considered were: the aeronautics complex at Sán José dos Campos; the telecommunications complex at Campinas; the science park at Sán Carlos in the State of Sáo Paulo; the technological pole at Florianópolis in the State of Santa Catarina which features microelectronics and precision mechanics; and the technological enterprise at Novo Hamburgo in the State of Rio Grande do Sul which is primarily involved with leather and footwear.

Based on our investigation, in this paper we identify the factors of success or failure which may contribute to a better understanding of the concept of industrial-technological complex, in order to be better able to indicate forms of promoting the creation of new complexes.

Technology Policy in Brazil

The technological culture of a country is a product of the evolutionary stage of its productive forces, and this includes the level attained by its scientific institutions in the technical areas. Since Brazil was chiefly an agricultural country until the beginning of World War II, its technological base was not very much developed in comparison with the progress which occurred in the countries of the centre during the first half of the present century. Thus, industrialization during that period and the accelerated industrialization which followed utilized technology obtained abroad. Such an industrialization process went through several interrelated phases the analysis and understanding of which may lead to an assessment of the present stage and thus to reflection about technology policy adequate to the country's present needs.

In summary, the interrelation mentioned above would have had to go through three phases (not necessarily sequential), two of them already concluded and the third one still in progress.

First Phase

The first phase is delimited by the industrialization which took place up to World War II and in the period which immediately followed. It may be characterized by the fact that interrelation with external technology mainly occurred through the importation of products. Not only consumer and capital goods were imported but also the human resources needed for the establishment and operation of local services.

Second Phase

The second phase took place starting in the 1950s and lasted through the beginning of the 1980s, which was the acceleration period of the industrialization process. It may be characterized by the fact that the origin of the technology employed was still external. However, the basic dynamic of this phase involved imports substitution. Gradually and sectorally, the country established its own foundations of previously imported goods, incorporating the technology available at an international level in several ways, basing itself each time less on the importation of capital goods, and increasingly investing in the transfer of foreign technological knowledge.

Third Phase

Beginning in the 1980s the third phase may be characterized by the fact that by then the country already produced most of its necessary products, both the consumer and capital goods needed for new investments. This phase is still going through its initial stages and has new characteristics, not yet sufficiently studied and clarified.

However, certain indicators can be identified:

1. Although the country still imports technology, this is no longer utilized exclusively in the internal market.
2. Several enterprises have started to compete in the external markets.
3. Sectors already consolidated have started to generate technology internally.
4. By means of explicit policies on the part of the government, through its agencies linked to technological policies, the bargaining potential of domestic enterprises is increasing vis-à-vis foreign suppliers of technology.
5. The evolving industrialization process has altered the productive forces context, not only forming a consolidated and diversified industrial base but also a block of capital whose owners are eager for new investment opportunities and profits.
6. In the new industrial sectors based as they are on knowledge areas related to high technology, such as data processing, bio-technology, chemicals and new materials, from the beginning the situation has shown its complexity with a potential for misunderstandings and difficulties that have not occurred in the previous phases.

It is possible to deduce that there are no objective conditions inviting the importation - technology transfer - full-competition cycle to again impose itself upon the already-existing structure. Thus arises the need to find new tools for a new technology policy.

The past two decades demonstrate that domestic enterprises have been increasingly intensifying their technological activities and, as a consequence, are attaining a relatively improved position in their potential power to bargain with respect to traditional technology suppliers. At present in the Brazilian case, however, only a small number of enterprises are able to incorporate R&D activities involving long-term re-imbursable investments; large government enterprises would be an example of this possibility.

Another aspect to consider is related to internal efforts of R&D activities in enterprises vis-à-vis the pace of technical progress which takes place within the sector in which the company operates. When the enterprise operates in a dynamic area, the pace of internal incorporation may not be sufficient to follow the evolution of competition. In particular, one should mention the situation of incipient or new enterprises in high-technology sectors which are strategically vital to the country's development.

It is important to define a new form of technology policy, capable of implementing in a complementary manner the human and financial resources available so that domestic enterprises may maintain and increase their competitive power in technologically more dynamic industrial sectors. It should also be emphasized that in high-technology sectors one can find all the limitations faced by new industries, including the inability to transfer substantial amounts to maintain a relative technological position, technological risks, and difficulties in acquiring suitable human resources.

Such considerations are responsible for the work that follows. A set of activities was organized to study some cases in which solutions were found through a special interrelation among several institutions, in a co-operative form, complementing resources and technology policy tools so as to make projects with high technological risks or requiring large financial amounts feasible, and in cases where institutions involved could not individually have met the goals desired. This form of co-operation was present in several forms. It usually comprised one enterprise or a group of them, one university or research institute and a specific and appropriate instrument on the part of a government institution. This new form of institutional co-operation is called an industrial-technological complex (ITC).

A sample of representative cases was selected involving traditional sectors, such as the footwear industry, and also high-technology branches, such as optical fibres and aeronautics.

Case Studies

Several cases were analysed and are the object of the descriptions which follow.

The Aeronautics Complex (Air Space Technology Centre)

The development of the air space technology centre, Centro Tecnológico Aero-Espacial (CTA/EMBRAER; Brazilian manufacturer of airplanes) should be appraised according to its time and evolution. Attempts to manufacture airplanes in Brazil date back a long time, but only in the 1940s did serious efforts get underway towards structuring an aeronautics industry in the country. Training and contacts generated the idea of creating the Aeronautics Technology Institute (Instituto Tecnológico da Aeronáutic, ITA), in Sán José dos Campos (State of Sáo Paulo), as an elite centre for training research engineers. In the 1950s, ITA's Research and Development Institute (Instituto de Pesquisa e Desenvolvimento) was created. Its aircraft department started, in 1965, the project which resulted in the construction of the first Brazilian-manufactured turbo-propelled bimotor airplane, entirely of metal: the Banderante. Such an accomplishment was possible beause the human resources trained by the ITA allowed the establishment and expansion of the CTA and, afterwards, of EMBRAER, being therefore the original nucleus of the complex which was formed later.

The establishment of the aeronautics industry in Brazil had its ups and downs. Although having the Ministry of Aeronautics support of CTA projects, as well as that of private enterprises, for some time it was not possible to consolidate the industry. In 1962, the CTA adopted a new philosophy - to develop aircraft to meet the needs of regional air transportation and, at the same time, bring renowned specialists to the project. This decision had an important effect and should be considered as fundamental, since it took the market into consideration, which is basic to any business.

At the time, the regional aircraft market for small and medium-sized airplanes was being disregarded by airline companies which concerned themselves only with the lines served by jet airplanes, creating difficulties for interregional routes. In addition, shortly thereafter came the oil crisis, imposing restrictions on the indiscriminate use of jets due to their high fuel consumption. From the standpoint of competition on the part of multinational corporations, it should be emphasized that the market was dominated by Cessna, which was not interested in the manufacture of airplanes in Brazil, since demand was very small. The other company was Piper, which later on made a licensing contract with EMBRAER, foreseeing technology transfer for the manufacture of medium-sized civilian aircraft. The fact that foreign companies were not interested in the manufacture of airplanes in Brazil was extremely helpful in the strategy adopted by CTA of taking an option on the manufacture of medium-sized aircraft, with a view to the regional transportation market in a country of the continental dimensions of Brazil.

During the 1960s, CTA personnel hired a foreign specialist on medium-sized and high-capacity aircraft to carry out the airplane design based on specifications made by the Ministry of Aeronautics. The role played by the hired specialist may be summarized as follows.

He:

1. Co-ordinated the project and put together an entirely professional staff
2. Transmitted to the CTA and its staff a mentality of always doing quality work
3. Gave reliable technical advice to CTA with regard to their capacity to design aircraft in Brazil

In the 1960s, taking into account the lack of interest on the part of domestic private enterprises with respect to aeronautics, the government created EMBRAER (in Sán José dos Campos), a mixed capital corporation, with the purpose of manufacturing aircraft in the country. (The government also utilized tax incentives with many companies in order to obtain financial resources compatible with the level of such an undertaking.) Within about ten years, it had become a large aircraft industry in terms of number of airplanes being manufactured.

During this phase two facts should be emphasized:

1. The Ministry of Aeronautics had immediately signed a contract with EMBRAER for the purchase of Banderante and Xavante airplanes, which enabled undertaking the start of the aircraft manufacture with sufficient resources.
2. The technology generated at the CTA, which originated the Banderante project, was taken to EMBRAER through a transfer of the entire staff which had worked with the foreign specialist.

Let's look at the consolidation of this industry: One can consider as the first phase of this consolidation the activities of ITA and CTA, during which technical and research capacity was formed and the CTA structured towards the study of aeronautics questions in general. The establishment of EMBRAER, as an industry, initiates the second phase and within a few years the picture changes. With the absorption of CTA personnel into the Banderante project, the success of policy adopted in the establishment of the industry, with the independence of its Projects Department and the expansion of manufacturing through licensing, with the creation of a network of enterprises manufacturing parts and equipment, and the overall success of its endeavours allowing its participation in the world market, EMBRAER consolidated itself as a large and important industry in Brazil.

Its relationship with CTA has changed and now is practically restricted to the use of aerodynamics test tunnels and the homologation of aircraft, and, naturally, to cooperative requests for occasional services originating from its own needs or the evolution of techniques requiring basic research. EMBRAER no longer depends on CTA for its projects and aircraft manufacture. Although this was basic during the first phase, at present CTA is dedicated to research of a scientific or technological nature in several fields - not necessarily of interest to EMBRAER.

As any industry, EMBRAER utilized the research institute or university in the development phase. With the establishment of the factory and the technology control required, its relationships with the research institute/university now tend to specialization or research of any type of innovation arising in the competitive market.

The Telecommunications Complex

TELEBRAS is the holding company in the telecommunications sector in Brazil under the Ministry of Communications (MINICOM). The creation of TELEBRAS in 1972 was the initial step in a long-range policy of telecommunications research and development with the objective of reducing foreign dependence in this sector. The enterprise started work in the standardization of operations, systems and services and handles the control of telecommunications as a holding of the entire system. At the time, due to the lack of an R&D and university infrastructure, TELEBRAS selected some groups with potential who had suggestions of projects of interest to the sector. Such groups received support from the company acting as technological development poles. One tried to allocate work to groups according to natural vocations. Therefore, from 1973 to 1976, several research groups in the academic area were hired for different projects: antennae and radio diffusion, temporal electronics commutation, rural telephony, semiconductors, optical fibres, data transmission and mircoelectronics.

In 1975, the industries started to participate in the company's R&D activities. One firm was contracted to develop a satellite communications antenna and others for the Brazilian standard telephone and the code pulse modulator (project of university origin). Such studies, the results obtained and the maturity acquired by the sector from 1972 to 1976, enabled the establishment of a telecommunications technology policy. Therefore, the adequate context was there for the creation by TELEBRAS of its R&D centre (CPqD) in 1976.

From its establishment, CPqD has acted systematically in the interrelationship between universities and industries, as an intermediary of the university-research institute-industry model, with the objective of providing the market with products adequate to the national situation. It should be observed that TELEBRAS controls most communications firms, including 97% of the telephone service in the country and all other public telecommunications services.

The integration of CPqD with the universities took place through support of basic or applied research of interest to TELEBRAS. Presently, there are projects involving the academic area in several sectors, including satellite communications, components materials, networks, digital transmission and optical communications. Through 1985, CPqD kept R&D contracts with more than 20 private enterprises. Among technologies already transferred to the industry, one can mention: satellite communications, digital transmission, optical communications and electronic commutation.

Originally CPqD had as a fundamental nucleus researchers from universities, especially the University of São Paulo. Its specific goals are:

1. Actions geared to the industry's maturity
2. R&D incentives aimed at the integration of the university and industrial segments
3. Assessment of national capacity
4. Bearable risk projects: outside CPqD
5. Risk projects: inside CPqD

Contacts with foreign countries are maintained through international agreements and there have been cases of technology purchase. Through international agreements some foreign experts have usually been kept at CPqD to follow up on projects or for personnel training.

The Transfer Process

Once a project has been defined and terminated it is advisable to transfer it to the industry. This process takes place after obtaining the laboratory prototype through the purchase of technology or from the beginning of the project, and the industry becomes involved by assigning its personnel to CPqD to participate in the development stage.

Thus, the contracts signed with industries are differentiated. Reimbursement is made in the form of variable royalties. Lower rates are applied when the industry invests in the project, that is, is involved in its development. Higher rates are used in the cases of technology purchase. Such policy of different rates functions as an encouragement to joint projects. Since the TELEBRAS system is monopolistic and only buys products homologated at CPqD, the interchange command is inserted in the definitions of the CPqD/TELEBRAS system. Most supplier industries in the sector are associated with large international groups; thus, the technology control of the sector is not yet internal in the country. However, the system's political objective is to gradually occupy areas through the development of domestic products at CPqD, which, once available, are purchased by TELEBRAS. This is how the market reserve concept for products is applied.

The Science Park of Sán Carlos

The Science Park of Sán Carlos, located in the State of Sáo Paulo, has as its agents the universities established there. As a consequence, the High Technology Science Park Foundation (PAqTc) of Sán Carlos, was created to act as an executor between the university and the creation or transfer of technology for enterprises.

The objective of analysing the PAqT was to observe its capacity for gathering and generating small industrial enterprises, similarly to other technology poles, with a strong link with academic research.

Created in 1985, with government support, industrial associations and the Town Hall of Sán Carlos, PAqTC seeks the conscious industrial utilization of the region's research capabilities. Both the Federal University of Sán Carlos (UFSCar) and the University of Sáo Paulo, have demonstrated substantial advancements in important knowledge areas, such as optics, mechanical and sanitary engineering, materials science and chemistry.

The background of research in Sán Carlos and its subsequent relationship with industry mainly originated in the Materials Engineering Department (DEMA-UFSCar), the Machine Tool Laboratory (LAMAFE-USP), and the Physics and Chemistry Institute of Sán Carlos (ISQSC-USP).

Materials Engineering Department

DEMA, if observed through the profile of its diversified faculty, constitutes a pioneering and innovative proposal for Brazil by developing interdisciplinary activities in the field of materials. Under its auspices research is carried out in the areas of ceramics, metallurgy and polymers, as well as of their interfaces, the "composite materials". Therefore, the importance of DEMA's research rests more in the materials engineering area than in the science of materials. On the other hand, this does not mean that there has been strong influence of this knowledge area on the department's formation.

DEMA's entire technological capacity was placed at the disposal of the productive sector and of the community since the creation of the department in 1982. This interaction occurred in two principal ways: by opening supervised training for the students at the firms and through the rendering of services.

The Machine Tool Laboratory (LAMAFE)

Since its creation in 1961 and throughout the 1960s, LAMAFE was dedicated to manufacturing and machine projects. During the following decade, with the support of government agencies, the laboratory became outstanding in tribology research, and up to now is the only such specialized group in Brazil.

The introduction of the study of tribology at LAMAFE has two aspects that should be mentioned. First, due to its interdisciplinary nature, this area of knowledge allowed a close link between research previously made in the two other conventional branches. Second, but not less important, the path was opened - already in the 1980s - to the fourth and last field of laboratory work, metrology. This means that today LAMAFE is one of the few complete research centres in the machine tool area in Brazil capable of rapidly entering the industrial automation area.

The laboratory's involvement with industry, although more recent, is being considered fundamental in metrology research. Several projects were carried out by the laboratory together with enterprises, such as cylindrical rectification of aerostatic bearing, test benches utilized in dams, devices for measuring dam deviations, hydrostatic bearing of a cylindrical rectifier headstock, pipe drillers for bridge pillars on rivers, and a project for a high-pressure hydraulic pump involving computer methods using finite elements.

The Physics and Chemistry Institute of Sán Carlos (IFQSC-USP)

Founded in 1972, the Physics and Chemistry Institute of Sán Carlos is an extension of the School of Engineering of Sán Carlos. Today, the IFQSC is composed of two departments, the Department of Molecular Chemistry and Physics and the Department of Physics and Materials Science.

The Department of Physics and Materials Science was initially dedicated to research in solid state physics, both theoretically and experimentally. Later on, new areas were included. The group consolidated itself and is now one of the most traditional in the country, working in the areas of atomic and molecular physics, solid state physics, biophysics, mathematical physics, theoretical physics and applied areas such as dosimetry, solar cells, fine films and optics.

Although several advances which possibly could have been transferred to the manufacturing sector have been made, this institute lacks the proper organizational mechanisms that would facilitate such transfers. Recently, the applied area has been concentrating on several projects of immediate applicability, including work in molecular biophysics, applied physics, growth and characterization of crystals, insulators and semiconductors, electronic instrumentation and optics. Among the areas most likely to be put to use immediately, one can mention glass and ceramics.

The High Technology Science Park Foundation of Sán Carlos (PAqTC)

In considering the background of high-technology research so far presented in the different university centres of Sán Carlos, one may observe the strategic importance of PAqTC with respect to the objective organization of the technology transfer process for domestic enterprises. Constant updating, through careful surveys of the existing potentialities, not only in the universities but also at institutes and even through independent research, seems to allow a more rational course of action in this entire process.

The foundation renders assistance to companies which may be created, providing them with basic information about legislation and their anticipated relationship with the public sector. On the other hand, the PAqTC tries to keep the research at the original institution so that no deviation from its major objectives occurs.

To date those who established the foundation continue to be linked to the extremely favourable atmosphere that exists with respect to the generation and dissemination of new technologies in Sán Carlos. Thus, historically, one notices that even before the creation of PAqTC, some companies were conceived and set up as a result of the individual initiatives on the part of former students or professors who today are at the foundation. Over the years many companies were thus created in the region now comprising the Sán Carlos Park. But of the forty enterprises which as new firms made up the basis of the foundation, ten were established after the creation of the Park, most of these in 1986 - a fact which demonstrates the dynamism of the Santa Catarina pole.

The Industrial Data Processing Complex

The Federal University of Santa Catarina (UFSC) and the School of Industrial Engineering were created in the 1960s, introducing the following concepts: obligatory training; rendering of services to industry; community integration with the school; encouragement of specialization; encouragement of training and specialiization of professors emphasizing strict post-graduate qualification.

UFSC now has a post-graduate programme in mechanical engineering, including five areas of concentration: manufacturing, projects, thermotechniques, industrial, engineering and production engineering.

Since 1975, two important events have consolidated the evolutionary process of the UFSC Mechanical Engineering Department: the technical co-operation agreement signed with the Federal Repulic of Germany and the agreement signed with a government development agency. The agreement with Germany made it possible to receive equipment and to have an exchange of professors who collaborated in the implementation of research lines, co-operation with industry and doctoral-level courses in Germany. With the resources originating from the Brazilian government, it was possible to purchase equipment, construct laboratories, and fund research and courses in the vibration and noise areas.

By the end of the 1970s the Metrology Laboratory (LABMETRO) had been created. In 1984, the Regional Foundation for Data Processing Technology was created (CERTI-SC). Among its objectives, one can mention:

1. Promotion of research making it possible to generate, adapt or install technologies according to the country's needs

2. Development of pioneering projects jointly with industries, engineering firms and the universities

3. Development of systems and products for industrial automation

4. Support of an expanded data-processing industry in the region

CERTI-Santa Catarina receives formal requests to design projects serving industrial enterprises. The link with UFSC is and will be important until the foundation is itself capable of generating the resources necessary for the purchase of tools, instruments and equipment for the execution of its activities.

CERTI-Santa Catarina's orientation is markedly connected with high-tech industrial automation, instrumentation and process control systems, and it is intimately associated with the research nuclei of the Mechanical Engineering Department of UFSC. The growing involvement of the Department with applied research of industrial interest has with time enabled a more careful selection of high-tech projects. New research groups have started to get organized, closer to these objectives, as is the case of the laboratory group working on computer-assisted engineering projects (CAD/CAE).

The experience with industry in the preparation of special projects has produced real advances in research. The maintenance of this relationship with industry has become a necessary condition of the academic performance that is being achieved by the department.

In 1986 an agreement was signed between the government of the State of Santa Catarina, the Town Hall of Florianópolis and the Federal University of Santa Catarina to establish an industrial complex, with the objective of the development of high-tech industry in Santa Catarina. The university has a strong role in providing skilled human resources and the results of new scientific and technological research. CERTI will act as a technology supplier of prototypes of industrial products and special systems of industrial automation. The complex intends to establish three distinct industrial poles:

1. The incubator Empresarial e Technológica (Entrepreneurial and Technological Incubator)
2. The Condomino de Indústrias (Condominium of Industries)
3. The Distrito Industrial (Industrial District)

Each project is analysed by CERTI and by the parties signatory to the agreements. For the technological evaluation the project content is analysed with respect to software, micromechanics, microelectronics and instrumentation. Up to the end of 1986, of 14 enterprises applying for participation with the incubator, only eight were accepted.

The Technology Centre for Leather, Footwear and Similar Items (CTCCA)

The footwear industry in the Novo Hamburgo region was started by a German-immigrant artisan. The industrial process began approximately in 1910, with the installation of cold-storage rooms for better utilization of hide. Mechanization started after World War II in the tanning establishments and footwear factories. During the 1960s the second development phase occurred, based on the importation of machines and equipment from Europe. Starting from about 1970, the substitution model of importation has strengthened the domestic industry with regard to equipment, by means of copying, a situation which still prevails.

The CTCCA is a non-profit organization which, according to its objectives and needs of the leather-footwear sector, is active in the areas of research, technical assistance, human resources development, documentation and information. The initiative to create CTCCA, successor to the Brazilian Institute of Leather, Footwear and Similar Items (IBCCA, founded in 1972), came from the Federation of Industries of the State of Rio Grande do Sul (CIERGS), and the National Service of Industrial Apprenticeship - Regional Department of the State of Rio Grande do Sul (SENAI-RS). The initial idea was put forward by the Technical School of Tanning at Estáncia Velha-RS, with the support of industrialists in the leather sector. The model used was based on the Leather Technology Centre (CTC) in Lyon, France, and similar establishments at Satra, England and in Germany.

In terms of research, CTCCA is carrying on projects in the areas of technical norms and quality standards regarding machines and implements, raw material and components, and industrial design.

Technical assistance rendered by the centre aims at the preparation of tests and issuance of technical results for the evaluation of the quality of raw materials, and final products, especially in the case of the exporting enterprises. Human resources development is attained through technical and practical courses at the centre or at the companies within the sector at their request.

Interaction between the manufacturing sector, research organs and technical schools is made on the basis of co-operative agreements. There is no formal relationship between the Federal University of Rio Grande do Sul-(UFRGS) and CTCCA. Recently, there has been a proposal for development in the graphic-computation area. There is also the possibility of joint work with CTCCA in the development of a design reader.

An industrial automation programme was begun in 1985. The first stage was based on pneumatic automation, with the direct participation of a company. The graphic-computation part is in collaboration with the UFRGS. In the PCP area there is an interchange with the UFRGS post-graduate programme in administration.

The technology generated by CTCCA is passed on gratis to the associated enterprises in cases where the resources needed for research originate from CTCCA itself or are received on the basis of funding. In cases where the CTCCA receives financing to execute new projects, the development costs are passed on to the buyer.

The CTCCA is characterized as a type of institution rendering services. The formation of enterprises fostered by the centre was not observed.

General Considerations

In addition to the cases just described other analyses were made. Based on these it immediately is clear that unlike the experience recently disclosed by the developed countries that high-tech enterprises have been established close to the universities, in the so-called science parks, the Brazilian case shows that technological parks have been only one form of what has been called the "industrial-technological complex". In fact, several forms of interrelationship have been observed between the universities, research centres and industrial sector.

It can be stated that, of the cases analyzed, the Science Park Foundation of Sán Carlos is the only complex which may be classified as an "orthodox" science park, a science park being understood as an environment whose essence is based on the existence of an academic specialization from which the enterprises can benefit, with support mechanisms to enable them to interface with the academic sector.

We discussed the significance of purchasing policies in government enterprises, which, traditionally, have always had a strong impact on the Brazilian economic environment, providing markets to new supplier companies of advanced technology, thus characterizing another type of complex. What can be observed is that research centres of these enterprises have developed products and processes that do not necessarily become part of their production. An alternative to production vertically has been to pass on the new technology to a private supplier, with a temporary guarantee. Evidently, this supplier has a different profile from the conventional enterprises since he possesses research experience which is a prerequisite to technological industrialization.

Another example we observed has been occurring in areas where conventional industries have been going through a rapid modernization process, based on development generated by the "technological co-operative associations". In several areas of conventional industrial production (such as footwear, furniture, clothing, etc.), in which there are small and medium-sized enterprises with scarce resources to carry on R&D programmes individually, several specialized technological centres have been established. With the growing participation of these industries in larger and more competitive markets (including internationally), there is now a greater modernization effort (for example, industrial automation). Some high-tech enterprises are being created in these regions in order to supply equipment (such as specialized-logic programmed controllers) to this conventional industry.

Factors of Success

The analysis presented showed that except for the leather and footwear complex, the proximity to or interrelation with an excellent university centre in technological areas is or was previously present. In the case of the aeronautics complex, there is the Aeronautics Technological Institute (ITA); in telecommunications, the University of Campinas (UNICAMP), at the Science Park Foundation of Sán Carlos, the State University of Sáo Paulo (USP) and the Federal University of Sán Carlos (UFSCar); and at the technology pole of Santa Catarina, the Federal University of Santa Catarina (UFSC). It should be pointed out that even at the Technological Co-operative Centre of Novo Hamburgo (CTCCA), the academic sector seeks contact, even if this is not done systematically. One could expect that in the future such a relationship will become more intense due to the urgency of modernization processes neccessary for the maintenance of competitiveness (that is, the introduction of automation processes) that will occur in the conventional leather and footwear sector.

Considering that the complexes described have been relatively successful, one may conclude that the presence of an excellent university centre in technological areas is an important agent in the complex. It should be observed that other experiences made or still underway in the country have had difficulties to consolidate in the absence of the "academic agent".

Another element common to practically all experiences described here seems to be the existence of a research centre mediating the transfer process to the industrial sector. Evidence can be observed in the role played by the Air-Space Technology

Centre (CTA) in the aeronautics industry; the role of TELEBRAS' research centre (CPqD) in telecommunications; the role of most specialized university laboratories (even if not isolated research centres) not only in the San Carlos park model but also as in the technology pole of Santa Catarina; and, finally, the role of the CTCCA in meeting the requirements of the leather and footwear industry. This means that the presence of an agent which can be characterized as an intermediary element in the process of support to technology transfer to the productive sector, either a research centre or specialized university laboratories, provides another indication of success with respect to ongoing experiences.

Another success indicator even if not noticed explicitly in all examples seems to be the different forms of contact with foreign countries. This is a dominant factor in the case of the aeronautics industry. As far as the data-processing experience is concerned this was also fundamental for the establishment of the industry manufacturing personal computers designed in the country. In both cases, specialists in pertinent matters were hired to work at the Air Space Technological Centre (CTA), in the case of aircraft, and at the University of São Paulo (School of Engineering), in the case of personal computers. In the other situations described, there is a natural contact made by the universities - training abroad, visiting professorships - and at the TELEBRAS' research centre (CPqD), with an almost permanent utilization of foreign resident consultants. At Santa Catarina, one could mention the agreement signed with a German institution for the establishment of the Regional Centre for Data-Processing Technology (CERTI).

The government's purchasing power is an objective factor which contributed effectively to the success of the aeronautics and telecommunications complexes, besides others, such as the oil complex that is not being described in this document.

In this analysis the first approach identified several factors which strongly contributed to the success of the experience related to the establishment of industrial-technological complexes:

1. The presence of an excellent university centre as agent in technological areas

2. The presence of the research centre or specialized university laboratories as agent

3. The contacts made with foreign centres in different forms

4. The presence of government purchasing power

These factors lead to an attempt to classify the different forms by which the complexes in the country are expressed, including:

1. The conventional science park model (São Paulo),

2. The model with a government research centre as its nucleus (aeronautics, telecommunications)

3. The model with a technological co-operative centre as its nucleus (leather and footwear, the Santa Catarina pole)

Difficulties

Some of the difficulties identified in the several experiences observed include:

1. The relationship of the university researcher with respect to participation in enterprise projects

2. The relationship between enterprises and the university

3. The acquisition of governmental support for research in high-tech enterprises

Conclusions

Even though the analyses presented have an exploratory character and, as a consequence, are preliminary, it can be stated that it has been observed that the initiatives of an innovative character, especially through the creation of high-tech enterprises, have not always received the necessary support from government agencies involved in technological development. The diffusion of advanced technologies is very recent in Brazil and the number of projects of this nature have started to multiply only in the past few years. Financing so far has been an instrument of limited efficiency with respect to incentives given to such initiatives and government agencies involved with development lack the appropriate support mechanisms.

The agencies have traditionally supported universities and technological research institutes through the management of federal resources. In parallel, the enterprises' own resources are utilized to finance R&D efforts. Even if there is an incentive for co-operation between enterprises and research entities, through differentiated interest rates, in fact not many are thus supported. Therefore, public institutions supporting the development of advanced technologies in recently industrialized countries should find original and more appropriate solutions to their specific realities to deal with high-tech enterprises within the framework of several existing complexes.

In summary, to overcome the present situation of relative technological handicap in which Brazil finds itself, especially at the level of insufficient capacity in the areas of product and process engineering, requires definition of incentive policies to increase technological efficiency in the industrial-technological complexes in general and in particular to support initiatives of an innovative character.

3.6 Innovation-Oriented Policy on the Regional Level as Well as in Border Areas of Southern Germany

Holger Haldenwang

The Problem

Research and development, new technologies and innovations increasingly are determining factors for the economic development of the nation. This applies to the regional level as well. High achievements in science and innovation are required in order to maintain international competitive power, qualified, crisis-proof jobs and a high standard of living.

The initial conditions for technological progress are a lot more favourable in agglomerations. This can be seen in the spatial allocation of university and non-university research facilities as well as of public funds for the promotion of science and technology in business enterprises. In particular project promotion by the federal Minister for Science and Technology tends to the "suitable" businesses, whose research facilities are most often located in agglomerations. In the rural regions, with their weaker structures and high rate of small and medium-sized enterprises (SMEs), there are clearly less favourable conditions for research and development.

Borderland and regional development policy must of necessity accommodate the goals of creating equal conditions of life and labour and of preferentially promoting the "Zonenrandgebiet" (area along the border between East and West Germany), and influence the development of technology in a spatial way, thereby reducing existing disparities between agglomerations and rural regions and avoiding new ones.

With regard to providing the population in rural regions with suitable infrastructures the situation has improved considerably. But, as before, there are still considerable differences in earnings, compared with the metropolitan areas. In the borderland regions and the regions with mostly weaker structures, unemployment, as a rule, is higher, the quality of jobs available and average incomes are lower than in the well-structured regions. As a reaction to the unfavourable conditions of employment in the weaker regions, about 10% of the younger generation moves away every year; the percentage of the well-educated moving away is likely even a little higher. This young work force is no longer available to the local job market, even though these regions in particular would need qualified workers, in view of the innovation potential that has to be increased.

Borderland and regional development policy, therefore, to accomodate a balanced job and population trend, must show interest in the spatial shaping of research and technology policy.

Because of the lower rate of mobility, compared with the 1960s, today's possibilities of bringing new jobs into the structurally weak and peripheral regions "from the outside", with the help of the traditional promotion of settlement, are limited. The regional policy, therefore, to continue to be successful, has to direct more of its attention towards the resident businesses and develop their competitive power and expansion. At the same time, the innovation-relevant regional infrastructure in the field of research and development has to be activated and extended as far as need be.

The spatial dimension of technology development and innovation support is mostly still being ignored in research, innovation and technology policies. This is, among other things, substantiated in the Federal Republic of Germany by the various reports of the federal government, like the ones on regional planning, the promotion of microelectronics, and the information and communication technologies of 1984.

The federal Minister for Regional Planning, Building and Urban Development had already picked up the subject of innovation, technology and spatial development in the 1970s and in the course of his "Mittelfristige Forschungsprogramm Raumordnung und Städtebau" (MFPRS, midterm research programme on regional policy and city planning) delivered several opinions.

The results of these examinations can only partially be applied to the situation in Bavaria. They either originate from surveys on isolated cases or relate to types of regions that e.g. summarize the rural areas of all states. Therefore, the special structural conditions in Bavaria are only taken into consideration in exceptional circumstances. The research studies that were ordered by the federal Minister for Regional Planning, Building and Urban Development have also shown that the results are more useful the more the economic and business structure of the examined area is standardized.

In order to obtain statements as accurately as possible for rural and peripheral regions in Bavaria, with justifiable expenditure, the region of East Bavaria, which is predominantly regarded as a structurally weak region, was chosen and examined, regarding innovation potential, innovation performance and innovation requirements.

In our definition, East Bavaria covers the administrative areas of Niederbayern and Oberpfalz. This area is mainly identical with the areas within the jurisdiction of the Industrie- und Handelskammer Regensburg and the Industrie- und Handelskammer für Niederbayern in Passau (Chambers of Industry and Commerce in Regensburg, and for Niederbayern in Passau). The delimitation of the regions Oberpfalz-Nord, Regensburg, Donau-Wald and Landshut, also provides a spatial correspondence - with the exception of the Mainburg/Kehlheim region and a small area in Oberpfalz.

The starting points for this study were the following questions:

1. How great are the differences in the innovation activity between big metropolitan areas and rural areas? What standing does East Bavaria have in such a nationwide comparison?

2. Can the reasons for the existing innovation gaps be led back to the influence of the structures of branch and business sizes, location factors, specific information bottlenecks or behaviour patterns, and how great is the influence in each case?

3. Which of the "new technologies" are especially important for the rural areas, regarding the local branch structures and company sizes? Can specific directions for technology development and distribution be determined in East Bavaria?

4. What is to be expected for the rural areas and especially East Bavaria under the assumption of a technology development and innovation activity, not influenced by regional policy?

5. How important are the research and technology policies as well as the education and campus politics for the regional innovation activity?

6. Are there possibilities for East Bavaria, through more extensive use of research and development capacities, to obtain a bigger part of the local, qualified potential of wages earned as well as to secure or create future-oriented jobs?

7. What initiatives as part of an innovation-oriented borderland and regional development policy seem to be appropriate, in order to develop the existing production facilities and to widen the innovation and information potential? How can the emergence of additional disparities, based on an unbalanced spatial distribution of new technologies, be avoided?

Procedure

First Partial Report

Based on an extensive analysis of the literature, the empirically verified differences in innovation between the metropolitan areas and the rural and peripheral regions were identified and the reasons for the differences in innovation brought out. The expected development under the present conditions was derived from that and evaluated.

The application and the distribution of new technologies was investigated in detail using the example of telecommunications. Furthermore, the generally determined results for the rural areas were compared with the specific situation of East Bavaria, as it appears in the available data on structure; clues for explanation of the low innovation performance in East Bavaria, compared with the metropolitan areas, were extrapolated from this comparison. A list of hypotheses that seemed appropriate for a survey with written interviews was formulated.

Second Partial Report

The next step was to interview East Bavarian businesses (written interviews). The results were given to experts in economics and administration, along with suggestions for a strengthening of the innovation potential, in order to be able to estimate their plausibility and the acceptability of possible measures.

Third Partial Report

From the results of the expert interviews and the knowledge of the innovation situation in East Bavaria, a catalogue of measures was derived that seemed suitable for an intensification of the innovation performance and that would have a positive effect on the economic development of East Bavaria.

Terms and Data Fundamentals

In this study all new products that are developed in a company as well as all technical improvements of products that have been already launched on the market (product innovations) and all technical improvements of the business's internal production or distribution system (process innovations) are called innovations.

Regional development policy is a policy that covers more than one subject, according to the regional economic planning law, which in the interest of a balanced development of the region and an efficient use of means has the task of co-ordinating the planning and measures that are important for the region. The goal of regional development policy is to create or preserve equivalent healthy living and working conditions in all parts of the state. Within the regional development policy, the development of the rural areas and the favoured strengthening and promotion of the "Zonenrandgebiet" and the structurally weak regions are of great importance.

The most important facts in this study were gleaned from written interviews with 207 companies in the manufacturing sector in East Bavaria. It was a representative sample of the 3101 companies that belong to the Industrie- und Handelskammer Regensburg and the Industrie-und Handelskammer für Niederbayern in Passau. Therefore, the survey, that was carried out in the spring of 1985, had a sampling fraction of nearly 7%; 87.4% of the interviewed businesses were independent and 12.6% were subsidiary plants or branches of non-regional firms.

In the description of nationwide regional differences in innovation, our report refers to the survey of the Fraunhofer Institut für Systemtechnologie und Innovationsforschung (ISI; Fraunhofer Institute for Systems Technology and Innovation Research), Karlsruhe, with the title "Erfassung regionaler Innovationsdefizite"(1) (Registration of regional innovation deficits). This survey basically relies upon two sources for data:

1. Data on about 8200 SMEs that conduct research and development and have participated in the federal wage subsidies programme for research and development

2. Data from the survey, carried out by the Kreditanstalt für Wiederaufbau (KfW) in co-operation with the ISI, on 325 SMEs, that have participated in the KfW programme

---

(1) Published as: Heft 06.054 in "Schriftenreihe des Bundesministers für Raumordnung, Bauwesen und Städtebau", Bonn 1984.

The data of the ISI survey are limited to SMEs with less than 1000 employees or with an annual turnover of less than 150 million DM that have participated in public programmes for the encouragement of innovation. The ISI proceeds on the assumption that about 70% to 80% of all businesses that conduct research and development are contained in their data. The ISI data refer to enterprises, while the data of our written interviews refer to firms. This difference has to be taken into consideration when it comes to the comparison of the ISI results with those of our interviews for East Bavaria.

Regional Differences in Innovation

The analysis of regional differences in innovation results from different indicators that have been checked for the Federal Republic of Germany for the first time in the ISI study. The most powerful indicators were chosen from the ISI catalogue, containing 25 indicators. They were presented with their special points for East Bavaria and enriched with the results of our own interviews as well as with government statistics.

Innovation Density

The indicator "innovation density" serves as a description of the innovation potential of a region; it positions the innovating businesses of a region in relation to the total number of businesses in the region. The share of innovating SMEs in the nation is about 16.4%, in the highly compressed regions it is about 19.4% and in the rural areas it is about 10.6%. The equivalent figures for East Bavaria are 11.4% for the Oberpfalz-Nord region, 15.8% for the region of Regensburg, 12.2% for the Donau-Wald region and 13.6% for the region of Landshut. Compared with that, Munich, with its share of 22.8%, is way above the national average.

The actual innovation differences between metropolitan areas and rural regions should be even higher than shown in the comparison of these innovation-density figures because the more innovating large-scale enterprises, that are mostly located in the metropolitan areas, are not covered by the ISI study.

Personnel Density in Research and Development

Similar restrictions are also valid for the indicator "personnel density in research and development", where the staff in research and development is set in relation to the total number of employees. Based on the results of the ISI survey, the personnel density in metropolitan areas is 4.7%, while it is 3.9% in rural regions. According to our survey, the personnel density in East Bavaria is only 1.9% and thus far below the average for all rural areas in the nation.

About 60% of the interviewed East Bavarian businesses indicate that they have employees who are developing or improving products or production methods. Compared with that, internal research and development is conducted by an average rate of about 70% of the businesses in the metropolitan areas and by about 65% in the rural areas nationwide.

Qualifications of Employees in Research and Development

According to the ISI study, the share of university/college graduates in the field of research and development is about 25% in the national average.

According to the results of the interviews in East Bavaria, the percentage of scientists in the field of research and development is about 30% and therefore above the national average. But the low personnel density of 1.9% in research and development also has to be taken into consideration.

Use of External Innovation Channels

Businesses can either conduct research and development themselves, or they can use research and development results that were acquired from outside the company. Some of the most important "external innovation channels" are:

1. Purchase of usufructuary rights and licences
2. Placing research and development orders with other businesses and research facilities
3. Use of results of joint industrial research
4. Purchase of innovative production facilities

In the national average, approximately 30% of the businesses use external innovation channels. In rural regions, the percentage of such businesses is about 34%, the purchase of innovative production facilities is especially crucial there.

The results of the interviews in East Bavaria indicate that the industrial plants buy external know-how to a large degree there, too, since internal research and development is conducted to a lesser degree. About 22% of the interviewed businesses have purchased usufructuary rights and licences. Also suggestions from employees, customers, suppliers and friendly firms are picked up to a large extent. But research in co-operation with other firms or facilities is very rare.

Innovation Level

This indicator covers the share of turnover of new products on the market. The East Bavarian industrial enterprises declare, that about 14% of their sales in the years 1983/1984 involved newly developed products. This is, compared with the results of the ISI study, an average rate. Approximately 37% of the East Bavarian industrial enterprises have launched new products and about 65% have launched improved products on the market in that period. Process innovations were carried out by less than two-thirds of the East Bavarian industrial enterprises during the last couple of years. A little more than half of the industrial enterprises spend less than 2% of their turnover on production and process innovation.

Applications for Patent

The proportion of businesses with applications for patents is, according to the ISI study, almost 33% in agglomerations, a little less, namely 30%, in the rural regions. The proportion of businesses with applications for patents is, according to the results of our written interviews, a lot lower in East Bavaria: Less than 12% of the businesses have applied for a patent.

All indicators show a wide gap in innovation between the regions with big agglomerations and the rural regions. The figures for East Bavaria are not only below comparable figures for agglomerations, but also below the nationwide average for rural regions.

Causes for Regional Differences in Innovation

A considerable part of the regional differences in innovation can be put down to structural factors (different structure of branches and company sizes). Also, "innovation bottlenecks" play an important role in the fields of personnel, financing and information.

Structure of Branches and Company Sizes

According to the ISI study, differences in the regional innovation potentials can partly be explained by different branch and company sizes. For example, the national average of innovating companies in construction and electrical engineering lies at over 40%. In East Bavaria the percentage of employees in the field of electrical engineering, compared with the total number of employees in the manufacturing sector, is below average. It amounts to only 16.7%, compared with 35.4% in Mittelfranken, for example. However, the percentage of employees in the general and luxury food sector in East Bavaria is above average with 7.3% (compared with Mittelfranken, with 4.4%).

Using the branch figures for the whole nation, "structure-adjusted" figures can be determined for the single regions. This leads to a reduction of differences in the innovation density. For the region of Oberpfalz-Nord, for example, the adjusted innovation density climbs from 12.2% to 13.4%. The comparable figure for Munich falls from 22.8% to 16.2%, when adjusted.

The differences in the structure of enterprise or business sizes explain less than the different structure of branches: Case studies have shown that different size structures explain about 5% to 10% of the differences in the innovation density between different regions.

Also beyond the direct effect of structures of branches and business sizes, the structure of branches influences the innovation performance. If, for example, only a few companies in the field of "key technologies" (i.e. communications technologies, construction and electrical engineering) are located in a region, there usually are also few complementary facilities, like planning agencies, consulting and engineering firms, technical laboratories, etc. This again has effects on the innovation behaviour of the resident companies in other branches. Such regions lack the advantages of contacts.

Personnel

The ISI study comes to the conclusion that only few businesses in rural areas see personnel problems as innovation bottlenecks. Contrary to that, the difficulties of getting highly qualified and specialized personnel in agglomerations are more commonly regarded as an impediment to innovation. As an explanation for these differences it is stated that businesses in a rural area need a lower rate of highly qualified personnel for their innovation. They predominantly recruit the staff for research and development jobs from their own company and acquire externally available know-how, mainly through the purchase of innovative production assets.

The interviewed businesses of East Bavaria do not regard personnel problems as a decisive innovation bottleneck either. The question "Where do the decisive hindrances or bottlenecks for the development or improvement of products and production methods lie in your company?" was answered with "Our employees are not qualified enough" by only 22.3% of the businesses, but 49.3% replied: "The market trend is too uncertain".

Financing

The interviews of the ISI study revealed that nearly one-fourth of SMEs have financing problems. Therefore, important innovation projects can not be started at the proposed time and/or can not be carried out in the required period of time or to the extent required. The other businesses did not state any, or only a few financing problems, and these did not have great influence on the innovation activity. Differences between metropolitan and rural areas were not detectable for the identification of businesses with financing problems.

Cost risk and the financing of innovations are of greater significance for the interviewed East Bavarian businesses than for those in rural areas nationwide. One-third of the businesses see insurmountable problems in the financing of product or process innovations. The cost risk is too high for almost 45% of the interviewed businesses.

Information

According to the ISI study, the acquisition of information on market potential is the most-mentioned hindrance for innovation. Businesses that rarely acquire information reckon with the fact that they only carry out developments when customers want them to or with the fact that they are working without rivals in a market alcove and therefore have a secure position.

Lack of information on long-term technical economic trends was seen as an innovation bottleneck by only a few businesses. The principle reason apparently lies in the fact that businesses mainly espouse development solutions that are practicable within a short period and, in addition, that are limited to the existing production range.

Information problems on the market trend are also the most-mentioned hindrances for innovation among the interviewed East Bavarian industrial enterprises. About 77% of the companies made this statement. The East Bavarian companies prefer talks with suppliers, manufacturers' agents and the exchange of experiences with other companies as information. Industrial magazines, technical books, patent filings as well as fairs, exhibitions, seminars and congresses are of lesser importance. Systematically conducted market research, like market and customer surveys, is conducted to a lesser degree. Counselling services, like the Ostbayrische Technologie-Transfer-Institut (OTTI; East Bavarian Technology Transfer Institute) or the Landesgewerbeanstalt are also used to a lesser extent by the interviewed businesses. The written interviews and the expert interviews show that a systematic acquisition of information only occurs in very few East Bavarian companies. Instead, the more randomized gathering of information by the company owner is the rule.

Innovation-Relevant Infrastructure

The appropriate reports of the government (regional planning reports, research reports, etc.) testify to a clear concentration of universities/colleges as well as public (Institutes of the Max Planck Society and the Fraunhofer Society) and private, non-university research and development facilities in the metropolitan areas. This is also the case with the regional dispersion of information bureaus and advisory boards. Most specialized information bureaus and data banks have their location in metropolitan areas. A spatial concentration in metropolitan areas can also be seen, regarding exhibitions, fairs and patent-specification bureaus.

Against this background of facilities that are unfavourable for the rural regions, the situation of East Bavaria can be described as follows:

1. East Bavaria has two universities and two colleges, which is favourable, regarding the nationwide distribution.
2. The University of Regensburg, that started its lectures and research in 1967, represents the largest scientific centre in East Bavaria with its 1700 employees. But the share of students in research and development-intensive scientific

subjects, compared with the total number of students, is only about one-fourth and therefore way below the rate at the universities / colleges in Munich or Erlangen/Nürnberg.

3. With the University of Passau, the administrative district of Niederbayern received its own scientific research facility. With the establishment of the faculty for mathematics and computer science in 1983, the first step into the field of science was taken.

4. The fact that neither of the two East Bavarian universities offer technical studies is to be seen as a drawback, with regard to innovation. Furthermore, there are no contact points for research and know-how transfer that organizationally and from the viewpoint of personnel would fit the needs of modern requirements.

5. The more practical-oriented colleges in East Bavaria (Regensburg and Landshut) offer more favourable possibilities for co-operation with SMEs. An example is the establishment of a CAD / CAM laboratory at the College of Regensburg.

6. There are practically no non-university or private research facilities in the East Bavarian region. The number of free-lance consulting firms is very low, compared with Munich or Nürnberg.

7. It is mainly the local branches and agencies of the Landesgewerbeanstalt and the OTTI that take the place of contact points and information bureaus in East Bavaria. Furthermore, regional advisory boards are run by the Chambers of Industry and Commerce and the Chambers of Handicrafts.

8. Larger fairs and congresses with a technological orientation rarely take place in East Bavaria. The University of Regensburg and the Chambers offer a limited range of events of importance for innovation activity.

Use of the Innovation-Relevant Infrastructure
About 8% of the interviewed East Bavarian companies stand in close contact and about 12% in loose contact with universities. It appears that there are more and closer contacts with universities outside East Bavaria. That can, on the one hand, be explained by the fact that some company owners have studied outside East Bavaria and kept up the contacts they made there. On the other hand, the lack of technical fields (for example, engineering science) at the universities of Regensburg and Passau has a hindering effect.

The regional orientation towards the colleges of Regensburg and Landshut is a lot stronger. About 6% of the companies are in close and 16% are in loose contact with the College of Regensburg.

About 80% of the interviewed East Bavarian companies do not have any contacts with university and non-university research facilities. The most -mentioned reasons were:

1. The branch or the production plan of the company does not enable such co-operation.
2. There is generally no need for co-operation.
3. The universities / colleges are out of step with practice.
4. There is a lack of information on fields of co-operation and contacts.

The unwillingness of the East Bavarian businesses to co-operate with universities/colleges could also be structurally conditioned. While about 75% of the businesses in the electronics industry, which is under-represented in East Bavaria, think that the use of the CAD / CAM laboratory at the College of Regensburg is important, this is so for only 35% of the businesses in the building trade, which is over-represented in East Bavaria.

The following results of the survey seem to be of importance for future co-operation between middle-level companies and the East Bavarian universities / colleges:

1. About half of the interviewed companies see the absence of contact persons as the main hindrance for co-operation with East Bavarian universities / colleges.
2. Only about one-third of the businesses think that the proximity of universities / colleges is important for their product or process innovations.
3. The businesses see the biggest chance for co-operation in the acquisition of additional information on technological trends and in consultation and assistance during periods of adaptation to new technologies.
4. More than two-thirds of the businesses consider the solving of management problems as an important starting point for a possible co-operation with the East Bavarian universities / colleges.
5. Only a few of the East Bavarian businesses attach importance to co-operation with students or graduates under the guidance of professors and teachers.

Regional Effectiveness of Research, Technology and Innovation Policy

Research and technology policy in the Federal Republic of Germany is primarily conducted by the federal government. In principle this policy is not regionally oriented. On the one hand, it covers a considerable promotion of "key industries" (electronics, data processing, nuclear energy, aeronautics). In these fields the innovation performance is high. The knowledge that is acquired there is supposed to trigger innovation processes in other production fields. The promotion of this main point of the programme is mostly to the advantage of the big companies in the metropolitan areas. The East Bavarian businesses only received 1% of the 1.3 billion DM that went to Bavaria within the scope of that programme in the years 1978/1980, while the companies in the metropolitan area of Munich received 77%.

Two other federal promotion programmes, even though they have fewer resources to spare, at least have the tendency of working against discrimination in favour of the metropolitan areas in research and technology policy:

1. Since the enactment of the "Gesamtkonzept zur Förderung von Forschung und Entwicklung in kleinen und mittleren Unternehmen" (Masterplan for the promotion of research and development in small and medium-sized enterprises) in 1978, the Ministry for Science and Technology has given more regard to SMEs. Here the contract research and pilot projects for advice on innovation are of special significance.

2. In 1979 the Ministry for Economic Affairs launched a programme that provides financial aid to compensate some of the expenses for research and development personnel in SMEs. This programme, with its financial resources in the range of 1.5 billion DM, mainly helps businesses in the rural regions.

In Bavaria, the federal programmes are being complemented by the aimed-at SMEs "Technology-Beratungs-Programm" (Technology Advisory Programme) and the "Bayerische Innovationsförderungsprogramm" (Bavarian Programm for the Encouragement of Innovation). Nearly 1200 items of advice on technology were sponsored by the "mittelständische Technologie-Beratungs-Programm", by defraying their losses with subsidies of 3.4 million DM; 1.4 million DM were available for supplemental measures. Almost two-thirds of the sponsored businesses were located in the borderland, structurally weak and other rural areas. In addition to the existing contact points at the Landesgewerbeanstalt Bayern and in the Chambers of Commerce, university teachers at ten Bavarian universities were named as contacts for industry. Also, technology transfer centres were established at the Universities of Munich, Erlangen/Nürnberg and Bayreuth and contact units were established in some non-university research facilities.

The "Bayerische Innovationsförderungsprogramm", that was started in 1981, promotes projects for the development of new products and methods, that are technologically and economically promising and therefore of importance for the national economy. With the help of this programme the innovation strength of the SMEs has improved, where their own equity has been insufficient for the realization of new ideas. In 1983/1984 the programme provided almost 16 million DM for 32 projects; 11.3 million DM went to the metropolitan areas, 1.4 million DM to the borderland and structurally weak areas and 2.9 million DM to the other rural regions. East Bavaria received about 3% of the funds.

The spatial allocation of funds from the "Bayerische Innovationsförderungsprogramm", since it is not an instrument that is oriented towards regional policy, reflects the regional differences in the innovation potential of the SMEs. The supernormal innovation efforts of the SMEs in the field of microelectronics in the metropolitan areas are especially reflected here.

Furthermore, the state provides a number of support programmes for Bavarian businesses, from which, under various conditions, money can also be requested for the strengthening of the companies' innovation performances. The interviewed East Bavarian businesses are familiar with these programmes to varying extents and they are called upon in varying degrees.

The interviewed East Bavarian businesses valued the following promotional measures as being especially important for the increase of innovation performance (given in the order of frequency named):

1. Investment grants

2. The GRW programme (Gemeinschaftsaufgabe "Verbesserung der regionalen Wirtschaftsstruktur", joint project for the "improvement of the regional economic structure")

3. The "Bayerische Mittelstandsförderungsprogrammem" (Bavarian programme for the promotion of middle-level businesses)

4. The "Bayerische regionale Förderprogramme" (Bavarian regional support programme)

5. The Credits from the European Recovery Program (ERP) funds

6. The "Bayerische Darlehensprogramm für Maßnahmen zur Luftreinerhaltung, Lärmschutz und Abfallwirtschaft" (Bavarian loan programme for measures to maintain clean air, protection against noise pollution, and waste management)

7. The special depreciation for research and development investments

The "Programm zur Förderung der externen Vertragsforschung" (programme for the support of external contract research), projects promotion by the Minister for Science and Technology and the "Programm zur Forschungskooperation" (programme for research co-operation) are less familiar to East Bavarian industry.

These results, for the rate of familiarity with (and use of) programmes for the encouragement of innovation, on the basis of the interviews with East Bavarian businesses, can be supplemented with the statement of the ISI study, that financial measures alone can not induce businesses to conduct internal or external research and development and to carry out technical innovations. Appropriate effects can, to a certain extent, be achieved with the help of innovation advice. But it can also be seen here that it is very difficult to reach SMEs without their own research and development, especially in regions with weaker structures.

Under present conditions, substantial changes in the regional allocation of innovation potential and innovation performance are not expected in the near future. This means that improvements concerning the innovation conditions for the rural and peripheral areas require well-aimed measures.

Telecommunications as an Example of the Use and Distribution of New Technologies

Possibilities and Opportunities for Rural Areas

The development of inexpensively producible microprocessors and the installation of extremely efficient communications networks have persistently changed the possibilities of information processing and communications in the past couple of years. Through the fusion of telecommunications and computer science into what has been called "telematics", new possibilities are being opened up that can have extreme effects on some regions.

There is disagreement among scientists about the expected regional effects. While supporters of the decentralization thesis expect the new technologies to bring more business activities and qualified jobs into the rural areas, others express the opinion that the new technologies will not spread any further than the border zones of the agglomerations. Another opinion that is often heard these days states that the new technologies will only have a very limited regional effect. Long-term developments that take place anyway are being supported: Depending on whether the technologies meet the tendencies of centralization or decentralization, they will be intensified.

We represent the opinion that the new communications technologies, with their technical possibilities, can contribute to the setting off of new activities. Against the background of the previously mentioned goals of regional planning policy this means that indeed there are opportunities for decentralization:

1. If SMEs in the rural regions could also be connected to data banks and centres for specialized information, and if information would be available everywhere without loss of time, the advantages of the agglomerations would be decreased.

2. The spatial unity of divisions that are connected by the intensive flow of information will not be of essential importance anymore, if new communications technologies are used. Thereby decentralized development and production locations are made possible, like the decentralized production control or teletype setting in the publishing industry.

3. The presently existing unity of the production centre and the individual work-place will be made unnecessary in many branches: information-processing jobs, for example, can be shifted to the livingroom.

4. At least a portion of the services that are still exclusively being offered in centralized places will soon be available everywhere. The best-known examples are "home banking" and "tele-shopping", which provide the possibilities of shopping and carrying out credit transfers from the livingroom.

If this decentralization potential of the new communications technologies comes to fruition, a wide range of effects on the regional structure become imaginable. The rural areas could make up the disadvantages of "living in the green". Disadvantages like the distances could be compensated with the new communications technologies and there would still be advantages for the rural regions regarding leisure activities and environmental amenities. This could lead to a change of location preferences for companies.

Whether the indicated opportunities for the rural areas can be utilized, basically depends on four conditions:

1. The expansion of area-covering, qualitatively equivalent telecommunications networks in cities and rural areas

2. The fact that no discrimination against rural areas takes place in the expansion of the new technologies

3. Analysis of the present state and of the status quo

4. Presence of telecommunications networks and services

The West German telecommunications networks, outside of businesses and households, are run by the German Federal Postal Administration. Presently there are three concomitant networks:

1. The normal telephone network (analogue technology), with over 24 million connections

2. The integrated text and data network (digital technology, IDN), with over 265,000 connections, covering Telex, Teletex, Datex-L and Datex-P

3. Local broad-band distribution networks for the transmission of radio and television programmes

The postal administration plans to expand and combine these networks in three steps. In a first phase, that has already begun, the analogue telephone system is being converted into a digital system. This enables the combination of the telephone and IDN networks into an "ISDN" network with which data and texts can be transmitted very quickly, using the already-installed copper cables. This way several services can be used at the same time. Experts expect considerably improved interfaces between the internal and external information fields of businesses from these innovations. Signs pointing in that direction can already be seen in the use of Btx (videotext). But the digitalizations will not be completed until after the year 2000. There is going to be an expansion of the broad-band distribution networks with copper-coxial technology for cable television and radio. By the mid 1990s, 80% of German households are supposed to be connectable. Furthermore, the postal administration wants to offer person-to-person connections with glass fibre cables, where needed, which will make make new services possible, like "video phone", "video conferences", fast transfer of documents and data, etc. The instalment of a glass-fibre connection between Hamburg, Hannover, Bonn, Frankfurt, Stuttgart and Munich has already begun.

In the second phase, beginning in 1990, the combining of the ISDN and the glass-fibre networks into a broad-band ISDN network is planned. In a third phase, which is to start in the 1990s and should reach far into the next millenium, the transfer to the "Breitbanduniversalnetz" (IBFN; universal broad-band network) is planned, whereby all sorts of individual and mass communications are to be possible.

Regarding the goals of regional development policy, the status and development of the telecommunications networks and services are to be judged as follows: Regional disadvantages with the presently existing networks are not as much caused by the availability of the communications-technical infrastructure, as by the existing structure of charges. The telephone network covers all areas. The only disadvantage for rural areas, regarding the text and data network (IDN), is the long waiting period for the installation of a connection. On the other hand, a long-distance call (over 100 km) of eight minutes length is 40 times as expensive as a local call of the same length.

With development of the networks, the regional gaps will broaden in the same way, whereby development in the agglomerations progresses faster than in the rural regions. According to the present plans of the postal administration, the rural regions will receive ISDN relatively late, because the postal service will first work on the metropolitan areas. This also goes for the other phases. Thus, discrimination against the rural regions, regarding the structure of charges, will continue.

The expansion of the copper-cable broad-band network has the tendency of favouring the metropolitan areas. By 1987, according to the plans of the German Federal Postal Administration, the degree of provision will rise to 32% in Bavaria. Then the region of Munich, for example, will be provided with cable connections to 51%, the Donau-Wald region to only 12% and only 23% of the Landshut region will be provided with cable connections.

Acceptance of Technologies by Businesses and Households (Diffusion of Innovation)

Uneven developments can already be seen in the acceptance of new technologies by businesses and households. In the metropolitan areas, for example, there is a far higher density in the use of Teletex and Telefax than in the rural regions. One exception in Bavaria is the Alpenvorland with its high number of innovatingSMEs. But the density of users in East Bavaria is way below the national average. The comparison of the intensity of connections for different services between the purviews of the Oberpostdirektionen (general post-offices) of Munich and Regensburg clearly shows a lower density of connections for almost all services in the purview of the latter.

There are indicators that under present conditions the acceptance of new communications technologies does not proceed at equal speed in all regions. So far, the applications are concentrated in the metropolitan areas. It is true that thereby the rural regions have the advantage of being spared the rationalization effects of the innovations of "telematics" for a longer time than the metropolitan areas. But in the long run, the late adoption of the new communications technologies is a disadvantage. Cost reduction and innovation potentials can only be used with an extreme time lag. Therefore, the competitive power of rural regions is being reduced and jobs could be jeopardized.

Such a trend seems possible in the present cicumstances, since the conditions for the acceptance of new communication technologies are more favourable in the agglomerations than in the rural regions. This is also verified by the results of our written interviews with the East Bavarian businesses. We discovered a large deficit of information on the possibilities of the use of modern communications technologies. Certain services, like Datex-P and Datex-L, are nearly unknown among East Bavarian companies. Telefax and Teletex are also less known than in the national average. The new communications technologies are seldom used by East Bavarian businesses: Teletex and Telefax are used by only 12% of the companies. Less than 2% of the businesses use the other services mentioned. There is no indication that the situation will improve very much in the next years: 18% of the businesses plan the use of Teletex, 9% have planned the use of Telefax and 13% the use of Btx.

One reason for the low frequency of use of modern communications technologies, is the low number of businesses with electronic data-processing (EDP) installations.

About one-third of the East Bavarian businesses make no immediate use of data processing. EDP installations that can be categorized as mainframe computers are being used by less than half of the businesses. The computers are mainly used in the field of business management. There is infrequent use of computers in the fields of production and development, according to the results of our interviews. The immediate future will probably not bring a thrust towards more frequent use of computers in East Bavarian businesses.

Conclusions for an Innovation-Oriented Borderland and Regional Development Policy

The results of our research have shown that there are strong elements of relationship between the innovation potential and innovation performance of a region on the one hand, and the provision of an innovation-relevant infrastructure and the spreading of new communications technologies, on the other. The opportunities for "regional compensation" that exist in the research facilities in East Bavaria as well as in the new communications technologies cannot be used to the full extent. There is a danger that innovations and new technologies pass by the East Bavarian region or can only be adopted very late.

Regarding the political need for action, the following questions arise:

1. How can the expansion of new communications technologies be influenced so that equal opportunities can be provided for the rural regions? How, in the interest of the expansion of innovation potential and performance, can the level of acceptance of new communications technologies be raised in the rural regions, so that a "competition of needs" with the metropolitan areas can be established?

2. How can the research and know-how potentials that exist in East Bavaria be better activated and how can the innovation-relevant infrastructure be further supported? How can the transfer of technologies and especially cooperation between the economy and advice or research facilities be improved?

Suggestions for Steps Towards an Expansion of the Infrastructure of Telecommunications (in Conformity with Regional Planning)

The expansion of the infrastructure of communications proves to be an important instrument for an innovation-oriented regional development policy. The makers of regional planning and regional development policy have already formulated their basic positions. For example, the federal government has stated in the "Programmatische Schwerpunkte der Raumordnung" (programmed key points of regional planning) in 1985:

> The new information and communications technologies can contribute to a reduction of long-existing disadvantages of location for peripherally situated regions in the field of communications and information.(...)Therefore well-balanced access to services and opportunities, that are possible through the new telecommunications technologies, has to be guaranteed in cities, states and individual regions... .

But the following modification is appended to this proposal:

> As far as this can be done with regard to demand and profitability.

Regarding the goals of the Bavarian regional development policy, there appear to be some problems. The advantages of the new communications technologies for the rural regions can only be developed, if together with the aspects of demand and profitability, that of development is taken into consideration. The consideration of the principle of development in, e.g. highway construction, is indisputable. The "Landesentwicklungsprogramm Bayern" (state development programme for Bavaria) also stresses the idea of development, regarding the expansion of telecommunications:

> In the interest of better satisfying information and communications needs, (we) should work towards the use of suitable new technology, especially for the peripheral areas of Bavaria.

The Ministerial Meeting for Regional Planning has commented on the new communications technologies and passed a resolution that covers the positions of Bavarian state development. There it has been demanded

> ... that a region wide access to the new information and communications technologies be established and that without any disadvantage in time for the peripheral and thinly populated areas. This has to be supported by the postal administration with an appropriate policy of charges.

> The regional planning interests are also respected in the "Medienerprobungs- und Entwicklungsgesetz" (Law for media development and testing). According to it, the "Landeszentrale für neue Medien" (state centre for new

media) is obliged, for example

> ... to work towards providing Bavaria with cable installations and the technical facilities needed for the supply of radio and television programmes, and especially towards an adequate provision to the rural and borderland areas.

It seems to be necessary to orient the expansion plans of the postal administration more towards the goals of regional and state planning. In that respect a regional planning clause, similar to § 16 of the "Bundesfernstraßengesetz" (federal highway law), could be included in the "Telegraphengesetz" (telegraph law). The practical realization of the demand for better co-ordination of the postal administration's plans with the goals of regional and state planning could be influenced by infrastructure plans for what have been called "telematics". The experts have suggested an exemplary instalment of such an infrastructure "plan for telematics" for East Bavaria.

It should take into account the expansion plans for networks and services of the German Federal Postal Administration as well as the expansion plans of the Landesstelle für neue Medien (Board for new media) and co-ordinate them with the goals of regional and state planning. In connection with the requests, regarding regional planning policy, for a reorientating of the scale of charges from distance- to time-dependent charges for all services and for a quick, region-wide expansion of the ISDN networks or a generous storekeeping of IDN facilities, the growth of technology-based disparities could be avoided.

With the instalment of new applications for telecommunications in East Bavaria could be realized that are suitable for raising the level of acceptance of these technologies among businesses and households. Especially the instalment of "Telehouses" new forms of "Teleconferencing", a master plan for the uses of Btx in the communities or communal special-purpose associations (e.g. tourism and a large-scale testing of "Telework" would be examples of such initiatives within the scope of an innovation-oriented policy.

A pilot project for the reception of new television programmes could provide additional interest and an appropriate demand in East Bavaria, so that the level of acceptance of new telecommunications technologies is raised and new forms of services, e.g. the realization of a co-ordinated information system in the health and social fields (help for the handicapped, sick and elderly people) is made possible.

Further Suggestions Within the Scope of an Innovation-Oriented Regional Development Policy

The conclusions from the research results can of course not be limited to the field of telecommunications. The task of an innovation-oriented borderland and regional development policy has to be the establishment of cross-connections between scientific developments, branch structure, innovation potential and innovation performance, as well as the age structure of the population, education and further education. Starting points for the accomplishment of this overlapping cross-connecting task will be shown, for East Bavaria, with concrete suggestions. In view of the observed information and co-operation deficits, the stronger use of the know-how potential in the university / college field seems to be of special significance:

1. Computer science education should, in the interests of the regional SMEs, be more practically-oriented. All East Bavarian universities should establish appropriate classes for computer science.

2. It is desirable to establish faculties for engineering and new institutes for semiconductor technology in East Bavaria and to more strongly support biotechnological research, which is partly conducted within the scope of special research fields by the "Deutsche Forschungsgemeinschaft" (German Research Association).

3. In combination with the building of the re-processing plant in Wackersdorf, research institutes, i.e. for special-process engineering, should be established.

4. A fund for initial advice should be established for the promotion of co-operation between East Bavarian businesses and the regional university/college facilities. This fund could also finance a pilot project for joint market research for SMEs and a business advisory for newly founded companies.

5. Access to the East Bavarian university / college facilities should be made easier for businesses. For that purpose, transfer centres that arrange contacts between businesses and university/college members in the fields of technology and economics, should be established at the universities/colleges. Also, the organization of the lending services of the university/college libraries should be improved, manpower requirements should be matched and co-operation with the computer centres should be intensified.

6. The information policy and the exchange of information between the universities/colleges and the institutions of the East Bavarian economy should be improved with a list of measures. Such measures are joint public relations for all East Bavarian universities/colleges, joint appearances at fairs, a common file with important addresses, joint events on important subjects from the fields of technology and business economics and the founding of working groups involving the participation of universities/colleges and representatives of industry.

For improvement of the regional competitive capability through the establishment of innovative businesses the following are suggested:

1. An East Bavarian technology park or ventures centre should be planned.
2. Support for so-called spin-off ventures from bigger businesses and university/college institutes should be intensified. The financing problems of such business ventures should be abolished with the help of a regional "technologieorientiertes Unternehmensgründungsprogramm" (TOU; technology-oriented business venture programme) and regional venture capital funds.
3. Through the regionalization of programmes for the encouragement of innovation and market launching, the financing of innovations could be made easier for the East Bavarian small and medium-sized enterprises.

Another basic precondition for the increased innovation performance of East Bavarian businesses is the improvement of the qualifications of the personnel active in the field of research and development. For example, the following measures could contribute to that:

1. The founding of an academy for technical and commercial managers and specialized personnel, where the knowledge of new technologies could be improved upon and the subjects of management and export could be taught.
2. EDP seminars, EDP courses and EDP competitions for young people should be held for the promotion and expansion of EDP use. In addition, an information centre and PC-bus should be installed and the appropriate courses at schools could be improved. In connection with the expansion of the CAD / CAM laboratory at the College of Regensburg, technical EDP applications could be tested and used more frequently.

3. The "Modellversuch Fachinformation in Fachhochschulen" (Pilot Scheme of Specialized Information in Colleges), that, in connection with the OTTI, offers businesses the possibility of getting "on-line information from data banks" on a variety of problems should be formed into a permanent facility.

All in all there is a wide range of possible measures in various fields for an increase of innovation potential and innovation performance in East Bavaria and for decreasing or abolishing disparities between there and the agglomerations in the process of development, use and distribution of new technologies. Application of the suggested measures could especially lead to improvements in the conditions of innovation and technology, the economic structure and an improvement of available jobs, in both quantity as well as quality, in East Bavaria and the rural regions altogether, if they are bundled (if possible) and co-ordinated within the scope of an innovation-oriented borderland and regional development policy.

3.7 Regional Development and Vocational Training

Maria Pierret

Introduction

Today, and even more so than in the past, there are marked differences among the regions in our community. In its resolution of 18 June 1987 in the 11th annual report (1985) of the Commission of the European Communities concerning the activities of the European Regional Development Fund (ERDF), the European Parliament:

> notes that the modest economic recovery achieved in the Community as a result of the favourable monetary and energy situation (that was in June!) has not led to a reduction in the regional imbalances as regards investments in products, productivity and employment.

In order "to develop the European territory", the Community has growing but still limited funds at its disposal. One example: the ERDF accounts for 7.5% of the Community's budget. It is attempting to improve its effectiveness by concentrating on certain regions and by co-ordinating the financial instruments including: the European Social Fund and the EAGGF (European Agricultural Guidance and Guarantee Fund), business creation and innovation centres, and the European Investment Bank. Priority is being given to the following three fields: basic equipment, enterprises and training of staff.

Role of Vocational Training

Training is one of the classic levers for adjusting the labour market but it can "initiate" development as well. Vocational training is being called on to participate both at the individual and collective levels, e.g. enterprises and local and regional authorities, in reseating projects which serve both integration and production. This applies in particular to the "poorly qualified" who are over-represented in depressed areas. In Lorraine (France), for example, a plan has been drawn up for the retraining of metalworkers which envisages stock-taking and orientation phases leading to new and permanent integration, possibly taking in more precarious forms of activity and training.

As far as co-operation between training centres and enterprises is concerned, we are moving away from the initial system whereby training bodies "sell" their practical training courses towards a service which analyses the needs of enterprises and elaborates their strategies for economic and social development. This service may produce not only a training policy but also cover other aspects such as the organization of work, technological modernization, and search for new products, markets and investment resources.

The various alternative training modules will cover both the technical aspects of training and the social aspects of the enterprises, including organization, participation, motivation and philosophy of the enterprise.

A new occupational profile is beginning to emerge, that of "development agents". Their training is important because they provide the link between the economy and the work-force. Italy and Spain have training programmes backed by the Social Fund.

When the social dialogue is lively trainers operate downstream, but where it fails in its mission trainers have to take technological and human aspects into account when putting together a training course. On the one hand, national training bodies establish a dialogue with representatives of the economic and social actors. On the other hand, local and regional authorities have to implement training policies.

In the field, various "partnership" formulae are developing and, at the regional level, coherence between the state, regions and enterprises has been reshaped. Whether we call these formulae "regional schemes for vocational training" or "state / regional planing contracts" as in France or "regional workshops" or "retraining units" as in Belgium, each seeks to co-ordinate the action of all those involved. Their aim is either to define orientations and priority target groups or to mobilize the educational resources in their area. The "grandes écoles" and the universities are ready to assist the local authorities in setting up substitute technologies. The COMETT programme has met with great success and this conference gives us an opportunity to assess the regional development prompted by the science parks.

Some Regional Achievements

Lorraine

In Lorraine, consultative structures have been set up under the aegis of the Deputy Prefect responsible for industrial redevelopment following the signing of a general agreement on social protection by the iron and steel industry and three trade unions. This agreement envisages, among other things, training-retraining contracts. Agents have been appointed to deal with the individuals who enter into these training-retraining contracts. Each of them plays the role of an employment guidance officer and is responsible for 20 people. Their task is to help individuals decide on a retraining scheme by giving them the necessary technical support and providing the necessary contacts.

Nord-Pas-de-Calais

In Nord-Pas-de-Calais, the public authorities wished to equip themselves with the technical tools needed to supply data on employment and training. The government and the Regional Council signed a contract for the 1984 - 1988 period which envisaged the setting up of a regional observatory for training schemes, qualifications and jobs. Government and regional authorities meet in a management committee which sets the annual priorities.

In order to combat illiteracy, the government, region and International Communication Crossroads (Carrefour international de la Communication) have elaborated a scheme for individuals to retackle their reading problem by means of computer-aided learning. Thousands of people have been using LUCIL (Lutte contra l'illettrisme, fight against illiteracy).

Northern Netherlands

In the northern Netherlands, the Chambers of Commerce offer courses for young entrepreneurs on setting up a new business. The region also has "Agences-Interim" and COAs. COAs are highly dynamic centres which provide a forum for contacts between education and work and which seek to co-ordinate all training activities. They organize courses for pupils in vocational education and for teachers and they provide a regular flow of information for enterprises. In principle, the COA management boards are made up of representatives of the provincial authorities in charge of the educational bodies, employer and trade union organizations, intermediary organizations and services such as the Chambers of Commerce. This variety in the composition of COA management boards enables better identification of economic needs and improved co-ordination of efforts.

Andalusia

In Andalusia, the problem lies in the inadequate training provided by firms. According to some top officials in SOFREA (public limited company for promotion and redevelopment in Andalusia), there are no enterprises, centres or mechanisms for training businessmen. Only INEM (national employment institute) offers courses to trainers in enterprises. INEM is the most active institute when it comes to training. It has signed a number of agreements which guarantee liaison between the various areas of economic and social life: There is an agreement with local corporations aiming to provide employment for the long-term unemployed which is based on a rural vocational training plan. Another agreement with the enterprises aims to meet the demand for skilled workers in each province, and an agreement has been made with the Junta de Andalucia concerning questions of financing.

Furthermore, INEM has considerably intensified its programmes for young people who drop our prematurely from school education. It gives them supplementary training within the framework of the INEM-Junta de Andalucia agreement. Under the INEM-enterprises contracts scheme, temporary work contracts enable the placement of trainees during or after training.

South Jutland

In this region, there is a shortage of higher education facilities. This forces young Jutlanders to go elsewhere for training. For that reason the local authorities have developed high-level training courses in the existing centres.

Saarland

The university and the Fachhochschule (technical college) of the Saarland have contributed to regional redevelopment by creating an advisory service in the field of technology transfer and in the setting up of new businesses. The university's equipment may be used for this purpose. In the Fachhochschule a centre has been established to promote the setting up of new businesses in order to improve the qualifications of "apprentice" heads of businesses.

Comment

All these initiatives run counter to institutions operating in a segregated manner. They are based on the theory that the local authorities involved in development are capable of promoting it. This desegregation policy, initiated by local actors, is the main achievement on the road to change.

The Community is experiencing the need to reinforce the co-ordination of its instruments and of its operations in the field. It would like to encourage regional and local partners to participate in the development programmes which it is financing. Hence, the strategy of "integrated development operation" (OIP, opération intégrée de développement), which promotes relations between the bodies affected by development. The preparation of integrated activities forces the various partners to consult each other and to work in "real time". Instead of a project being passed on from one institution to another, both in vertical and horizontal directions, preparing an integrated regional programme leads to the simultaneous involvement of all those responsible for its implementation. As a united force, the community offers the local authorities themselves greater financial security.

Such co-ordination is by no means easy. Financing by means of programmes meant that (in 1985) only 6% of the appropriations of the Regional Fund could be used. Considerable ground has still to be covered before we can reach the objective of 20% envisaged by the Commission for the end of 1987. The regional authorities never have full command of all the financial and technical tools being used on their territory. Their level of autonomy varies according to the areas (economy, regional development, initial training, continuing training, etc.) in which they are active. As local authorities are aware of these shortcomings, they are participating in operations to integrate these initiatives.

In Northern England, the Tyne and Wear Committee has joined forces with local enterprises and associations providing guidance on and assistance in setting up new businesses, in order to develop, with the help of the European Social Fund, the Tyne and Wear Enterprise Trust (ENTRUST). This association, in turn, has set up a business development unit and a training unit providing training in self-employment, new products, new production processes, organization of work, management, etc. It works in collaboration with the MSC (Manpower Services Commission) and with the Sunderland Polytechnic on elaborating training programmes. It organizes the placement of unemployed engineers and technicians in small local enterprises in order to help them to diversify their products and modernize their production processes. The same kind of operation has been set up for unemployed women as office employees.

Eighty SMEs have benefited from the services of ENTRUST, with 50,000 training hours being provided in 1985. A certain number of job-seekers lent out in this way (about 50) were subsequently hired by the enterprises.

In the Saarland the municipality of Saarbrücken has mobilized all its resources (its own funds, resources of the Land and the Federal Institute for Employment, as well as assistance from educational bodies) to draw up an integrated training and employment programme (launched under the heading of the "programme to combat occupational misery in the town of Saarbrücken"). Its objectives are vocational preparation courses, retraining and further training courses as well as job-promotion schemes. It has mobilized the social services, the youth service and the associations for the protection of young people and Protestant charitable works. Of its achievements, we should like to mention the taking over of a factory with a view to transforming it into a training workshop.

In Ireland, the Youth Employment Agency has proposed, in order to improve co-ordination between the bodies responsible for the work-force at the local level, the creation of local intermediate agencies (COMTEC) which would offer young people integrated training and employment programmes, improve the links between the employment agencies, and give local authorities a more important role in the provision of services for young people, etc. Two COMTEC's have been set up on an experimental basis in the southeast area.

Thus, it can be said that what Mrs. Colette Gadioux from the European Parliament described as ideal at the 11th Inter-regional Forum of CEDEFOP in Seville last May, is being realized here and there:

> It seems in fact quite desirable that the various social partners be involved in defining and implementing training activities. The bodies which represent employees and employers, the Chambers of Commerce and Industry, the representatives of craftsmen, and agricultural organizations could be consulted on the projects, could formulate criticisms, observations and proposals and could participate in the implementation of the measures taken and thus contribute to their success. Of course, decisions would remain in the hands of the public authorities, but it is quite certain that regional development depends on the dynamism of the overall population and on the willingness of elected representatives and administrative heads. It is,

therefore, appropriate that the dynamism of the social partners be allowed to take on a concrete form in these procedures.

4 Instruments of Regional Policy for the Furthering of New Business Ventures
(Working Group 2)

4.1 Conceptualization of Technology Centres and Regional Venture Capital Funds in Conformity With Market Conditions

Klaus-Dieter Otto

What Can Technology Centres Achieve?

For regional structural policy, the technology centres will be one of the vital cornerstones for the foreseeable future. This is so, even though there is the tendency in the public to discuss such projects to death both when they are planned and when they are realized, all because there is an absence of obvious visible success. Of course there are legitimate reasons for this critical discussion that apply for many projects and can be summarized briefly: Too much mediocrity and not enough professionalism and orientation towards private enterprise. That starts, to begin with the external characteristics with the structural element: In many places it is apparently believed that an unused and empty old factory building, outfitted with the nowadays required sanitary facilities, in an area in which freight trains and trucks rumble by, ought to be an appropriate location from which young high-tech businessmen with their employees will bring future technology to market maturity and successfully carry out their first transactions.

It is assumed here that the young businessmen need nothing more than just a few inexpensive rooms, perhaps together with a minimal range of services, like a typing and telephone service. But the proverbial garage, where some American high-tech business heroes once started out, is available everywhere under reasonable conditions, just as typing and telephone services are nowadays offered by private service businesses at reasonable prices. Furthermore, it is assumed that such a centre attracts crowds of entrepreneurs and - even worse - brings university and college graduates to set themselves up as businessmen. In the end there is surprise when the two or three really useful persons float off to a technology centre after a short period of time, while the other "businessmen" turn out to be very costly for the state, without creating jobs for the future, as had been hoped.

An entrepreneur who has a really good idea, and also personally provides the most important qualifications, will try to reach independence one way or another - either with or without technology centres. Perhaps, to him the proximity of a university, or a private or public research facility, because of the possibility to use such facilities, - in order to obtain and exchange development results and especially to acquire new, highly qualified employees - is important. Nonetheless, he himself will probably not be a newly fledged university graduate, but will have several years of industrial experience - which by the way is in many ways the case in "Silicon Valley". And this business founder, sooner or later, has one or more products, methods or services to offer and depends more on a representative address than a company that is established on the market. Not only for the high-tech, but also for the low-tech field, it is a valid comment that something must be foul with the principle when the price for a few square feet of factory and office space poses the decisive hurdle.

Thus, it can be stressed, that a technology centre must offer a lot more than a provisional joint roof over the various young businesses: It must have a first-class address in a functional structural arrangement, various joint interaction effects and contacts, and additional opportunities and far better conditions for growth than any other location. Experience shows that such facilities can quickly be profitably operated because high performance earns high wages. Even though the various aspects of technology centres and technology and research parks can not be dealt with in detail here, some important principles, based on practical experience, are discussed in what follows.

A technology centre should offer a clear technological emphasis, and be linked to the potentials offered by a university, a research facility and/or the local/regional industry. This does not at all mean restricting itself to some "fashionable streams of technology", but rather, fosters the desired joint interaction effects and the realization of a marketing concept, with the goal of making this facility regionally competitive and helping its businesses to better results. Only then can a technology centre become attractive to non-local, maybe even foreign, businesses and investors.

The profitability concept of a technology centre should be applied in such a way that the facility can turn a profit or at least be cost-covering within the medium-term (a period of ten years for this is normal in the commercial real estate field, with a view to economic efficiency). With the high-tech "general store" this can hardly be achieved, whereby the emphasis can be varied in the course of time. As the market demands a permanent and flexible willingness to adapt, this also - and especially - goes for a technology centre.

The support base can not be large enough. The participation of public agents or organizations can be sensible in the starting phase, under the rubric of acceleration. If need be, the public agent has access to and the possibility of use of properties / buildings that are not available to private users (e.g. the university grounds) and can set the course for the future, with regard to matters of planning law (new developments). The participation of banks, companies and important users of the technology centre in a sponsoring organization is especially important. Public agents and organizations should from the start restrict their engagement in a sponsoring organization to a limited time, so that the facility can be run like a private business as soon as possible.

As well as newly founded businesses (not more than about three years old), established medium-sized businesses (that relocate certain development projects and sections, in order to, e.g. take part in joint projects with a university and / or other companies and also to qualify their own employees in that area) should also belong to the target group of tenants. Especially joint projects, in which developers, users and science, in co-operation, bring new products or methods to market maturity, offer a great potential for growth businesses: As experience shows, the participating partners will probably develop a new business for each market that most often starts on a solid basis and can be tied to the location because of the cross-connections of personnel and science. At least one-third of the companies involved should be well established because the newcomers can develop better in a professional surrounding than all by themselves.

Factors to consider in planning a technology centre:

1. The technology centre should have a first-class location. That means proximity to a university and service businesses, as well as being in a favourable urban and infrastructure situation.

2. The planning concept and its structural conversion should be in close correlation with the most important needs of future users. Its realization should only begin when enough serious and interested parties have been canvassed.

3. Because of the wide range of possible uses, there can not be a said structural design. In any case, there should be enough possibilities for expansion; a move can be expensive for a growing business - in many respects. A representative and smart appearance can only help, but often cuts are made at the wrong places.

4. The technology centre should, to a certain extent, provide better possibilities for application of research material for the professors and their colleagues than the nearby university itself can (for understandable reasons).

5. The rents should be in conformity to the market and at least marginal.

6. In technical and (most of all) security respects (valuable and/or irreplaceable equipment; undesired transfer of "know-how"), the technology centre should be run absolutely professionally, like any comparable industrial facility.

7. The whole range of services (from typing services to business, finance and legal advice) should be supplied by private businesses, while, of course, the use of any service is on a voluntary basis. In this way, quality at reasonable prices is readily guaranteed. Certain key functions of advice (business and technical advice, marketing and financial advice, data-bank service) should also be represented in the centre. It should not be overlooked that young, technically oriented businesses are often in great need of help when it comes to of project presentation and documentation. The advisers, residing in the centre, should not be at all subsidized, but should earn their way competitively.

The management of the technology centre has three main tasks:

1. The technology centre has to be represented adequately and convincingly.

2. The requests of the participating businesses are to be taken care of in a fast and unbureaucratic manner.

3. Important contacts to advisers, banks, other businesses, authorities and associations should be made, if requested by the businesses.

A small management team is enough for these purposes. It should be chosen carefully and paid adequately (second-choice solutions could be very harmful).

The businesses should be able to develop freely, under the principles of free enterprise. Therefore, it is unnecessary and in fact harmful, if an overblown management cadre permanently interferes in business matters, thinking it could provide the advice itself - maybe even for free. Third-class advice and high-tech do not mix. It should be made a principle for the businesses to buy the best advice - perhaps with the help of the centre management's mediation - that is available on the market, on a competitive basis. If the participating businesses regard co-operation, joint marketing, technology transfer, etc. as useful, they will be involved with these themselves. It is also important for development that the businesses not be unnecessarily disturbed; it is inadequate and harmful to run a technology centre like an "open house" with constant tours.

A technology centre must be marketed professionally. Therefore, a sufficient budget for marketing, advertising, international co-operation etc. should be included in the plan, not only for the launching phase.

With consideration to these principles, technology centres can make an important contribution to structural change - if a professional service and financing infrastructure is built up at the same time. Also, the "aura" of a successful technology centre cannot be valued highly enough, with regard to concern for the existing regional structure. If important local industries - especially the most innovating businesses and the ones most capable of growing - are included in the planning and implementation early enough, fruitful discussion can be initiated. Such a facility produces a lot of self-confidence: "High-tech is possible here". In this environment, the low-tech and service businesses feel better than in a surrounding in which the deficits in the industrial policy are always lamented.

A technology centre offers great possibilities for an active policy of "industrial colonization" - if a convincing setting of priorities is put into practice. After all, the arrival of non-local and foreign companies (that can play the role of an idol) serve also to nurse the existing structures. As "highlights", a few successful models can offer better motivation than the continuous entreaty for more structural changes, technology transfer, readiness for innovation, etc. in the public discussion. If concept and realization are compatible, an increase of jobs can be reckoned with. Here the technology centre of Dortmund might serve as an example. When the centre, which is located near the university, opened in May 1985, it was already fully occupied by about 40 domestic and foreign firms, which led to 150 to 200 new highly qualified jobs in the centre itself. Presently the City of Dortmund is in negotiations with 30 seriously interested firms wishing to settle in the new technology park that is to be connected to the centre and will also be smartly built. All of those involved believe that by 1989 at least 1000 to 1500 new jobs will be created in this complex.

The Significance of Venture Capital and Public Means of Promotion

The structural change - especially, regarding the high-tech businesses - has to be financed. There is little doubt about the fact that the large sums necessary for the continuous building of a great number of high-tech firms can and should only be provided by private risk capital. And there is little doubt that the Federal Republic of Germany limps years, if not decades, behind the American venture capital market. The most important difference between the two countries here lies in the fact that venture capital (VC) is a natural and established financing instrument in the United States, next to other classical financing instruments. The difference from investment capital, as it has existed in Germany for over a century, is the fact that it is available to those businesses that have the strength to grow, in connection with management support - venture management. The goal of the participation is, first of all, the realization of a high profit, through the sale of the (in most cases) minority shares after five to ten years. During that time, possibly incurred annual proceeds stay in the business, in order to provide favourable conditions for growth. Many factors favour the effectiveness of this financing instrument as it is in the United States:

1. A broad public acceptance of the private initiative of the independent businessman, who quickly and efficiently earns money, even with smaller businesses, with the use of technology that is new and in conformity with the needs of the market

2. The far lower social significance of a bankruptcy, compared with the Federal Republic of Germany

3. A relatively high readiness of entrepreneurs to take financial, management, industry and marketing partners into the business, in order to succeed as quickly as possible or at least to survive in the market

4. A high rate of venture management at the VC companies and a functional network of services in connection with VC, like business, financial marketing and legal advice

5. Good possibilities of finding top managers and first-class engineers and

technicians, who are willing to give up a career in a multicorporate enterprise and to move to a small, young business

6. Good possibilities and an efficient services market for selling of shares, also with the selling of stocks to the public with admission of shares to quotation; the stock market is more accessible to the public

7. Government support for young, growing businesses (e.g. Small Business Investment Corporation, SBIC), a wide range of services provided by the government, especially, regarding market surveys and information services, as well as good tax laws

8. The willingness of governmental institutions to give high-tech contracts (e.g. in the aerospace industry) to small and smallest firms

9. VC funds' spreading of risk, by participating not only in the high-tech field, but also in the low-tech and services areas and by taking part in the high-risk phases of a business (seed-financing, start-up financing) as well as in the less risky phases (second-stage financing, third-stage financing)

10. Finally one of the most important (objective) factors: The U.S. market is a lot bigger than the West European domestic markets, which means that the minimum piece number, that is so important for the marketing of high-tech products, can be accomodated by the domestic market. This is a very big advantage of American businesses, regarding marketing and sales as well as the guarantee of and compliance to national standards and thus a lower risk for VC commitments

Even if meanwhile there is a risk capital of about 1 billion DM on hand in Germany, experience shows that there are great problems in getting entrepreneurs and VC companies together. Really professional VC companies, that are capable of enforcing real venture management, are rare; they are only a handful. Of all the hundreds of requests that reach those companies every year, only three to five are given closer consideration. That has something to do with the fact that businessmen often present poor business plans and have wrong ideas of the VC company's expectations regarding business. That again has something to do with the fact that VC companies still are rarely willing to take risks at a time where the VC market is just beginning to stand on its own feet because of the fear of investing in a flop and therefore suffering a loss of image in the eyes of the industrial and institutional investors.

Since this market barely works in Germany at this time, it is sensible that the government is trying to help the country to keep up with the international leaders in the high-tech field with supportve measures. Japan, France and Great Britain, for example have realized that the young high-tech businesses and small and medium-sized enterprises (SMEs) in general, play a key role and are, therefore, trying to secure their countries' competitive power, not only in the field of basic and large-scale industry research, but with special firms and middle-level oriented technical programmes and measures for the building up of VC markets.

Especially the Bundesprogramm Technologieorientierte Unternehmensgründer (TOU, Federal Programme for Technology-Oriented Entrepreneurs) and the various state programmes for technology (which barely differ) are in principle suitable for the creation of new funds, since they grant the recipient compensation for lost benefits in the extremely costly phases of development and marketing. They can - as experience has shown - also contribute to the acquisition of more funds for themselves in the forms of silent partnerships or venture capital. But there are a few problems:

1. The staffs in the technology-advice centres are often overtaxed, when it comes to evaluating future technology and especially the degree of market orientation and the entrepreneurial qualifications of the management.
2. Most programmes are very production-oriented, which means that it is very difficult or almost impossible to receive grants, e.g. for future software or services.
3. The extent of professional business and legal advice and support that is necessary in order to push through a project with a starting volume of, say, several million DM is often underestimated and its cost is insufficiently taken into consideration.
4. Businessmen often let themselves be led to "bet" on certain programmes and their limitations and adjust their projects accordingly, instead of working out a concept that first and foremost is oriented to the market and the management possibilities. Experience shows that in spite of professional planning, the actual volume of financing most often exceeds the planned volume. There are examples of high-tech businesses that after one or two years were more or less insolvent despite considerable subsidies and public participation. This is probably the most serious problem.

5. It takes more than just money. Often management support, contacts, additional distribution opportunities, etc. are more important than the appropriation of funds - and that is what the VC idea is based on. This is confirmed by the fact that even though the use of foundation subsidies is rather good, there is an unbroken bankruptcy boom among young businesses. Or putting it another way: If the young businessman can not exploit a good range of services, he is in danger of starting with the wrong concept and maybe even the wrong money.

For professional VC organizations it is, therefore, only natural to invest a lot of work in the preparatory phases of planning and analyis. But often public subsidies are used to fill up personal accounts, unfortunately even with the help of a few "advisers", who have "specialized" in the procuring of subsidies.

We can only plead for a further "professionalization" of public technology subsidizations, that are so important for acquiring international competitive power, especially due to the lack of an expanded and well-adjusted private capital market. This means a better integration of private services into planning and management connected with the goal of mobilizing more private capital with the use of public means. In this context it should be said that the promotional measures of the present regional economic policy, especially the task force Verbesserung der regionalen Wirtschaftsstruktur (improvement of the regional economic structure) has experienced a push in another direction. The primary goal used to be to regionally influenced new installations or developments of subsidiary plants, while nowadays conservation is the main issue (promotion of capital mobility in a region, promotion of expansions, reorganization, rationalizations, relocations). This probably leads to a high rate of dead weight, even if the regional investment support, under otherwise similar conditions, works more as a factor for the location than the mostly by far overestimated factors of real-estate price or business tax. Regarding the structural-political challenges of the future, which require growing investments in human capital, software, etc., the weapon of regional investment substitution, in its present form, will probably turn out to be too blunt.

Regarding the regional structural policy, some important conclusions can be mentioned:

1. Structural change can only work within the framework of an efficient and sophisticated structure of finance, in addition to a technological infrastructure. Since young high-tech firms, as a rule, show an especially

high growth rate, their own funds - even those that can be derived from (highly taxed) proceeds - are often too low, so that additional funds are needed. At the same time, especially fast-growing high-tech businesses place great demands on management, international marketing, etc. Next to the traditional forms of outside financing and, if need be, public technology promotion or regional investment aid, the private capital market will gain importance with the participation of venture capital (VC) companies and other forms of capital involvement, which in the long run, will be an indispensable requirement for the financing of a great number of growth businesses. Even, if VC companies are location-independently ready to transact investments, they are very interested in concentrating their scarce and cost-intensive capacities for management support. Since the risky, but lucrative participation in high-tech firms requires especially close teamwork, the locations, where they are concentrated will provide far better conditions for the fast-growing low-tech or service companies as well.

2. Since the West German VC market is still in its beginning stages and some important conditions as compared with the U.S.A. do not (or barely) exist, there are possibilities to influence the further development of this market, and especially its spatial shaping, through well-aimed regional measures.

Meanwhile, there are several regionally active risk-capital funds, mostly carried by savings banks or the state sector, that in the risky phases of seed financing and start-up financing provide young innovative growth businesses with additional own funds, in the forms of silent partnerships or risk credits. This can definitely be a solution for certain businesses, especially those that do not (or not yet) qualify for venture capital. But still the restriction has to be made that these funds, as a rule, cannot provide professional management support.

But in terms of regional policy, it is important that the participation of such funds can make commitments easier and possible for private investors. This so-called co-venturing - meaning the participation of at least two investors - is common not only in the U.S.A., but can also be deemed to be a trend in the Federal Republic of Germany. The example of Berlin with its Senate's innovation fund shows that in connection with other activities for the promotion of technology, the establishment and concentration of private VC companies at one location can be achieved; at present there are more than ten private companies in Berlin, which will probably make public funds unnecessary.

A regionally oriented fund will realize the expressed goals more successfully, the more it is oriented and organized professionally and in terms of private enterprise. This especially means, that it should be carried by respected businessmen of the region, with a clear aim at long-term profits and the opening up of additional trade opportunities for the investors. Regional activity based on higher-level, economic intentions is of course, desirable, but a clear aim towards private enterprise is a better guarantor for a market-conforming and professional conception, organization and realization of a regional fund.

Then of course the question of professional management of the fund arises. Here, the local weakness of not having enough qualified personnel can be formed into a strength of industrial location policy, if the main staff is kept small and co-operates with the best supra-regional consulting organizations for technology, marketing and business management. This opens up the possibilities for contacts and multiplier effects and, at the same time, takes into account the fact that it is a lot cheaper to thoroughly examine ten projects with the best (and therefore most expensive) advisers, than to ruin one project, because of a rash decision - not to mention the regional and supra-regional loss of image.

A regional fund, by the way, should not only be oriented at high-tech, but also at low-tech and service businesses. There are also possibilities for use of the finance-market factor, in conformity with regional policy, below the measure of "regional funds". Together with regional or local promotion programmes - that for example, grant founders of very innovative firms and businesses that are extremely capable of growing, location-specific subsidies or credits (which they only have to repay if they are successful) for market studies and especially for professional management advice - access to private capital, VC venture capital and outside financing or even programmes for the promotion of technologies can be facilitated or made possible, and the decision on the question of location can be influenced. Of course, the principle that the recipient of a grant has to provide his own appropriate part has to be in effect here, too.

Such regional or local promotion programmes have the goal to help businesses to help themselves and therefore do not have to burden the government budget too greatly. But they do provide an access to the regional network of advisers, service suppliers, banks and businesses for the interested businessman, at a comparatively low price. The time advantage and the project itself, if the regional conditions are relatively fair, leave other locations far behind.

4.2 Models for the Creation of Business Ventures in the Vicinity of Science Parks and Universities

Harry Nicholls

We talk about models for the creation of new business ventures in the vicinity of science parks and universities. I think many people who are interested in developing a new business near to universities or other technological institutes, when first called upon to undertake this task tend to look around for a model to follow, an idealized set of conditions, processes, procedures which, if implemented, will lead to success. I agree with some of the comments made earlier that there is no single model.

Anyone building new companies in relation to a university or polytechnic needs to have a thorough appreciation and understanding of the economic, political, technical, social, cultural, legal and all other environments in which the project will be operating. It is neccessary to understand the context and then to be quite clear what the objectives are in trying to generate these new companies. There can be different reasons, different motivations, and the key task, it seems to me, the key identification that needs to be made, is what the objectives are in relation to that environment. If one is not clear about what the objectives are, and one takes on responsibility for the creation of these new enterprises, then one is in a very exposed position. The backers of this process can, at any time, accuse you of failing to meet the objectives which they had in mind when they provided the funding for the project. Thus, first of all find out what it is that you are supposed to be doing. Even so, I do not believe it is entirely possible to be clear in these objectives initially - I think you should have some broad objectives, but I also believe that when you go out and start to operate and move towards the achievement of those objectives, you will find that there are differences in the environment, differences in your own or your organization's abilities, differences to what you expected before you embarked on the process, which will require minor, if not sometimes fundamental reappraisal of what the objectives are, or if not a change of objectives, then a change in the working processes needed to achieve them.

I would like to briefly describe our experience in Birmingham, at Aston Science Park. I am not concerned to offer it as a model to anyone, unless the model happens to fit your own particular circumstances - it is certainly not an ideal model. My intention is to use it as an example against which to examine the statements made above in a practical context.

When you look at objectives, it seems straight-forward enough, but when you look at the experience of parks around the world, there are surprising differences in the objectives. It partly depends upon who the owners are, or who the primary, paramount, or most powerful owners of the process are. In some situations, the science park is a means by which a university interfaces with its local environment, in some cases a means by which a university tries to make some money in a harsh and hostile funding environment. In other cases, it is an example of where a university is trying to demonstrate its academic excellence. I can think of examples around the world, particularly in North America, whereby science parks have been extremely successful in creating new business ventures alongside the university, only to find that the majority owner, which is the university, decides that the firms which have been established, although generating wealth and creating employment, are not respectable in terms of the level of the technology applied, they are not respectable in terms of the activities which they carry out in relation to the activities which are carried out in the university, and that can cause fundamental reappraisal.

So, what do we do in our own situation? Our own objectives are to create wealth and employment, and help to regenerate the industrial base of our city. What we have done at Birmingham is accept the fact that even the largest university, and our own university is a relatively small one, is not going to be generating a week by week, day by day or, in some cases, even month by month, flow of superb ideas in the laboratories just waiting to be transformed into wealth and rapidly growing companies - simply by moving the operation into attractive science park premises and offering a little business advice. I do not think it is as simple as that. The process of transferring ideas generated at university into wealth-creating businesses, profitable businesses nearby that university, is not a simple one. It is not a direct line, but a diffused process, working through the whole infrastructure of the organizations around.

Thus, what we have done is to simply take some of the ideas coming from the university and other ideas coming from elsewhere which have technology elements, high-technology elements, which relate activities carried out by other firms on our park. We have tried to do this by providing (a) venture capital; (b) very flexible space, which moves and adapts to meet the needs of the company rather than the needs of the property owner; and (c) common services, business advice and so on. All these work organically with the companies in the creation of a community of companies, whereby the members of that community can learn as much from each other as they can from the managers of the park, although it is the responsibility of the managers of the park to create that learning environment, to create that community environment. What we do, quite simply, is to work with them through time to help them achieve business success.

We do not have any formal programmes in management training. Our feeling is, if you have somebody with a "hot" idea that they want to translate into a profitable business, if they are going to be able to do that successfully they are impatient, dynamic people who want to be getting on with the job. If you say, sit down and learn about cash flow management, marketing, personnel management and then start your business, their enthusiasm will go but, more importantly, a significant part of the business advantage will be lost. Six months in the life-time of a project that might only be two or three years, given the short life-cycles of high-tech products, is too long a time to spend. So, we have worked alongside our companies to help them to grow, to help them to learn from their experience. To date we have acquired about 40-50 companies in just over four years. Of those 32 were start-ups, of which 30 are still alive, and two have died. Meanwhile, we have learned a significant amount in that time.

We have tried some very short programmes without any major success. I was a professor of management for 20 years, so I am not without interest in formal programmes or knowledge of formal programmes. What we would ideally like, and it will be a long time before we get this, is maybe some kind of interactive computer/video-linked training with some kind of expert system designed behind it, so that a manager can access it, at any point of lack of knowledge relating to a real business problem and, from that introduction, enter into a world of learning. It might be a small world, depending on the amount of time, but it could lead into the whole body of knowledge in relation to successful business practice in small companies. That is wishful thinking. It is going to be a long time before we get that but our experience is that when someone has a real problem they will devour knowledge very quickly and apply it, although having said that I do not think the managing of a business is a totally rational, intellectual exercise. I often say that when a company is experiencing cash-flow problems, then it will learn about cash-flow management - there is a delay in my experience. Say you have a rapidly growing company that sees the job as new orders coming in, and they take the new orders. You say to them, "Are you aware of the financing implications of accepting that business?" They say "sure" - but they are not: they probably do not have sufficiently up-do-date financial information of where they actually are, let alone adequate forecasts of cash flow that will tell them what the implications are of the growth in business. So, we say to them, "You really ought to be, perhaps, considering re-financing the company to have an appropriate capital structure to deal with this growth." They say, "Sure, but we do not have time because we're too busy running the company." So, we say, "OK, then factor your debts" and they say, "Factoring is very expensive" (about 25% of the amounts collected). It is, but the alternative is even more expensive because it might be business debt. So even when they have accepted the business reality of the problem intellectually, it might still take several weeks or months before they actually implement the solution.

4.3 Four Years of Innovation and Technology Centres in the Federal Republic of Germany: An Evaluation

Karl Heinz Wodtke

Let me start with a few general remarks about the situation in the Federal Republic of Germany, then I will try to give you an outline of our four years of experience with technology and innovation centres.

When the first innovation centre was established here in Berlin, we went through a so-called start-up period. The Bremen Progress Institute at the time called it "Silicon Valley fever". Since then many new centres have been established under a wide variety of names like technology and innovation centres, technology factories, innovation centres, and technology and development centres - to mention just a few.

In 1985 we founded the Society of German Technology and Innovation Centres (Arbeitskreis Deutscher Technologiezentren, ADT) of which I am the director. I myself come from Syke, a small town of 20,000 inhabitants near Bremen. We were the first place in the Federal Republic of Germany, just after Berlin, to build a technology park and that is why I feel qualified to talk about this matter. The society is at the moment not registered with the authorities, but will be in the future and this will be a great advantage. We arrange conferences twice a year at which the overwhelming majority of participants are managers from other technology and innovation centres.

There are 12 such active centres in North Rhine-Westphalia and, as far as I know, plans have been drawn up for 18 more. In Baden-Wuerttemberg there are ten, in Bavaria four, in Lower Saxony ten, in Berlin at least one, one in Bremen, one in Hamburg, four in Schleswig-Holstein, two in Rheinland-Pfalz, one in the Saarland and one in Hessen. That makes about 50 altogether in Germany and there will be around 70 centres, once they are all open. Recent surveys show that these centres at the moment are used by an estimated 750 companies with about 5000 employees; this has been stated in recent studies which claim that the centres have a positive effect on the labour market.

Our society, as mentioned above, meets twice a year and mainly serves to exchange information. It was the first society in West Germany to publish a list of all technology centres, and in response to the heavy demand we are now preparing the second edition. In this second edition the information which is relevant to planners and businesses has been made more concise and repetition has been avoided. Thus, the really important information about our enterprises will be given more emphasis, especially the figures about the number of employees, the first year of operation, the financing and, if possible, the annual turnover figures. Last, but not least, we want to cover current developments in the U.S.A., Europe and the Federal Republic and to encourage the discussion of and initiatives for further development.

The ADT, together with other international organizations, is preparing an information system, a data bank, which we consider to be very important. As soon as this ADT Information Centre is established in Berlin - and we are assuming that it will be established in Berlin - we will be able us to expand the products and services available to firms in the centre on an interregional and international co-operative basis.

One final comment on ADT: We are very interested in co-operation with national economic associations and also with international organizations like the EBN in Brussels or the United Kingdom Science Park Association, the European Section of the International Association of Science Parks and the Club de Technopole. As I said we are very interested in these relationships and will nurture them accordingly.

To summarize:

1. Every technology and innovation centre is unique and an instrument of regional economic assistance. The enterprises derive their strength from being located together and the centres put this strength to good use.

2. Every technology and innovation centre must adapt its concept and activities to the local circumstances, resources and aims.

3. The centres here in the Federal Republic of Germany have all developed differently. This development is influenced by strongly independent regional structures, different concepts and different requirements of the target groups.

4. The state of development of the technology and innovation centres in West Germany does not yet allow us to make any generalizations. If the individual centres make good use of their potential and use their opportunities realistically, they will develop in strongly individual directions.

5. A point which I consider to be very important is that the public expectations - raised by politicians, managements and the media - are far too high. This especially applies to the effects the technology and innovation centres are expected to have on the labour market. As far as these expectations are concerned, all parties involved should show patience and restraint.

6. If we want the innovation centres to expand at the expected rate, we will require a large, highly specialized staff. Central management in that respect might prove rather limiting.

7. It is necessary to establish a network in order to provide qualified advice by external specialists and to mediate between potential future users of the centre. The more economists, scientists, banks, Chambers of Commerce and managers co-operate, the better it will be for the new enterprises.

8. The anticipated synergy effects, the inter-relationships among the user-companies, have not yet fully materialized. This is in spite of the fact that companies share an infrastructure, their staff and their experiences. In my opinion it is not really feasible to construct an internal network, linking businesses within a technology and innovation centre. This does not affect the external co-operation between the firms, of course.

9. The managers of technology and innovation centres must not see themselves as real estate agents. It is immensely important that the centre itself be an autonomous enterprise right from the start. Thus, the management has to be actively involved itself. This often presents the chief executive with an unsolvable problem. On the one hand, there is the public and especially the politicians, who are impatiently waiting for results, and on the other, the centres are expected to be self-financing.

10. In my opinion the costs which are directly incurred by the enterprises should be shared between the users. At the same time it is unrealistic to expect the centres to be completely self-financing.

One last remark: Even though my view of technology and innovation centres is very optimistic, it is obvious that in the long run only the market can determine the future of these centres. Only the market can decide whether the development of particular technology and innovation centres, as part of regional economic assistance, will remain an experiment or prove to be a lasting innovation.

4.4 Assisting Businesses in Problem Areas

Gerhard Burian

Introduction

Politicians are continually confronted with the special needs certain areas in their countries might have. Regional policy therefore has to deal with a variety of problems, such as the setting-up of new factories, promotion of investment, supply of skilled workers, permissions for new factories, environmental questions and problems caused by the tourist industry, to name just a few. The federal ministries constantly are being asked for help in promoting investment. This requires exact and scientific definitions of problem areas that would then qualify for government aid. Exact definitions are particularly important because federal policy - in order to support regional policy - will need guidelines which are valid for the whole country yet allow scope for regional differences. In Austria these guidelines for regional assistance were not developed *a priori*, but in accordance with their economic practicability. They were always supported by scientific tests and surveys.

In Austria four different kinds of problem areas can be distinguished and these will be discussed.

Economical Weak Regions

Underdeveloped Areas

Underdeveloped problem areas are known for a stagnating or decreasing number of new jobs. They are usually situated in peripheral areas, for example, in the northeast, where Austria borders on the COMECON countries Czechoslovakia and Hungary. The infrastructure is not well developed, the population density is low and decreasing by the year. There is little industry or even tourism.

Industrial Areas with Structural Problems

Industries in these areas did not adapt to the new market situation. They are either dominated by mining or iron and metal works. The industrial structure is basically unilateral.

Tourist Problem Areas

In these regions there is hardly any tourism at all. The infrastructure and public transportation network are underdeveloped and profitability is extremely low.

Urban Areas in Need of Renewal

The alleged need of renewal does not only refer to the housing situation - flats in particular - but also to enterprises. Firms sometimes have structural problems as well as facing difficulties with the neighbourhood, which might feel disturbed. Public assistance and often the environmental conditions, too, are bad.

The Austrian Raumordnungskonferenz (Conference on Land-Use Policy) has worked out these definitions and then assigned problem areas accordingly. Members of the conference are the Chancellor, the federal ministers, the Landeshauptleute (local authorities) and the "social partners".

Assistance

In Austria special funds have been set up for helping weak regions. In order to qualify for them, a region must be situated within one of the defined areas. Thus, the financial assistance is meant for underdeveloped areas and those with little industry or tourism.

Regional assistance can be divided into four types. Specific regional assistance includes special job and investment bonuses and tax advantages. There is a fund for the general promotion of investments. From this fund small and medium-sized enterprises (SMEs) can obtain financial help to modernize and restructure their firms or to buy new machinery. Problem areas get a higher financial subsidy. The same applies to financial assistance in tourist areas, where the help is meant for the modernization of enterprises and restaurants. Independent regional co-operatives are encouraged and people who are just setting up a new business are given special loans with low interest rates; businesses in problem areas get a bigger bonus.

Counselling services offered to businesses have been intensified over the past couple of years. So-called regional counsellors were hired to comprehensively advise entrepreneurs and at the same time co-ordinate the co-operation between different enterprises.

Our experience with regional assistance allows us to make the following generalizations:

1. Regional policy must be comprehensive.

2. It is important not only to create new jobs, but also to improve the general standard of living. Therefore, the cultural, social and transportation infrastructure must be integrated into the whole programme. An example of such a comprehensive view is the money that is put forward for the renewal of old villages.

3. The programme wants to encourage areas to make good use of their "local" resources. In order to achieve this, new confidence has to be built up and out-dated attitudes have to be overcome.

4. The integration of economy and culture has to be intensified, otherwise certain regions might develop into peripheral areas. One way of avoiding this is the setting up of big shopping centres which also provide facilities for leisure activities.

5. There is an emphasis on non-material assistance. Open information deficits have to be regarded as structural problems. This deficit can be overcome, if counselling, professional training and further education are given more emphasis and the transfer of qualified staff is intensified.

Regional assistance cannot be restricted to entrepreneurs who are just setting up a new business, but should also enable existing enterprises to compete in the market. Crucial to the success of newly established enterprises are the local circumstances. This does not apply to new branches of larger existing firms, however.

In order not to isolate new enterprises, existing firms, training centres, universities and colleges have to co-operate with each other better than they have done so far. Furthermore, the mediation of new contacts and joint activities abroad must be encouraged.

4.5 Enterprise Creation in Italy: The Role of SPI

Giovanni de Felice and Claudio Fornari

The crises which have hit areas of traditional industry during the last few years have not spared Italy. A large number of workers who were employed in heavy industry have since been made redundant or layed off. More than 50% of workers in shipbuilding, for example, have lost their jobs. This problem, which has affected the previously thriving developed areas in the north of Italy, is aggravated by the existence of our traditionally underdeveloped areas in the south. Naturally the Italian government has not turned a blind eye and, thus, possesses in the IRI group (Istituto per la Ricostruzione Industriale) a means of facing these problems. In fact the IRI group is by its very nature heavily involved in the problem of unemployment, first because of its vast investment and ownership in traditional industry (steel and shipbuilding etc.) and second because of its state-financed character which obliges it to take into consideration Italian social problems.

Recent experience has amply demonstrated that reliance only upon traditional forms of government intervention is insufficient. Rather, it has shown the need for special instruments to carry out planned and organic action in the fields of job and enterprise creation. It is in this context that the IRI group has entrusted its own financing company, SPI (Promozione e Sviluppo Imprenditoriale), with the work of research, promotion of, and assistance for, entrepreneurial activity, particularly in the areas affected by the reorganization and reconversion of industry. The company has been given the necessary means to do this (80 billion Liras of stock capital and 50 billion Liras credit).

In order to fulfil its mandate, SPI follows two main strategies. The first is in the form of technical and organizational assistance for entrepreneurs, and the second is in the form of direct financial intervention. The assistance offered has been shown to be essential for our work in encouraging new entrepreneurial activity. Time and time again we meet individual would-be entrepreneurs with a good idea but no real knowledge of how to develop it. These are the people who are in need of the kind of technical advice which our organization is able to offer, and they are the very people who, experience has shown, we must encourage. This is because in today's world an industrial venture is not created on a large scale. On the contrary, in order to create new industrial activity we must support small and medium-sized enterprises (SMEs). For example, around Terni (an area of iron and steel industry near Perugia) we have had to stimulate the growth of about a dozen small projects each with from 5 to 30 people working in them, in order to prepare the ground for the future development of this area while at the same time offering immediate opportunities for jobs. The type of assistance which is offered to those entrepreneurs chosen by SPI consists in the usual drafting of a business plan, help in fund-raising, and in assessing the economic viability of the project, etc. In the help given in fund-raising SPI can intervene directly, which brings us to the second strategy of the company.

We have chosen to use risk capital as a means of investment in this field. This is because loan capital is already available for businesses in the form of traditional bank loans, government grants, tax concessions, etc. and it is here that fund-raising comes into its own as an essential part of our advisory service, in so far as we are able to suggest the best method of approach according to the individual needs. Furthermore, in Italy it is difficult to find risk capital and SPI is in a position to provide it.

The instruments used by SPI in this kind of financial activity include:

1. The acquisition of share stock: this, for us, is a temporary and minimal investment, i.e. a maximum of 30% of the share stock, except for special cases, and for a three- or four-year period, after which time we expect our private partner to acquire that stock so as to enable us to reinvest in other new ventures.

2. The use of bond loans, either convertible or non-convertible: our normal conditions provide for a maximum period of nine years, of which during the first 3/4 year only the interest is paid, and not yet the capital. This kind of financing enables SPI to offer the new business venture capital at a considerably lower rate of interest than the current market rate, especially when the loan is convertible.

3. Special partnerships: this kind of investment already exists in Italy but is uncommon. This is because there is a high risk element for the lender, in so far as a certain sum of money is given to a company for a certain period (four or five years) during which we cannot ask for it to be reimbursed. However, SPI shares in the results of the company, whether they are positive or negative. Of course, should the company consistently lose money during that period SPI would not get its investment back. In spite of this risk we have used this method because it is the fastest, the least bureaucratic, the best and most practical for those small ventures which we are specifically interested in promoting in certain areas.

In the first two years of this activity our company has invested in over 50 new ventures, about half of them in the form of acquisition of share stock, and the other half divided more or less equally between bond loans and special partnerships; moreover about half of our investments have resulted in the setting up of new enterprises. The precise data are presented in Table 1. It is worth noting that in Genoa, for example, which is in a shipbuilding area that has been severely hit by the industrial crisis, employment has already been found for 314 people in the 16 new enterprises which SPI has helped to launch. The total number newly employed is now well over 1000 in more than 50 new enterprises.

Table 1: Results of SPI's investment activity (mid-1985 to mid-1987)

Area	Number of enterprises	Number of employed
Genoa	16	314
Trieste	13	249
Terni	11	184
Naples	5	131
Others	6	152
	51	1030 *)

*) The employment data for Trieste Sincrotrone and the BICs are not included

These results, when compared with the dimensions of the "unemployment problem" may at first seem negligible, but, considering the short period in which SPI has been operating in this field, they are in fact an extremely positive pointer to future development. Our hope is that these small enterprises will grow into larger concerns employing more people. However, in order to achieve better results, experience has shown us that intervention in the form of government aid is essential. This is above all the case in those depressed areas where we wish to encourage entrepreneurial activity, because external entrepreneurs must be encouraged, or even enticed, into those areas.

Meanwhile, as far as SPI is able to act in this field, it is already using another strategy to prepare the ground in these areas through its serious involvement in business innovation centres (BICs), which are an invaluable factor in turning individual entrepreneurs (especially young ones) into real businessmen. SPI has in fact promoted the foundation of the Genoa, Naples and Trieste BICs, which it runs, and is putting the finishing touches to the feasibility study of the Taranto BIC. It is also on the promotional committees for those of Terni and Livorno-Piombino. Recently a plan has been drawn up for a network of centres for new entrepreneurial activity in southern Italy, adapting the BIC model to the real situation and needs of the south.

4.6 Results and Requirements for Promoting Technology-Oriented Enterprises in Infrastructurally Weak Regions: The Example of Eastern Bavaria

Eberhard Auchter

A well-known thesis of regional policy says that establishing enterprises in the field of new technologies may lead to positive effects, from the creation of jobs in growth industries to a permanent improvement of the "innovation climate" of a region. Examples which can help to support this thesis are: the agglomerations of Munich, Stuttgart and Berlin for the Federal Republic of Germany, the region around Nice in France, and the famous "Silicon Valley" in California. These regions have in common the fact that from the point of view of economic policy, they may be described as structurally weak regions. The question arises: Are there in structurally weak areas technology-oriented enterprises which deserve our attention and what kind of basic conditions are conducive for the founding of such enterprises in structurally weak regions?

The Initial Situation:
The Regional Economic Structure of Eastern Bavaria

The region of Eastern Bavaria covers an area of about 150 km by 250 km in the southeast of Bavaria (see Fig. 1), with the "Regierungsbezirke" (administrative districts) of Niederbayern, Oberpfalz and Oberfranken.

Characterizing the region are the facts that it borders on the eastern neighbour states of Czechoslovakia and the German Democratic Republic (GDR) and the disadvantages of location which arise out of this position as well as the absence of financially efficient agglomerations. The regional economic structure of eastern Bavaria can be generally described as follows:

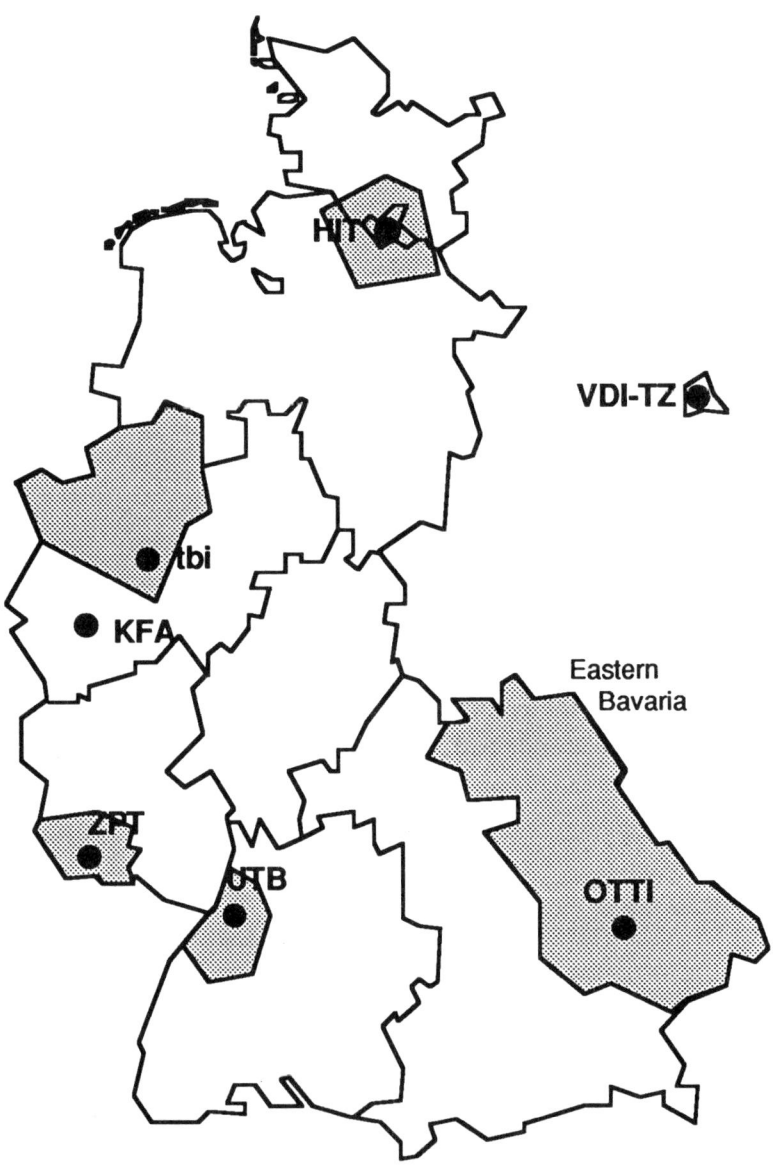

Figure 1: Regions includet in BMFT projects

1. There is a dominance of economic branches with poor future prospects, e.g. basic materials industry, food, beverage and tobacco industry, and agriculture.

2. There is low "innovation density", i.e. the ratio of innovative enterprises in proportion to the total of enterprises in eastern Bavaria, is compared with the average of the Federal Republic lower.

3. There is a one-sidedness of industrial structure. In some areas of eastern Bavaria there are industrial monostructures, which, due to changing market conditions, can lead rapidly to considerable structural problems (fine ceramics / porcelain, toy and furniture industries) or have already led to them (steel and glass industries).

4. The border-area situation imposes itself. Due to the long border with the Eastern-bloc countries, the GDR and Czechoslovakia, formerly important markets and transportation connections have been cut.

5. There is a weak innovation-relevant infrastructure. Innovative enterprises need an infrastructure (for example, universities, research institutes etc.), which promotes technology transfer and supplies important input factors (qualified personnel, qualified ancillary suppliers). In eastern Bavaria there are, however, no universities with technical departments; no research institutes; only a small number of technical consultants, engineering offices, etc.

Promotional Measures for the Innovative Creation of Enterprises in Eastern Bavaria

The importance of economic policy in creating technology-oriented enterprises has been perceived in politics and partly realized in promotional schemes of the federal states or of the whole Federal Republic. For the region of eastern Bavaria, innovative entrepreneurs can, in the first place, obtain state aid from a number of federal programmes (e.g. BERP, Bundesentwicklungs- und Raumordnungsprogramm development and regional planning programme; aid from private capital). The financial volume of these programmes, however, is often limited and based on a system of collateral credits.

These aids which are quite appropriate for "normal" setting-up processes are not sufficient for setting up innovative enterprises, as the financial needs and the start-up risks are higher.

For these groups of entrepreneurs in Eastern Bavaria the two Bavarian schemes Bayerisches Innovationsprogramm (innovation programme) and Bayerisches Technologieeinführungsprogramm (technology introducing programme) are available. Both are support measures of the Bavarian state for the promotion of small and medium-sized enterprises (SMEs) for the development and market entry of innovative products or processes. It is exclusively a matter of financial aid which is granted in the form of subsidies - up to 40% of the total sum of the project - or as loans.

Pilot Project Förderung technologieorientierter Unternehmensgründungen (TOU, Promotion of start up of technology-oriented new firms) of the Bundesminister für Forschung und Technologie (BMFT), Federal Ministry of Research and Technology)

More than four years ago the BMFT had already realized the importance of technology-oriented new firms and designed a promotion programme to improve the starting chances for such firms in the field of technology. This promotional programme is especially geared towards this target group and offers support for young technology-oriented enterprises, in the form of:

1. Grants for preparing a concept for evaluation (up to 75% or 108,000 DM)

2. Grants for the development and building of prototypes

3. Research and development (up to 75% or 900,000 DM)

4. Non-collateral venture capital (credits) for the building-up of production plants and the financing of market introduction, in amounts up to 80% or 1.6 million DM (banks granting the credits have to risk 20% of their invested capital)

This promotional scheme is a pilot project, i.e. the BMFT first tests the promotional instruments with respect to feasibility and prospects of success. For that reason at first only certain regions of the Federal Republic or selected technology fields like microelectronics or biotechnology without regional restriction were included in the pilot project. Moreover, all enterprises financed by venture-capital companies as well as enterprises from 12 selected technology centres can apply. In addition to five other areas of the Federal Republic of Germany (see Fig. 1) Eastern Bavaria is the only region of Bavaria that has been included in the pilot project.

Significant for this regional variation of the promotion of technology-oriented enterprises is that within the regions so-called technology-consulting offices prepare the selection and financing of the enterprises to be promoted and - besides financial help - assist and consult the promoted foundation projects. This additional service for newly founded enterprises is lacking in nearly all the other promotional programmes which only offer financial project-related support.

The BMFT Programme TOU in Eastern Bavaria

The technology consulting office responsible for the region of eastern Bavaria is the Ostbayerische Technologie-Transfer Institut (OTTI; technology transfer institute) in Regensburg. The institute is a "self-help organization" of the eastern Bavarian SMEs and aims at the problem-related imparting of know-how from universities, institutes and other knowledge institutions to medium-sized enterprises. The main tasks when implementing the BMFT programme TOU are:

1. To evaluate and select promotable projects

2. To assist and consult the projects currently being promoted

Evaluation and Selection of Start-up Projects

Since the middle of 1983, the OTTI has received about 300 project proposals, out of which approximately 20 technology-oriented enterprises have come into existence. The selection criteria are mostly similar to those of private investors, i.e. the enterprise or the products to be placed on the market have to be entrepreneurially promising. The chances of success should be based on a high technical and qualitative standard of the products as well as of the technical and business capacities of the founders/group of founders. In addition to the above-mentioned criteria - market, product and founders' qualifications - which also apply to private investors, there are some formal restrictions laid down by the BMFT. For example, there is a technical minimum level of the products to be developed and placed on the market, or a limit on the age of the enterprises to be promoted. The high rejection quota of about 85% indicates how carefully the several project proposals are chosen.

196   *Eberhard Auchter*

Due to the technical preconditions of choice by the BMFT the 20 promoted enterprises, without exception, deal with products of advanced technologies. Examples worth mentioning are microcomputers, the manufacture of special computer-controlled machines for cutting hollow glass, and the development and manufacture of plants for purifying flue gases for small power-stations.

Comparison of the Promotion of Technology-Oriented Enterprises by Federal States and Regions

Figure 2 gives interesting evidence of the endogenous innovation potential of structurally weak regions. Here the number of enterprises promoted by the BMFT programme TOU is demonstrated according to federal states and regional variations. It can be clearly seen that the number of promoted enterprises in the structurally weak areas, e.g. eastern Bavaria (19 promoted enterprises) or the problem region of North Rhine-Westphalia (18 promoted enterprises) in comparison with the so-called structurally strong regions, e.g. Baden-Wuerttemberg (24 promoted enterprises) does not fall off dramatically, but instead shows remarkable results. However, when comparing those data the different sizes

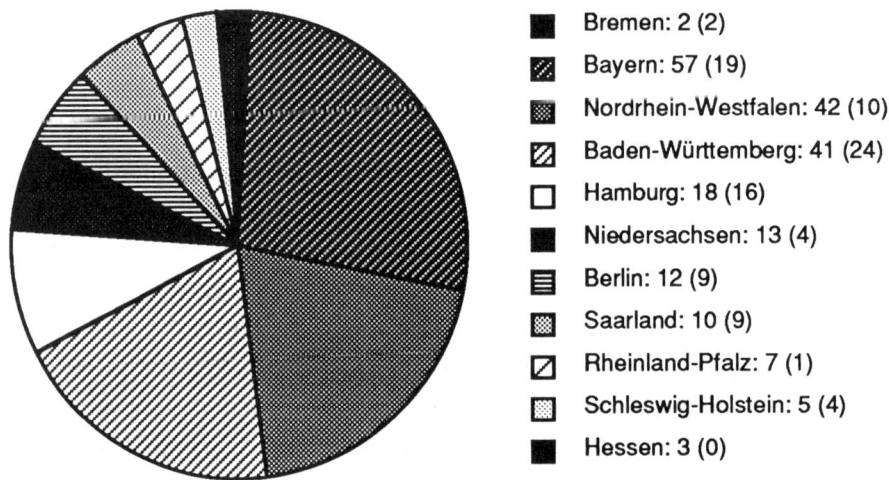

Figure 2:   Proportion of promoted new technology-oriented enterprises by federal state. (Figure in paranthese gives the regional variation)
Source: ISI / FHG Karlsruhe, 6/87

of the areas, which are included in the regional variation of the pilot project, as well as the distribution among the several federal states must be taken into consideration. Beyond that, when viewing the total number of promotions per state, one must consider to what extent technology parks chosen by the BMFT for the pilot project are represented there.

For example, the strong position of the electronics branch in the metropolitan area of Munich as well as the importance of the Munich technology centre are reflected in the high number of grants in Bavaria beyond the regional variation. From the above-mentioned figures an important conclusion can be drawn: In structurally weak regions there are a considerable number of "innovative cells". The existing stock of enterprises is equipped with the innovative potential of its enterpreneurs, who are prepared for spin-offs. Preconditions for this are concrete help and basic conditions, which compensate for the deficiencies of the structural weaknesses of the regions. In the following some - partly well-tried - measures are proposed.

Requirements for an Effective Promotion of Innovative Enterprises in Structurally Weak Regions

The effective promotion of setting up innovative enterprises in structurally weak regions calls for measures at three levels:

1. Financial and consultative support
2. Short and medium-term compensation for disadvantages of location
3. Long-term strategies of revitalization of structurally weak regions when implementing economic policy measures

In comparison to the setting up of "normal" enterprises, innovative setting up distinguishes itself by its complexity and by a high technical, financial and market risk. The financial engagement of a third party, the public sector or private investors, is generally the rule. The state is called upon especially when development costs, so-called seed capital for technology-oriented enterprises is to be provided, for in the nascent stage of development the reluctance of private investors to grant credits is very noticeable.

Especially in structurally weak regions the financing of prospective technologies by the state should be obligatory. Before and while financing innovative enterprises, appropriate assistance (as needed) and consultation must be made available to them. Because of the above-mentioned reasons, this accompaniment is seen to be necessarily independent of whether the enterprises are settled in structurally strong or weak areas, but the structural deficits of the latter make assistance even more urgent.

In eastern Bavaria these requirements are met by the OTTI, in as far as it offers management and technical advice and services to the assisted entrepreneurs concerning introduction of planning systems, arrangement of financial matters, preparation of the market entry, and solving technical problems. The demand for these services verifies the need for them.

Technology-oriented enterprises setting up in structurally weak regions are confronted with a number of hindrances, which are to be traced back to the structural weakness of the area. Such impediments are, for example:

1. Contact problems with customers, enterprises in similar branches, cooperative, partners, financiers, etc.
2. Remoteness from research institutes, ancillary suppliers, and institutes of further education
3. Shortage of qualified personnel

The OTTI in Regensburg tries to reduce these structural deficits with the following measures:

1. Compensation for the information deficits brought about by location is being made through an intensified offer to use data banks. The OTTI has access to more than 800 data banks throughout the world. This data bank includes information on subjects ranging from technology and management to patent research.
2. In these structurally weak areas the supply of courses for further training is rather limited for this target group. Therefore, the OTTI offers a wide range of various courses in relevant management and technical subjects.
3. Requests for regional cooperative partners can, as a rule, be followed up quickly by the OTTI's technology transfer activities, for there are contacts with more than 1000 firms within the region. The technology transfer activities of OTTI also include contacts with research institutes and other "know-how" institutions throughout the Federal Republic. Within the scope of a programme by the EC the OTTI co-operates with public

institutions, chambers of commerce, and private enterprises in Italy, France, Spain and Ireland. The goals of these co-operative efforts are to initiate and mediate between joint distribution and development undertakings as well as licensees.

A greater problem for young technology-oriented firms is the recruitment of qualified personnel. Especially in the field of microelectronics, many young entrepreneurs cannot find staff for their established posts. Particularly the large enterprises in the "microelectronics centres" of Munich and Nuremberg try to cover their great demand for qualified electronics experts by high financial incentives.

The consequence is a migration of qualified engineers also from eastern Bavaria into the metropolitan areas. OTTI tries within the scope of the project "technical-scientific junior staff" to interest engineering students during their studies to work in young innovative enterprises; OTTI mediates between these students and smaller projects, working on development activities of innovative firms. The students then carry out project-related work during their summer vacations in young enterprises. One aims to please the young engineers during their work in small dynamic enterprises so that they do not migrate to the metropolitan areas after their studies, but remain at the firms.

The above-stated first steps can only be successful if they are included within the framework of an innovation-oriented regional policy. A lengthy discussion of those innovation-oriented strategies of revitalization for structurally weak regions would be beyond the scope of this article. Therefore, some important items should only be mentioned:

1. Creation of an innovation infrastructure by, for example, providing research capacities in the technical fields at the universities and research institutes; improvement of the infrastructure of transfer and consultation by the extension of a network of technology consultation offices; and expansion and extension of the supply of initial and further training

2. Financial help for activating the endogenous potential, for example, special promotional measures for technology-oriented enterprises or the initiation of regional venture-capital companies on a private-enterprise basis

To sum up, the following conclusions can be drawn. Structurally weak regions are provided with an endogenous potential of "innovative cells". Only within the scope of an appropriate innovation-oriented regional policy can this potential be activated. The measures for setting up technology-oriented enterprises in eastern Bavaria are showing the first signs of moving in this direction. If these preconditions are not taken into consideration or if the effect which an innovation infrastructure should produce is still not achieved, isolated activities are not going to be successful. Unsuccessful examples are some technology centres which because they were built up without attention to an existing innovation infrastructure, now can not live up to their proclaimed objectives.

4.7 Mobilizing Higher Educational Institutions as a Source of New Technology Based Firms

Andrew J. Gould

During the past ten years in the U.K., as elsewhere in Europe, there has been a dramatic increase in the start-up of new technology based firms. In some localities the formation of such firms is providing the basis for transformation of the local economy through exploitation of its technological base.

This technological base encompasses, in addition to higher educational institutions, large firms, research establishments and small and medium-sized high technology businesses. In any locality a higher educational institution is unlikely to be the most important source of new technology based firms: the process of "spin-out" of new businesses from existing, and usually small, firms is quantitatively more important. But higher educational institutions are increasingly seen as a local resource of exceptional potential in stimulating the growth of a high-technology business sector.

There are multiple reasons for this change which I will not elaborate. But the desire of higher educational institutions to operate in a way that is more relevant to industry and the wider community, and their need to generate income from new sources and to be seen to be doing so are common factors in the U.K.

What evidence is there of higher educational institutions acting as a source of new technology based firms? Perhaps the best know case in the U.K. is that of Cambridge where a flourishing high-technology business sector has developed with origins directly and indirectly in the university. The essential feature of what has become know as the "Cambridge phenomenon" is growth of high-technology industry on a broad sectoral base in which the leading role is being played by the start up and growth of small locally formed independent businesses. The firms are mostly engaged in research / design/development or in low-volume production.

The origins of this development are long-standing with two companies which still exist having "spun out" of the university in the nineteenth century. But significant growth is recent. There are now over 450 high-technology firms in the area, about one-half have been set up in the last seven years. They employ about 17,500 people (which is 13% of total local employment) but their overall impact on the labour market has been much greater because of the multiplier effects.

The beginnings of these businesses mostly lie in individuals leaving existing organizations ("spinning out") to start their own business. The indirect role of the university can be seen in this process. Only 60 or so new technology based firms have been set up by individuals coming straight from the university, but the university has indirectly been the origin of well over 200 firms as these spin-out companies have themselves spawned new companies. Even where firms have no origin in the university, it has been a key reason for the company to be located in the area.

While there have been multiple causes for this development it is worth stressing that it has happened spontaneously in an unplanned way and ultimately derives from the presence and policies of the university. The university has an outstanding record of scientific research and the sectoral composition of high-technology firms in the Cambridge area can be traced back to research undertaken in the university.

As regards exploitation of results of this research, the university has adopted unusually liberal policies. The essence is that intellectual property rights are regarded as belonging to the individual and that academic staff have considerable freedom as to how they spend their time. The unplanned consequence of this approach is that academics have been able to exploit their know-how through formation of new technology based firms. Cambridge, of course, presents a highly unusual set of circumstances and the phenomenon has evolved over a long period of time. Is it possible to create conditions for the formation of new technology based firms in a structured way?

Evidence from the United State shows that specific programmes within higher educational institutions to foster entrepreneurship may not be important. In fact, it appears that the harder the university has tried to encourage firm formation the less successful it was likely to be! This clearly has not been the case at Chalmers Institute of Technology at Gothenburg in Sweden, which has a high rate of spin-out. This is thought to be largely the consequence of a liberal policy towards ownership of intellectual property and of structured efforts to encourage entrepreneurship and to teach business management.

What are the key factors then, that influence the role and impact of a higher educational institution as a source of new technology based firms? The institution makes itself attractive:

1. Through being a centre of excellence of research and teaching and through this and other means contributing to the creation of an environment where talented people want to live and work

2. By allowing academics the freedom to pursue business ideas and by helping to foster a business culture in which new firm formation flourishes

3. By providing active support for academics to establish themselves in business through reducing the level of risk at start-up, for example, through assistance with patenting or market research

4. Through supporting new technology based spin-outs once they have been established. A few science park schemes, for example Aston, combine the provision of accommodation and common service with business advice and support, including venture capital

5. Through encouraging geographic clustering of new technology based firms, this agglomerative effect helps give confidence and the impression individually and collectively to young and small technology firms, as well as to other bodies inside and outside the area, that something significant is happening by way of new business development

Now I would like to address the role of a science park. Clearly such initiatives are not a necessary condition for higher educational institutions to spin-out technology ventures. In most cases neither will a science park be a sufficient condition - other "non-property" ingredients must be present already. On the basis of quantitative criteria the impact of science parks is small - they will never represent more than a small proportion of new technology based firms. However, as an element in approaches to creating conditions which are conducive to spin-out of technology based firms, a science park can play a number of profoundly important roles:

1. It can become the focal point of joint local university-industry and high technology activity.

2. It can serve as a visible symbol to both the academic and the outside communities that university-industry links are important. And in doing so

it can change the culture and attitudes within the higher educational institution towards establishing businesses.

3. It makes it easier to achieve visibility and a critical mass of new technology based firms, which in some cases would not occur if the businesses were spatially dispersed.

4. It can support growth of established firms through providing more appropriate and higher quality property than may be available elsewhere locally.

To conclude, it is clear that there is no single approach to promotion of the spin-out of new technology based firms from higher educational institutions. That which has worked with considerable success at Cambridge is not easily transferable to other institutions. Nonetheless, there are measures which may encourage and support the process through removing constraints on academics wishing to pursue business ideas and by providing active assistance for them to do so.

4.8 Dutch Spin-Off Companies as a Means for Successful International Technology Transfer: The Case of the University of Twente

Dick van Barneveld

Introduction

Twente, The Netherlands

Twente is a district in the northeast of Holland and has a population of 400,000 with a work force of 45,000, 25% of which is employed in the manufacturing sector.

Having suffered from the decline of the textile industry in the area and an unemployment rate of 23% in 1984, falling into 16% in 1987, the region has made determined efforts to rejuvenate its industrial base through encouraging the start-up and development of high-tech companies.

The University of Twente

As one of the three leading technological universities in The Netherlands, the University of Twente (UT) has been heavily involved, since 1980, in supporting and promoting the formation and expansion of new innovative businesses.

The University of Twente has also operated a Transferpunt (or industrial liaison agency) since 1979 and has established a good reputation for assisting local small and medium-sized enterprises (SMEs).

Industrial Liaison Agencies (Transferpunten)

In 1980 Transferpunten (TPs; transfer points) were founded in The Netherlands at the three technical universities, having as a main aim the enhancement of the flow of knowledge from the universities to the SMEs. At that time the growth of the economy and the lowering of unemployment were expected to be linked strongly to new entrepreneurship and the flow of knowledge to SMEs with a product or service based on new technologies. In the subsequent years TPs have been started at all Dutch universities; the TP of the university of Twente - although it started as a regional TP - has developed as a nationally oriented TP that attracts about 50% of its clients from parts of The Netherlands outside the province.

Transferpunt University of Twente

The technology transfer mechanism at Twente is carried out by the TP and is part of a network of such centres established in universities by the Dutch government. The TP at the University of Twente is still extending its range of activities which are focussed on generating and extending contacts between academic staff and industry, particularly SMEs.

The main aims of the TP-UT are:

1. Improving and developing conditions through which co-operation between SMEs and the UT will be stimulated

2. Participating in projects through which the UT will contribute to the economic development of the region/province

3. Stimulating entrepreneurship within the UT

Stimulating Entrepreneurship

The encouragement and training of technically qualified young persons with entrepreneurial potential are essential factors for economic development. New technology based business enterprises are required, particularly in regions suffering significant unemployment levels. The formation and growth of such enterprises depend on qualified and highly motivated innovators who have access to adequate resources, facilities and expertise - notably those resident in universities and other higher education establishments.

Support of several kinds is required, and a structured methodology is essential to provide appropriate assistance, together with relevant training in commercial skills to complement technical capability.

The Temporal Entrepreneurial Jobs Programme (TOP)

TOP was launched in 1984. The programme is operated by the TP - UT. In summary, the programme has focussed on the skills and resources needed by the graduate entrepreneur to effect the transition from a product, process or service concept to a successful business. Contributions of expertise and access to facilities are provided by the university and this institution is the key source of enterprise ideas.

New product, process or service concepts are generated within university research groups or through the interests of individual academics and consultancy activities. The "liberation" of ideas with commercial potential from the academic environment and their exploitation by young graduate entrepreneurs in collaboration with the innovating academic staff members are the key strengths of TOP.

General Structure

The TOP programme provides graduates from all universities and higher technical schools in The Netherlands, who want to become independent entrepreneurs, a place in the University of Twente, in a research group for one year.

To those who are in the "incubation" stage with their firm the TOP programme provides:

1. Support by university experts with know-how and expertise
2. Use of technical facilities and accommodation
3. Housing and office facilities
4. A living allowance. (Dutch guilders 30,000 for one year)

Funding support is provided by the Ministry for Economic Affairs and the University of Twente. The social fund of the European Communities has sponsored the programme for a certain period and a limited number of companies.

Successful entrepreneurs who have left the TOP programme after one year have to pay back 50% of the grant over five years. Thus, a revolving fund has been built up which allows the university to establish new TOP places in the future.

Procedure

Graduates who want to apply for a TOP place have to develop a business plan and are invited to discuss their plan with a TOP advisory board. People from industry, consulting and from the university are members of this committee.

Usually an experienced mentor from industry is assigned to the young entrepreneurs, thus being a help in the background and covering any weak areas in the business plan.

All young TOP entrepreneurs are advised to join the course "How to become an entrepreneur" developed by staff members of the faculty of business management of the university. This course gives them the opportunity to develop their own business concept and provides feedback on their plans from all the other young entrepreneurs.

The TOP advisory board regularly evaluates the development of the new company. Frequently young entrepreneurs apply together for more than one TOP place. It has been proved that new firms established by a partnership have better chances in the market, especially when they cover a combination of technical and business management areas.

Developments and Achievements of TOP

Since January 1984 a total of 45 young entrepreneurs have made use of TOP start-up facilities (Table 1).

These 45 new companies are employing approximately 250 people at the moment. The forecast (within two years) is good: there should be approximately 400 work places.

The entrepreneurial climate at the university has proved to be very positive: 80% of all university start-ups have settled after the TOP year in the business and technology centre close to the university.

Spin-Offs in The Netherlands

It has been shown that in The Netherlands every new firm established by a graduate engineer gives new employment to eight persons, on average.

The growth figures of new high-tech companies compared with the average start-ups in the Netherlands can be seen in Table 2.

Table 1: Analysis of users of TOP start-up facilities since 1984

Number	Line of business	Consultancy	Production
4	Chemical engineering	1	3
2	Energy	1	1
2	Environment		2
4	Mechanical engineering	2	2
3	CAD/CAM	3	
1	Laser technology		1
2	Bio-medical		2
2	Materials		2
2	Robotics	1	1
1	Automation	1	
5	Electronic engineering		5
2	Software	2	
3	Photography	1	2
1	Agriculture		1
2	Trade	2	
5	Business consultancy	5	
2	Education	2	
2	Publishing		2
45		21	24

Table 2. Growth rates of new high-tech companies (%)

	HIGH TECH	AVERAGE
Employment	21.8	3.2
Sales	33.2	7.4
Profits	37.3	16.5

Thus, it can be seen that this way of setting up a new firm is very successful. Only 12% of all university spin-offs have ceased operating after two years. The average failure rate in The Netherlands for the total number of start-ups is over 60%!

University of Twente Spin-Offs

The total number of 134 new companies which have started from the university since 1965 are now employing 800 people (see Table 3).

Table 3: Number of University of Twente business formed

Year business started		Defunct
Before 1977	12	3
1977	6	2
1978	8	1
1979	8	3
1980	11	2
1981	10	1
1982	14	1
1983	14	1
1984	15	2
1985	15	3
1986	12	-
1987	9	-
Total	134	19

Of these companies 75% have settled in the vicinity of the university. The technological fields of these high-tech firms are:
- Acoustic and audio visual systems
- Applied education and training
- Automation in industry and offices
- Chemical analysis
- Energy and environment
- Management consultancy
- Medical technology
- Micro-electronics
- Operating systems
- New materials
- Planning and logistics
- Process technology
- Product development and innovation
- Quality control
- Special working techniques

One-third of these firms are in consultancy. Over 60% bring a product to market.

Recently we have started with an initiative, the "Business and Science Group Twente", in which we bring together a great deal of our university spin-offs to promote mutual contacts and to present them to the bigger companies as a source of know-how and to the international market. A directory of these high-tech firms will be available in 1988.

Methods and Means for Successful International Technology Transfer

Internationalization of universities is a strategic issue that will become more and more important in the coming years. For The Netherlands it is obvious that education and research do not have a sufficient international orientation. This counts even more when seen against the background of a very internationally oriented Dutch market situation and the importance of competitiveness between Europe and the U.S.A., on the one side, and the Pacific area, on the other.

The Dutch government has therefore decided that further internationalization between Dutch regions and regions abroad has to be encouraged. Thus, the ITP project has been established.

The International Transfer Point Project (ITP)

The hypothesis of the ITP project is that it should be possible to identify regions in other countries that have a similar infrastructure and network between industry, authorities and an "entrepreneurial" university and that - having identified such regions - it will be possible to develop a network of networks which will enhance the international technology transfer within this network. The net result of the project would have to be the enhancement of the economic development of our region.

We started with already existing international contacts and some new ones in Norway, Sweden, Bavaria (Federal Republic of Germany), Ireland, Minnesota (U.S.A.) and with the "triangle cities area" (Ontario/Canada).

The working method of the ITP centre is to have a transfer consultant active in gathering offers and requests for new products, technologies and markets in the regional firms. He then selects a number of projects. The selection criteria are:

1. Unique selling points for the international market
2. State-of-the-art technology or product
3. Economic feasibility of the business development

A marketing expert should be connected to the transfer centre. He should conclude service contracts with the companies selected.

The entrepreneur should make a marketing plan for the transfer project. A consultant could assist him with this work.

Conclusions

In such a project one has to learn by doing; learn from one's own mistakes and from the experiences acquired by others. It is for this reason that we are very much interested to communicate with colleagues who already have worked in this field.

Up till now we have found that it takes much effort to initiate such forms of interregional co-operation and to set up an effective network of networks. It presupposes active involvement of both parties on different levels and even then it takes time before results will become apparent. It will take an even greater effort to reach a situation where co-operation is initiated and supported by the individual partners themselves, leaving only a minor role to the transfer points.

Programme of Work

In order to achieve co-operation between The Netherlands (and the European market) and the Pacific-rim countries, our International Technology Transfer Centre offers the following:

1. Locating of Dutch (SMEs), identifying their needs for new technologies and linking these SMEs with those in regions abroad
2. Business information exchange between the regions
3. Advice foreign companies entering the Dutch and the European market
4. Advice to foreign companies about subsidies available on different levels of government and in the European Community
5. Mediation in arranging joint ventures and licencing agreements
6. Access to university know-how and expertise in The Netherlands

Summary

Based on our own experiences and from what we have learned from others, the best practice to stimulate the international transfer of technology based businesses in a region could be the establishment of an internationally oriented transfer centre. This transfer centre should be well known to trade and industry in the region. The best way to start up international transfer activities is to start with high technology. However, this high technology has been introduced in the vital, traditional sectors, too. Even the textile industry is high-tech nowadays!

The time needed to start up a well-organized network for international technology transfer is at least three years. During this period such a network needs the extra support of a start-up grant. In the third year this grant could be decreased. After this period, local and regional support should still be available. This could take the form of a general support system for business innovation in the region, including training facilities and venture capital.

The best selection criteria should be marketing criteria. The most important elements in international business transfer are "mentality" and the right marketing approach. Small and medium- sized industries have no staff to communicate with time-consuming Community agencies. Therefore, the best way to stimulate the smaller industries in Europe is to stimulate the vitalization of business life in the region by stimulating regional, industrial innovation programmes.

The conditions necessary to operate a successful international transfer centre are:

1. Suitable number, size and pattern of existing (spin- off) firms
2. Business development services, training and consultancy firms
3. An "entrepreneurial" university based on technology and/or research centres (technical colleges, industry)
4. Financial agencies
5. Involvement of local and regional authorities

Let it be borne in mind that the university and industry are allies: the university needs money to make knowledge, industry needs knowledge to make money.

4.9 The Twente Centre for Innovation and Entrepreneurship: An example of public-private partnership for the development of business opportunities

Willem E. During

Introduction

The Twente Centre for Innovation and Entrepreneurship (CIOT in Dutch) was initiated by the department of graduate studies in management of the University of Twente, in close co-operation with the Business and Technology Centre (BTC) Twente, the Rabobank (a major Dutch bank) and a firm of innovation consultants. The ministry of economic affairs provided, through a programme of the regional authorities, part of the funding to cover initial expenses of the centre.

The centre's aim is to strengthen the quality of entrepreneurship as one of the major conditions for successful development of business and business opportunities in knowledge-intensive industries. By training, consulting and development of course material the CIOT offers its services to:

1. Independent entrepreneurs of new businesses and of existing small and medium-sized businesses (SMEs)
2. Entrepreneurs within larger organizations (intrapreneurs)
3. Educational institutions and government organizations

The first part of this paper presents an overview of this, for The Netherlands unique, co-operation of the partners in CIOT. The importance of the bank as a medium to communicate to the target enterprises will be demonstrated. The second part describes our view of entrepreneurship and the opportunities for training in this field. The third part of the paper discusses the centre's activities for start-up companies and some of the results to date.

The Structure of CIOT

CIOT has opted for a small and flexible organization. The policy of CIOT is to bring together persons from various organizations who see an interest for themselves and for their organization in developing and stimulating entrepreneurship. We call this "networking".

It will be obvious that for different activities we will not always find the same persons or institutions interested. The specific role of CIOT up to this moment has been:

1. To define a topic of interest and design an outline of possible activities
2. To communicate the planned activities and search for interested partners. In particular we look for people who are prepared to
   - Invest time for developing an idea into a feasible action plan
   - Participate in the activities proper
   - Invest money to realize the necessary stages of design development and try-out
3. To "direct" and organize the development of the planned activities
4. To market, provide and organize the activities proper

The resulting structure of CIOT is represented in Fig. 1. Up to this moment the CIOT is part of the department of graduate studies in management, which is ultimately accountable. In the near future CIOT will become an independent foundation. To ensure participation of the business community an advisory board of three people was formed. The members are a business manager, a bank manager and the former dean of the faculty.

Specific activities of CIOT are organized on a project basis. The small business management course is a joint development of CIOT, Rabobank and the Business and Technology Centre Twente, in close co-operation with six independent entrepreneurs. Together with the university, the bank provided the money to develop this course. Furthermore, the Rabobank plays an important role in marketing the course to its clients. The course is meant for owners-managers of small and medium-sized companies and has a total duration of ten days (5x2 days with 2- to 4 week intervals). A steering committee (one faculty member, one entrepreneur, two from the Rabobank) provides assistance in further development of the course.

The course "becoming an entrepreneur" is a joint development of CIOT and Van der

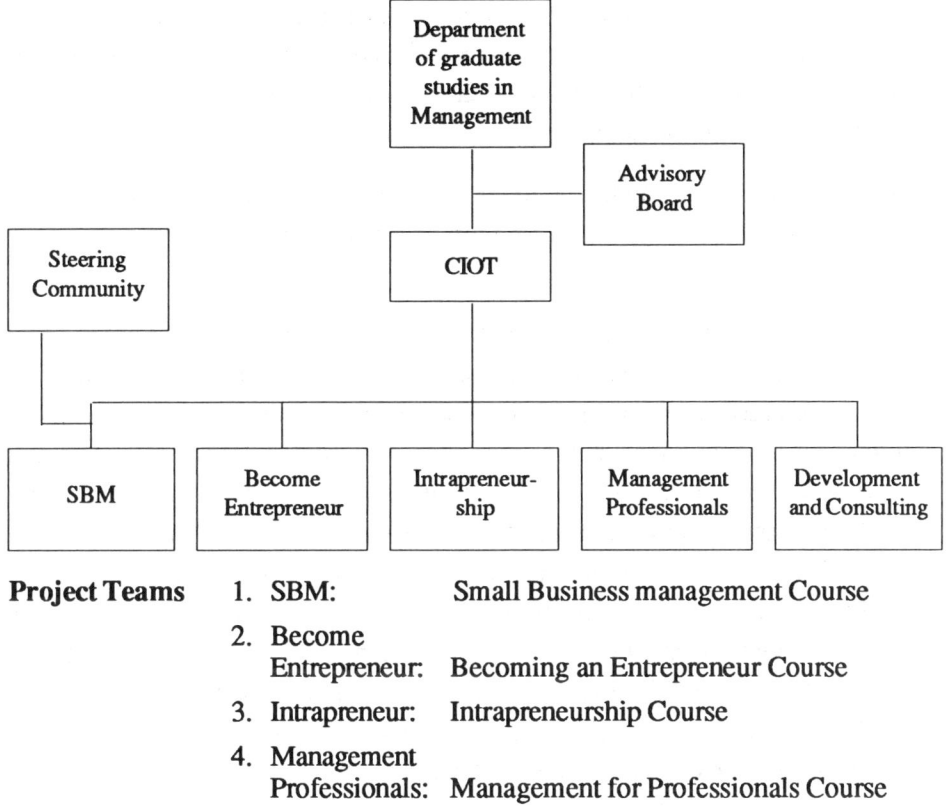

Figure 1: Structure of CIOT

third part of this paper. The "intrapreneurship" course is still in the development stages together with a large company. The "management for professionals" course is meant for medical professionals in large hospitals; this course is a development of CIOT, a foundation for postgraduate medical studies and a large hospital near the university.

A last activity of CIOT consists of the development of course material and of consulting with regard to entrepreneurial problems.

Entrepreneurship: What It Is and How To Teach It

Entrepreneurship is difficult to define as is also the case for complex notions like innovation and quality. A definition like "to initiate, maintain, or organize a profit-oriented business unit for production, or distribution of economic goods or services" (Cole 1959) may illustrate this. There is a wealth of literature in which important elements of entrepreneurship become clear. An excellent overview is given in the encyclopedia for entrepreneurship (Kent et al.1982).

Entrepreneurship is closely linked to the notion of individuals seeing and seizing opportunities. The prototype of an entrepreneur is the founder of a new business firm.

It is the independent entrepreneur who by means of "neue Kombinationen" (new combinations) creates new economic possibilities. In a broader perspective we may state that entrepreneurship is dependent upon the interaction between an entrepreneuring individual and his/her environment (Cooper 1986). For the independent entrepreneur the environment consists of customers, financing institutions, suppliers, government and so on. For the "intrapreneur" (Pinchott 1985) the organization itself is the environment, e.g. the department head, the finance department, the company regulations, and so on. The common feature of independent intrapreneurship and entrepreneurship consists of detecting and realizing new opportunities to serve potential customers, while taking a personal risk of loss (financial or "status"). The difference is that an independent entrepreneur may choose his own environment while the intrapreneur has ultimately to comply with the company constraints.

Although it is difficult to give a clear definition of entrepreneurship, consensus exists about several elements which are essential (Timmons 1982). Perhaps the best way to illustrate these is to describe a situation which is typical for a lack of entrepreneurship. In this case we see that:

1. There are no initiatives to set new goals or to execute tasks in a new way.

2. There is little or no reaction with regard to new developments in the environment.

3. People do not dare to get outside the given rules.

4. The organization has little feeling for actual problems of the "people in the field".

5. Norms and motivations are system-oriented instead of client-oriented.

From this illustration we can now formulate some conditions for individuals and for organizations that are conducive to entrepreneurship.

Condition 1: Individuals and organizations alike are opportunity-directed. A strong orientation to the environment is an important element of this condition. On the individual level "all" people are evaluating their experiences in the light of possible opportunities instead of mere problems that have to be solved.

Condition 2: Individuals and organizations alike are initiative- and action-oriented. When you see an opportunity to improve present functioning, act on it. Do not lose time in lengthy studies. Given rules are not meant to hamper initiative; rules can be changed.

Condition 3: When developments impede on present operations, new goals are formulated and implemented. Flexibility in company activities and individual tasks is part of company life.

Condition 4: Individuals have the freedom to search for the resources to realize an opportunity, and to decide with whom they will try to realize it.

From our past research it is clear that making use of new opportunities is hampered if present operations are not managed properly (During 1986). This leads to another condition.

Condition 5: Entrepreneurship is supplemented by good management. To realize the potential of an opportunity all activities must as much as possible be goal-directed and efficient. Hardly ever does an opportunity exist that involves only all new activities. What is already known must be used to full advantage.

When all five conditions are met, the organization may acquire excellence in entrepreneurship. For all kinds of organizations we can define a "line of excellence" (see Fig. 2).

In the next section of this paper we will give some examples of how the conditions can be better met through education and training.

Opportunities for Education in Entrepreneurship

In the Introduction we learned that a growing demand for entrepreneurship has manifested itself. The University of Twente saw this as an opportunity to stimulate and develop sound entrepreneurship through training activities. Parallel with the

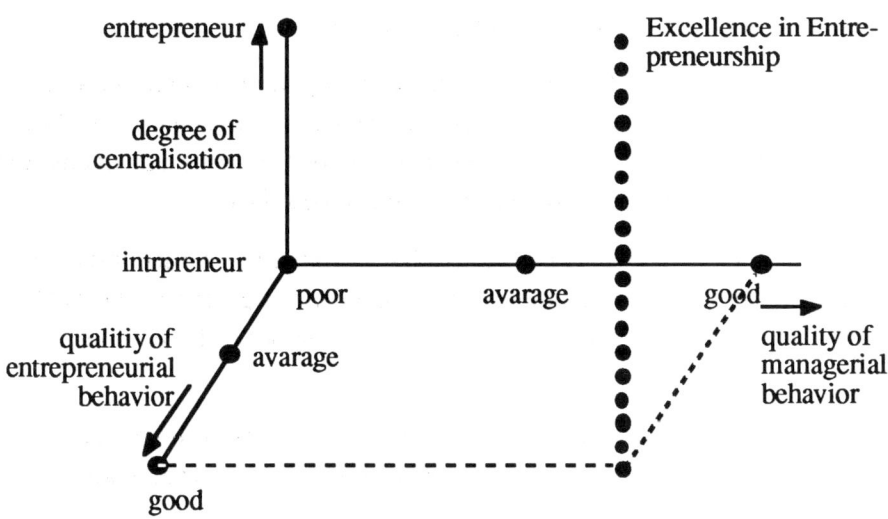

Figure 2: Relation between entrepreneurship, management and centralization of decision making. Good management and good entrepreneurship gives excellence.

development stages of a young company a number of objectives have been formulated (Table 1).

Table 1: Objectives of a young company

Development stage:	Course objective:
Incubation	Raise awareness
Formal beginning	Develop business plan
Try-out	Develop marketing and finance plan
Early growth and extended growth	Develop management and entrepreneurial skills

As stated before, CIOT runs courses for students of the university and engineering schools, for entrepreneurs starting their own business and for managers of existing innovative companies. The courses for students have as their main objective to create an interest in and understanding of entrepreneurship. The other courses are directed at acquiring entrepreneurial and managerial skills concurrently.

The different courses of CIOT have some common features. All the participants have to develop a business plan, most cases are derived from the participant's own situation; all teaching staff is actively involved with business practice, the focus is on practical value. The course "becoming an entrepreneur" may serve as an example.

The Course "Becoming an Entrepreneur"

Participants

People who take this course all have decided to start a company. Mostly they have an engineering degree and the core of their business idea is some invention or special development of their own. These people take part in a special programme with the university. Development of the business idea takes place from the university grounds. For technical development university facilities may be used during one year. The majority install themselves in the BTC after this year, if they are successful.

Course Organization

The training programme for young innovative entrepreneurs has been developed in close co-operation with a firm of innovation consultants, who are also active in the field of business start-ups. A project team (university teacher and consultant) is accountable for the course organization and teaching.

To attain the necessary practical orientation, many business consultants, managers, accountants and banking institutions participate in the teaching of special topics, in presenting real-life cases and in screening the business plans. All contributions are on a contract basis.

We have no "permanent structure" for this course. Financial means are for the most part provided by the local office for the unemployed, the university and the European Social Fund on a year-to-year basis.

Course Structure

The training programme consists of a common core for all and optional coures in accordance with individual needs.

The common core centres around four topics; the structure and problems of a start-up process, marketing, finance and conditions for start-up products and drawing up the business plan of the individual's venture. This core is worked on in six half-day sessions. In between the different sessions individual needs for special topics and for drawing up the business plan are dealt with by several people from the university and businesses. The course ends with a presentation of the business plan to a panel of bankers, accountants and business consultants. Afterwards individual consulting is possible. Both during the regular course and during the consulting, elements of entrepreneurship and management are incorporated.

How does the course help to achieve the five conditions for entrepreneurship we formulated?

1. Opportunity direction. Participants in the course are generally technology-oriented by nature and by education. Apart from further technical development, emphasis is put on the recognition and evaluation of realistic market opportunities for the different product or consulting ideas. Participants are strongly stimulated to interact with representatives of potential client organizations, business societies and market specialists. Special exercises are developed for getting into contact with these kinds of people and for analysing data thus gathered. Another topic is the analysis of competitors' activities in the light of meeting customers' needs.

2. Initiative and action orientation: Generally there are no problems in this field with the participants, who are determined to start up there own business. Special activities are related to cases and to drawing up action plans for the participant's own business creation process.

3. Flexibility in goal orientation. Most start-up companies have to change their original plans in the light of unanticipated events or developments. To prepare the entrepreneurs for the necessary flexibility, we use exercises in contingency planning and in drawing up action plans for sudden (simulated but plausible) events.

4. Directed search for resources: Although the freedom for choice is left to the participants, we place a lot of emphasis on the choice of a business partner. Especially the basic ideas about the way of doing business, the personal goals for becoming an entrepreneur and the intention with regard to business growth have to be comparable.

5. Good entrepreneurship and good management: Participants are confronted with basic managerial techniques with regard to: marketing and sales; financial accounting and control; negotiating; bidding for and finalizing contracts; and management for development projects.

For students of the university and engineering schools we offer a comparable programme. The main difference is that only a small number of the students will actually start a business after completing the plan. The emphasis in this course is more on entrepreneurship than on management.

Course evaluation results show that the strong points of the course are: number of sessions; presentation of plans to outside panel; co-operation of management, students and entrepreneurs; exchange of experiences by participants with different backgrounds and experience; use of guest lectures; and practical orientation towards a business plan. Participants would prefer more attention to the following topics: personal consulting between course sessions; practical skills like negotiating, selling, cost accounting; cases; and government regulation with regard to financial support. About 70% of the entrepreneurs who participated in the course are interested in follow-up activities or courses in the following subjects: marketing and selling techniques, promotion, and management of a small firm. Furthermore, former participants are interested in personal consulting with regard to actual business problems.

Results of interviews with former participants show that:
1. Entrepreneurs find the course was useful for solving problems during start-up and early growth (83%).
2. Drawing up the business plan is very important. Entrepreneurs become aware of many aspects they would have overseen. Every year the plan is updated (75%).
3. Entrepreneurs learned to be less one-sidedly technically oriented (75%).

A comparison between starters who followed the course and starters in the same period who did not is presented in Tables 2 to 4. Most course participants percieved the university as a stimulating environment for starting their own business. All participants completed a business plan, compared to 56% of non-participants.

A marked difference exists in the main problems perceived by participants and non-participants. The latter see finance and selling as major problems. Participants see marketing (market strategy) as their most important problem.

Table 2. Role of the university in starting a company and completion of a business plan for participants and non- participants of the course "becoming an entrepreneur"(%)

	Non-participants N=30	Participants N=28
Role of the university		
Stimulating	33	85
No role	67	15
Uncertain	--	--
Business plan		
Yes	56	100
No	44	--

Table 3. Main problems felt during start-up by participants and non-participants (%).

	Non-participants	Participants
Finance	29	20
Orders	23	15
Time management	3	15
Marketing	3	30

Participants are more aware of the usefulness of entrepreneurship courses then are non-participants. "Catching" entrepreneurs in an early stage is important for their development towards better entrepreneurship.

Table 4: Interest in follow-up courses on entrepreneurship by participants and non-participants of the course becoming an entrepreneur"(%)

	Non-participants	Participants
Yes	60	82
No	40	18

Conclusions

Entrepreneurship is of growing importance for the successful operation of organizations. A growing demand for entrepreneuring people creates an opportunity for education and training for graduate and post-graduate programmes.

A training course centred around core topics for developing a business plan and optional courses geared to individual needs has proven to be successful in meeting the requirements for:

1. Opportunity orientation
2. Initiative and action orientation
3. Flexibility in goal orientation
4. Directed search for resources
5. Balance between good entrepreneurship and good management

Joint efforts of the university, business community and (local) government have resulted in a successful training centre for entrepreneurship around the University of Twente. It may be expected that the activities of CIOT will help to raise the quality of entrepreneurship in this region.

References

Cole, Arthur H., Business enterprise in social setting Cambridge, Harvard University Press, 1959

Cooper, Arnold C., Technical entrepreneurship: what do we know? In: The survival of the small firm, vol.2, James Curran et.al. eds. Gower ,1986, pp. 100;113

Dekker, W., De implementatie van innovatie: een zaak van ondernemers. In: Innovatie en Strategie, H.O. Goldschmidt ed. SMO, 1986, pp. 120-146

During, W.E., Innovatieproblematiek in kleine industriele organisaties Van Gorcum, 1986

Kent, Calvin A., Sexton, Donald L., Vesper, Karl H., Encyclopedia of entrepreneurship,Prentice-Hall,. 1982, pp. 425

Keuzekamp, T.M., Management van Creativiteit. In: Ondernemen met Voorsprong Kluwer/COB, 1986, pp. 21-90

Pinchott, G., Intrapreneuring Harper and Row, 1985

Timmons, Jeffry A., New Venture creation: models and methodologies. In: Kent, Sexton and Vesper 1982

5 Initiatives in the Context of Regional Policies in Order to Intensify R & D Activities and Technology Transfer as well as to Improve the Qualification Structures

5.1 Are Science Parks Effective?
A Proposal for Cross-National Research

Hans-Dieter Ganter

Introduction

Most of the science parks in the countries of the European Community and particularly in the Federal Republic of Germany appear to have a number of structural and functional deficiencies. Some of them were existent from their very beginning, others emerged during their development.

The most obvious structural deficiencies are the following:
- Science parks came into existence without taking into account the aims and contents of current regional and / or local structural development planning.
- Science parks were originally planned only under the aspect of opening up local high-tech industry.
- The development targets of science parks are at most medium-term (for the coming 5-6 years).
- Financing science parks guarantees neither their structural expansion nor their functional innovation.
- Science parks with but only specialized companies face the danger of a "one-crop system", which may be harmful in the long run.

Among functional deficiencies of science parks are especially the following: The viability of most of the science park companies is interfered with by insufficient capitalization and unstable future financing capabilities. The provision of services for science park tenants covers their needs in tactical, i.e. administrative tasks rather than in strategic aspects, i.e. management tasks. The follow-up care of companies once they have left the science park appears to be insufficient. Co-operation between science park tenants appears to be underdeveloped. New companies for science parks are predominantly recruited without taking into account the situation of national or international markets. There is no satisfying mediation between the provision of products or services of the science park tenants and the potential demand of local or regional markets. Should there be no possibility of overcoming these deficiencies science parks may fall into a marginal position in national economic contexts.

Starting Points for a Development Model to Overcome the Deficiencies of Science Parks

The required development model implies a number of starting points, which are outlined in the following.

Factors of Economic Success of Science Parks and the Firms Within Them

Firms in technology parks must be installed in close fit with the provision of loan capital. This again depends on well-defined prospective product chances. To reach this aim it is necessary to have an institutionalized integration of the science park with local or regional banks and co-operation with public authorities on a local or regional level. Public authorities should provide specific credit guarantees and subsidies. Moreover, contribution to the expenses by science park firms should depend on corporate earnings. Management of science parks must be in the hands of managers in order to perform the necessary tasks required.

Know-How Logistics for Companies in Science Parks

Universities and colleges as well as - if possible - private research institutes within the region should provide research and consulting capacities for science park tenants at accommodating terms. This requires an intensive formal co-operation between science parks and the institutions mentioned above.

Integration of Science Park Firms into the Regional Economic Structure

Both embedding of science park tenants and their developments should be carried out within the guidelines of the regional economic structure. This requires, on the one hand, using the strength of the regional economic structure with regard to product demand, dynamics of research and development, investment focuses, etc.

On the other hand, the weaknesses of the regional economic structure provide a starting point to stimulate the establishment of firms in science parks, adding to the provision of services and complementing industrial policy within the region.

Encouragement of "Company Pluralism" in Science Parks

To create a solid structure of high-tech companies in science parks, it appears absolutely necessary to recruit corporations for the park that are technology and science-oriented as well as oriented towards "social techniques" such as management consulting firms, companies specializing in professional training or in ergonomic design. Besides firms with an academic background, also those with a handicrafts background should be accepted in the science park if they specialize in production or maintenance of high-tech products. Such a mixed structure encourages the co-operative realization of R&D results in production, selling and service.

Consideration of the Science Parks' Demands in Developing a Regional Infrastructure for Transportation and Communication

An infrastructure must be designed that not only adapts to current needs but also anticipates future needs of the science park. This implies high-grade means of transportation and communication for the region, both quantitatively and qualitatively. It goes without saying, furthermore, that an adequate material-technical supply must be assured to science parks aiming steadily at furnishing a certain excess capacity.

Moreover, regional policy planning for the surroundings of science parks must be open to developing their technical and spatial requirements. It is also necessary to contribute to an intensive promotion of available manpower in order to meet the demands of the industry being encouraged.

Encouraging Companies Leaving Science Park sto Stay Within the Region

To encourage firms that have left the science park to stay in the region, it is necessary to create commercial conditions with a fully developed infrastructure in order to enable companies to establish themselves at low cost. Such conditions should also be offered to those firms which, for various reasons, have not been accepted by the science park. Moreover, it is necessary to increase the quality of life in the region in order to make staying attractive to highly qualified staff as well as entrepreneurs. This implies not only the development of leisure facilities but also the installation of schools, training and further training institutions in the region. Beyond that, it appears to be necessary to offer a complete supply of high quality residential facilities in the region.

Promotion and Protection of the Long-Term Development of Science Parks

To promote and protect the long-term development of science parks, it is highly important to establish some sort of permanent advisory board that represents political interests. Its task is to integrate the development of the science park into all relevant regional and local planning. Furthermore, the planning of industry and its authorities as well as universities should be adjusted. The integration of industry and retailing associations and trade unions fosters the protection of long-term development. The management of science parks should participate on all boards on all levels.

We are planning a comparative study of various science parks. Since this concept in general implies a number of kinds of fostering companies in economic, technological, and regional terms, it is necessary to form groups following existing categorizations such as:

1. Industrial parks

2. Technology parks

3. Science parks

Although industrial parks are not to be subsumed under the term "science parks", they are included in this study as a means of regional structural development and of co-operation between the university and companies. We intend to perform case studies in two units of each category. A further criterion of selection will be economic development of the region in which the science park is located. We are studying science parks in both well-developed regions and regions which are poorly developed. This kind of differentiation also makes it possible for other countries to take part in this study, including Italy, Ireland, the United Kingdom, Denmark, Sweden and Belgium.

Working Perspectives

Working perspectives for the intended projects are:
1. Evaluation of the science parks within their region
2. Drafting aims in connection with development and planning for the long-term future of science parks within the boundaries of regional development
3. Strategic consulting by science parks in realizing long-term development models

The following questions will guide evaluation:
- What was the political and institutional context of the inception of the science park?
- What political intentions guided the founding a science park?
- What is the current development perspective of the science park like?
- How is the science park funded?
- What is the structure of firms within the science park like?
- What is the experience with regard to the viability of former and current firms in the science park?
- What is the structure of the supply of services by the science park to its clients?
- What kind of co-operation exists between the science park and the industries in the region?
- In what way are contacts with institutions of the region and communities established?
- What is public opinion on the science park like?

Concerning future planning of science parks the above-mentioned approaches are valid. Experiences from other science parks as given in various research reports may be used. One might also think of a co-operation with science parks of research teams evaluating them in various countries.

Strategic consulting can only be designed in combination with future planning, which has to have come first.

5.2 Tecnopolis: Between International Tendencies and Regional Development

Umberto Bozzo

Tecnopolis Novus Ortus is a science park which was founded in 1984 in Valenzano-Bari. Its operative programme is based on the cooperation among the scientific, productive, financial and political-administrative systems and it aims at the development of a new town model, according to the Japanese concept of "technopolis". It is characterized by a double and wider goal: on the one hand, it offers itself as a "technological bridge" towards the developing countries of the Mediterranean and, on the other, as a "technological observatory" for the new Mediterranean markets. The Tecnopolis program represents an evolution of the experience of integration between the R & D activities, education and technical services, led since 1969 by the C.S.A.T.A. consortium, which was founded in that same year as an association among universities, industries and southern development agencies.

The C.S.A.T.A. consortium has acted as a promotional element in the Tecnopolis programme, proposing some lines of intervention based on the experience gained during 15 years of activity in the information technologies' sector: an experiment which was directed both towards constant comparison with the evaluative trends of the economy on an international level and to a careful analysis of the new models of technological development, in particular of the growing phenomenon of science parks.

An "incremental" approach has allowed for the planning of the next stages of development in which the complete realization of C.S.A.T.A.'s goals, which had been expected only in one stage, made access to a further and wider level of intervention possible. In particular, Tecnopolis Novus Ortus aims at promoting:

1. The development of specific technical services to support the production apparatus
2. The revitalization of both production activities and of service activities in the traditional sectors
3. The creation of new production and service activities
4. The call for high-tech production initiatives
5. The increase of skilled jobs
6. The testing of cultural promotion models and the organization of leisure life

On the present six hectares, there are 20,000 square metres of infrastructures, including research and demonstration laboratories, a large processing and communications centre, an education centre, a congress centre, offices and services and leisure facilities.

Over 400 people are presently employed in the park working on research programmes led in collaboration with industry; educational programmes and on programmes at the international schools; resarch programmes of the new, small enterprises centred in the park; and in the different service activities devoted to local enterprise. These initiatives arose out of the contacts the park has established with industry, with the university and with the research institutions.

Different multi-year research programmes are already in operation, in collaboration with large industrial companies, both Italian and foreign, on subjects of common interest, such as multimedia documentation systems, the development of advanced sensorial systems for factory automation, the production of multimedia training packages, the intelligent planning of space robotics operations.

The university has been involved in testing new curricula at a high level of specialization, such as those which the two international schools, SASIAM (for training mathematics engineers) and ASMIT (for training new technologies managers) are aiming to emulate. Professors and university researchers have been asked to give the results of their own scientific activities for use in "enterprise plans".

Also planned with the university, is "Zeus", a type of multi-tenant building, which will include educational, innovation and interdisciplinary research programmes.

Furthermore, it has been proposed to specific national research institutions that new laboratories be built, and new programmes be initiated. One of these institutions is the National Research Council which is going to found an important research centre in the Tecnopolis area.

As regards local enterprises, besides a Business Management Training School founded by the Associazione Industriali of Bari, Tecnopolis includes a series of advanced services addressed to the SMEs: the Microelectronics Centre works on failure analysis, homologation and certifying of electronic components; while, the Reliability Circle aims at collecting, processing and spreading data concerning electronic components, and the Centre of Electronic Publishing aims at producing technical documentation for enterprises.

Tecnopolis has also planned a complex programme according to the Community's directives and in the meanwhile is aiming at the promotion of a specialized information market in southern Italy. The expected future interventions are addressed to the industrial tertiary sector users, as well as to the local public administration. They aim at promoting the demands of specialized information while tailoring their offers of advanced services to favour increases in local enterprise capacities. This is a meaningful example of a strategy whereby the international dimension is constantly being joined to the regional one.

All the initiatives of the park, which have as their goal emulating the EEC's programmes in the field of research and innovation, aim at joining quality with the present face of research in the international field, through cultural stimulation and through current initiatives for the diffusion of information technologies within a local context.

5.3 Technology Transfer: Enhancing Scotland's Competitiveness (Summary)

David Lightbody

The principal focus for the Scottish Development Agency's initiatives which support the generation and commercialization of technologically advanced products and processes is its Technology Transfer Division (TTD).

TTD's main tool is its Company Programme which aims to sharpen the international competitiveness of Scottish companies by introducing new products and processes principally through licence and joint-venture agreements with foreign partners. Companies of all sizes are guided through a business development process involving five main phases:

1. Strategy Formulation: Identifying the company's key competitive strengths and deriving the criteria for business development
2. Market Opportunities: Examining a new selected number (generally five or six) of product/market areas which match the company's strengths and ranking these against the business development criteria
3. Market Focus: Analysing in detail the most attractive product/market areas (generally one or two) and identifying and selecting potential foreign partners
4. Exploitation: Establishing the basis of agreement for a license or joint-venture arrangement with a foreign partner
5. Feasibility: Determining the full implications of the technology transfer venture and defining a detailed business plan for the company

Using this structured approach to technology transfer the Scottish Development Agency is registering notable successes with its client companies.

5.4 Pilot Projects as an Instrument for Technology

Hermann Kösters

Introduction

ZENIT (Zentrum in Nordrhein-Westfalen für Innovation und Technik GmbH), based in Mülheim an der Ruhr, was established for the promotion of economic activity in technical fields. The major areas of activity of ZENIT are consultancy services and the initiation of pilot projects in the areas of computer science, production engineering and environmental engineering.

Nearly all organizations working for the promotion of regional development focus on new technologies as a main object of interest. Frequently putting new products including modern technologies on the market increases turnover only very slowly. With respect to work done in developing the new products by the producers, often with the aid of developing agencies, this occurrence is rather disappointing. The reason is quite clear: customers usually require references and obviously new products have little references as they are new. In this situation therefore, there is an urgent need for pilot projects to test the effectiveness of new products or new processes.

This paper reviews some practical experiences we made with new processes for soil reclamation. All industrial regions in Europe have land that has become contaminated by substances that can present hazards to future users. These areas are a serious handicap for economic development in general.

Aims of the Pilot Projects

Against this backdrop, the aims of the soil reclamation pilot projects were:

1. To define the objectives of soil reclamation in the light of problems posed by specific areas

2. To create a basis for the practical testing and improvement of innovative environmental engineering processes on the basis of these objectives

3. To test combinations of various possible solutions

4. To ensure that development and testing are adequately financed

As these aims indicate, the major objective of the proposed pilot projects is to promote technological development.

Various cities in the Ruhr area have already made available test areas which pose quite varied pollution problems. In view of the importance of abandoned coking plant sites in the Ruhr area, it was decided to approach a location of this type first.

Test Programme

A major element of the pilot projects proposed by ZENIT was to give interested companies an opportunity to have an influence on the analysis of the test area with regard to specific processes.

By their very nature, investigations of polluted soils by public bodies tend to concentrate on risk assessment, i.e. on analysing the toxicology of the pollutants and the possibility of pollutant escape. Such investigations must also attempt to determine the extent of the polluted area. On the other hand, the procedure proposed by ZENIT, concentrating on technological development, offers the possibility of analysing a large number of parameters which are relevant from the process-engineering point of view, although initially on a rather small area. The programme, therefore, includes investigations which are relevant both for in-site processes and for on-site processes with regard to the thermal, extractive and microbiological features.

The major points of the programme are as follows:

1. Investigation of the geological and hydrogeological situation

2. Determination of the particle size distribution of the soil

3. Determination of permeability and ion exchange capacity

4. Detailed investigation of the anorganic pollution of the soil

5. Detailed investigation of the organic pollution of the soil

6. Determination of the biological activity of the soil and the biodegradability of the evaluates

Results - Reclamation Processes

On the basis of the results of these investigations, the following processes have been proposed by ZENIT after discussion with the various companies interested.

Air Extraction Harnes System

The extraction of air from the soil is a frequently practised method of removing volatile organic compounds, particularly chlorinated hydrocarbons, from polluted soil. In view of the results of the analyses made, it was clear that it would not be feasible to reclaim the test area by this method, as organic substances with very high boiling points represent the major source of contamination. However, we believe that there are various points in favour of this process.

First, the extraction of air from the soil would make a contribution to the reduction of acute hazards. The results of the investigations have shown that there is no risk of contamination escaping via the ground water. Air escaping from the soil, therefore, represents the major environmental risk. For this reason, action to seal the area has already been discussed. As this would represent a serious obstacle to further reclamation work, we propose that the extraction of air from the soil should first be attempted. We do not believe that this process has already been tried out at an abandoned coking plant site.

Furthermore, the extraction of soil air would facilitate the subsequent removal of soil for on-site processing, as it would reduce the extent of safety precautions required to protect workers in this area. Finally, this process is interesting from a technical point of view as a preliminary stage to solvent extraction. The extraction of air would remove substances which could later form an azeotropic mixture with the solvent and which it would not be easy to separate from the solvent, at least not by distillation.

Extraction of Pollutants (Kresken-Wessling Process)

The reclamation plant consists in principle of two cycles, one carrying the polluted soil and one carrying the solvent. Whereas the polluted soil only passes through the cycle once, the solvent can be recycled almost indefinitely. This offers the possibility of extreme concentration of the pollutants.

It is proposed to use amyl ether or petroleum ether or another substance with a similar low boiling point as the solvent. Such solvents combine the advantage of high efficiency with a high evaporation rate which would mean that pollutants could be removed almost 100% without leaving any solvent residue in the soil. In addition, due to the high evaporation rate of the solvent, it would be possible to operate the process as a closed evaporation - condensation - extraction loop and to concentrate the pollutants by repeatedly using the same solvent.

The polluted soil is transported to the plant and then passes through an inlet chamber which is operated at a vacuum and is carried to the counter-current extraction chamber by a screw conveyor. The extraction chamber itself operates on the principle of a rotating drum spiral elevator. As the drum rotates, the polluted soil passes upwards through the chamber. Solvent passes downwards and is collected at the bottom of the chamber.

The soil emerging from the top of the extraction chamber still contains solvent and is passed through a drying or degassing section before it emerges through an outlet chamber operated at a vacuum for replacement. The drying and degassing section is connected to the solvent condenser in order to minimize the loss of solvent vapour.

The solvent, now containing pollutant, is fed to a vaporizer in which it is cleaned by distillation before passing to the condenser. In the condenser, the solvent is condensed and then returned to the solvent tank which in turn feeds the extraction chamber. The pollutants removed from the solvent by distillation are fed to the system outlet for disposal.

The only method suitable for the disposal of the highly concentrated solutions of pollutants collected in the collection tank of the plant will be extremely high temperature combustion.

This leads us to the third process proposed.

Thermal Treatment (Deutag-Von Roll Process)

The functioning of the Deutag-Von Roll runs thus. In the upper section of a rotary tubular kiln, soil is intensively mixed by the rotation of the tube and ignited by an oil burner with a capacity of 185 kg/h installed in the end of the kiln at an average temperature of 800° C, which is sufficient to obtain the temperature of 650° C required for the complete combustion and evaporation of the organic substances in the soil. Gas velocity in the drum is limited to ensure that the soil passes through the drum very slowly. The drum has a length of 10 m and a diameter of 2 m.

The flue gases from the rotary kiln are fed to the combustion chamber. The combustion chamber has an internal diameter of 2.2 m and a height of 6.5 m. In view of the flue gas flow rate involved and the temperature of 1200° C and a gas velocity of approximately 2.2 m/s, the flue gases take approximately 3 s to pass through the combustion chamber.

The ashes are removed in a dry state and carried by a conveyor belt to a water bath with a temperature of approximately 70° to 80° C for cooling. The water requirement is approximately 0.5 m^3/h. The hot vapour produced during the cooling process is extracted and mixed with the pre-heated combustion air.

The flue gas emerging from the combustion chamber is cooled in an evaporative cooler to a temperature of approximately 470° C by the injection of water.

For passing through a cloth filter, the temperature of the flue gas must not be higher than 250°C. For this reason, the flue gas is cooled by an air-flue gas heat exchanger with the additional admixture of air before it is passed to the cloth filter. In order to prevent excessive fouling, a double cyclone separator to remove solid particles is installed upstream of the heat exchanger.

The flue gas leaving the heat exchanger, cooled with fresh air down to 150° C is filtered by a cloth filter which can reach an efficiency of up to 99% depending on the solid particle content of the flue gas.

5.5 Promoting Research Advancement in the Lagging Regions of Italy

Stefano Boffo and Francesco Gagliardi

Manufacturing today has become more complex and needs the support of "advanced" service activities upstream and downstream of the production process. It is well known that in the present dominant technical and economic paradigm, science and research can not any longer be considered as part of a separate sphere independent from production and economic relations.

"Upstream" investment in science and research has become indispensable for the long-term maintenance of production processes and the renewal of products and techniques. As a result, the fixed form that capital embodies in the production process now tends to be relatively less important, while what Professor Christopher Freeman has called the "intangible forms of capital" become more and more determinant. It is therefore to be expected that a higher concentration of research institutions could influence the economic growth of a region in a positive way. The recent three-year programme for the south of Italy, approved by the Italian parliament, places priority on the development of research activities and the dissemination of scientific and technical knowledge in the Mezzogiorno: "the technology issue has to be the hinge of the new discretionary public policy..."; it has to be the main set of guidelines by which to set up the local and central policies and to develop behaviour patterns of the social actors, tuned to the new technological transformation processes". The directions indicated in the programme have been taken up in part in the 1986 Law 64 for the Mezzogiorno which establishes, together with other incentives, special provisions for the development of advanced business services and technological and scientific innovation (see Table 1).

Table 1: Incentives in the Mezzogiorno

Type	Present Laws	New Law (no. 64/86)
Financial	- Grants for up to 40% of capital expenditure depending on size of investment in new initiatives (a)	- As before but enlarging the potential users (b)
	- Cheap loans for up to 40% of capital expenditure in new initiatives (a)	- As before but enlarging the potential users (b)
	- Support on interest rates for loans on restructuring and recovering manufacturing plants (reducing to 30% of current interest rate); restricted to some industrial sectors	- As before
Tax	- Ten years exemption of profits from 50% tax on new initiatives	- 100% exemption
	- Ten years 70% tax exemption on manufacturing plants (buildings)	- 100% exemption
	- Negative VAT	- As before
Labour costs	- 100% exemption on company's social security contribution in some industrial sectors	- As before
Scientific research	- Low-cost loans from IMI funds (for applied scientific research)	- As before on IMI funds
		- Grants of 50% - 75% of expenditures of research project, scientific and management services (up to 500 million lire, limited to SMEs)
		- Low-cost loans for purchases in high-tech investments
Other	- Reductions in railway and sea freight rates and in the tax on electricity consumption	- As before
	- Support to state enterprises in return for obligation to make 60% of total investments in Mezzogiorno	- As before
	- Obligation to public administration to disburse 30% to 45% of its expenditure both in investment and purchases in the Mezzogiorno	- As before

(a) Grants and low-cost loans can cumulate to 70% of total capital expenditure
(b) Grants and low-cost loans can cumulate to 75% of total capital expenditure

At present, the R&D activities either private or public, are largely located in the centre-north of Italy. A few data can describe the significant features of the current situation in the Mezzogiorno:

1. Only 24% of Italian private and public research institutions (apart from universities) are located in the Mezzogiorno and its share of total research funds is 18.5%.

2. In 1986 it had 9000 employees in R&D (comprising 8% the national total), 90% of them in the public sector.

3. Only 5% of the southern researchers work in firms either public or private, whereas the national average is 50%.

Nevertheless, it should be emphasized that there is no significant difference in the scientific productivity of southern research institutions compared with the national average.

The present contribution focuses on the role of scientific institutions in the development of the lagging regions of Italy and the initiatives undertaken in this field by our agency, the FORMEZ (Training and Studies Centre for the South of Italy).

But prior to discussion of this role let us briefly introduce ourselves. FORMEZ is a government agency which was set up in the 1960s within the broader context of the special intervention plan designed to help Italy's less-developed southern regions. It specializes in planning, promoting and organizing training scheme studies and pilot actions. FORMEZ provides organizational support to public and private bodies and, in particular, public administration and small and medium-sized enterprises. The aim behind this is to foster a continuous process of modernization in the south.

These programmes are designed to promote innovation, improve management expertise, create new professional profiles and set new standards of management in the public institutions. Particular attention has been given to specific projects designed to spread technological innovation throughout small and medium-sized enterprises (SMEs).

Within this general framework, FORMEZ, in collaboration with the Ministry for the Mezzogiorno, provides southern universities and research institutions with financial, technical and organizational support in order to encourage the general advancement of these institutions.

In the seriously underdeveloped southern scientific and technical system, an important feature to be pointed out is the relative strength of universities, whose numbers have increased considerably since the late 1970s. Today, there are 19 universities in the Mezzogiorno (37% of the national total), fairly equally distributed among the different southern regions, with over 6000 professors and researchers (30% of the national total) and 351,597 students.

Universities are an intellectual resource that may influence in a positive way the economic and technological potential of the regions in which they are located. In addition they can provide a neutral forum for discussion and act as a catalyst for both ideas and action. It has also to be mentioned that universities can (or should) represent a potential source of "spin-off" by researchers wishing to start their own firms.

Southern universities can thus play an essential role in policies for the development of the Mezzogiorno, by contributing through training and research as well as through direct intervention in the innovation process. But this requires a significant change both in attitudes of the academic community and in the organization of scientific institutions.

In general, the interaction of the Italian university with its industrial environment is relatively limited. Actually, up to now, it has been mainly carried out by individuals holding an academic position. This is largely due to present regulations and procedures and the organization of the university administration. The situation is even worse in southern universities, where to the insufficient ties with the external environment are added:

1. The limited availability of technical personnel capable of experimenting and, furthermore, putting their experimental results in strategic areas into operation

2. The lack of information on access to financial means available in the local, national and international system

3. The poor information about new developments in research and technology

In order to overcome these limitations, a twofold apparatus has been set up by FORMEZ. The first part relates to the universities', administration. A pilot project has been developed in the largest universities of southern Italy (Naples and Palermo), aiming to re-design the organizational structure of the administrations and to increase their productivity. The objective is to adequately administer a range of activities better and more widely with in the local socio-economic environment and to have more efficient administrative management of scientific research. Five more southern universities will shortly be included in this project, so that within 1988 nearly 40% of southern universities will have a new organizational architecture in managing scientific research.

The second part of the plan has been developed to enhance, through an International Fellowship Programme, the research capacity of southern universities in disciplines considered strategic for the development of the Mezzogiorno. The programme involves an increased exchange with the international scientific environment. Seventy scholars from 18 public research centres and a southern university have been awarded grants to carry out research in academic centres of nine foreign countries. At the same time, 28 scholars from 10 different countries have spent from 2 to 12 months researching and teaching in 14 scientific institutions in southern Italy. A further three-year fellowship programme is now on the way to being realized. It will include nearly 400 additional grants as well as many seminars and various activities aimed at spreading the results of funded research.

The basic assumption of this initiative is the idea that contemporary social and economic development can be launched and sustained only in the presence of a relatively strong cognitive and scientific cultural research system. Admittedly, such a context is not easily created from scratch. However, putting southern universities into communication with outstanding research institutions, for stering the exchange of scholars and establishing links of mutual co-operation in research seems to be the right intermediate step.

Even if the two initiatives seem to have reached the goals they had for themselves FORMEZ is conscious that they are only part of the major objective of a development policy that is to foster a deep interaction between the university and its social and economic environment. In order to encourage active co-operation in this field, various initiatives have been set up in the Mezzogiorno. Among them, it is worth mentioning here the Special Project for Scientific Applied Research in the Mezzogiorno (Progetto Speciale no. 35, 1979), a state provision which aims to strengthen the research and technical system in the Mezzogiorno by setting up and improving research- and service-oriented consortia with the participation of the southern universities and by financing the training of researchers. The project, which is run by FORMEZ, will provide 1000 new researchers; this is 12% of the present number of research workers in the Mezzogiorno.

The management of this project has become particularly complex since a majority of the research centres have been deliberately located in areas lacking an "environment" already fertilized by similar previous actions. The main difficulties met by FORMEZ here have essentially been two:

1. The recruitment of managers in the area able to catalyse the local actors (university, local authority, firms, etc.)

2. The selection of individuals possessing the necessary knowledge and capacities to be trained as researchers

At present, 13 consortia in various areas of scientific research, such as computer sciences, "teledetection", laser manufacturing, solar energy, pharmaceutical products and food production have been set up (see Table 2) and about 110 staff researchers have been trained.

It is worth pointing out that acting only on the supply side of research is not enough, at least at the beginning, to fill the gap between university research and the needs of the local economic environment. The strengthening of the universities and their administrative bodies and the widespread diffusion of research institutes is a useful, but not in itself sufficient, tool for cementing the interaction between the university and its local society. Unless these actions and structures emerge through the organic regional planning of applied research, there is the risk that they will tend to be under-used and not satisfy local requirements. The need for such planning is felt all the more in areas where the relative weakness of industry may lead to an insufficient level of demand for applied research or where the local demands often tend to remain unspoken. Any such planning should be promoted and co-ordinated by local authorities through the creation of specific structures established in collaboration with different indigenous social actors (university, research centres, science parks, unions, entrepreneurial association, etc.). Any such planning should enhance the capacity of local resources through the diffusion of scientific and technological knowledge and the growth of human capital.

Throughout Europe the lagging regions present serious and difficult problems. Thirty years of communicating policy have been able to reduce the distance from the more developed areas, but not to overcome it. In this context science and research policies cannot be conceived of as a "panacea". However, it is important to start with concrete, even if limited, initiatives based on the involvement and strengthening of local resources in research activities. This has been the philosophy followed by

Table 2: Research and service-oriented consortia in the Mezzogiorno set up and improved with the 1979 Special Provision no. 35

Name and site of the Consortia (a)	Field	Research staff present end 1985
CRAI Rende Cosenza (Univ. della Calabria)	Computer science and manufacturing automation	50
CSATA Valenzano-Bari (Univ. di Bari)	Computer science and manufacturing automation	90
CONPHOEBUS Catania (Univ. di Palermo)	Solar energy	20
Stazione Sperimentale per l'Industria delle Conserve Alimentari Angri-Salerno (Minist. Industria)	Agricultural and food production	27
Mario Negri Sud Chieti	Pharmaceutical products	40
Stazione Sperimentale per l'Industria delle Essenze e dei Derivati Agrumari Reggio Calabria (Univ. di Messina)	Agricultural and food production	14
CRIAI Napoli (Univ. di Napoli)	Computer science and manufacturing automation	55
CRES Monreale-Palermo (Univ. di Palermo)	Computer science and manufacturing automation	22
CSEI Catania (Univ. di Catania)	Development of water data bank	3
BONOMO Castel del Monte-Bari (Univ. di Bari)	Agricultural and food production	29
CO.RI.SA. Sassari (Univ. di Sassari)	Application of "teledetection" in agriculture	57
LASER Bari (Univ. di Bari)	Laser manufacturing application	12
AGROBIOS Matera (Univ. di Potenza)	Biotechnology	30

(a) In parantheses the university participating in the Consortia is reported

FORMEZ and we will continue to promote indigenous actors in their own development. However, any such policy can not at all be thought of as effective without being planned and co-ordinated at either the national or the EEC level.

5.6 Information Technology Centres as Instruments of Regional Policy to Promote Information Technology in the Federal Republic of Germany

Norbert Tüschen

The Concept of Information Technology Centres (Informationstechnik-Zentren)

In recent years we have had to acknowledge that there is no homogeneous diffusion of information technology in the Federal Republic of Germany. The process of diffusion is characterized by a slow adoption of information technology in small and medium-sized enterprises (SMEs) and by regional imbalances. Therefore, the concept of information technology centres was developed in order to:

1. Dampen the effects of the disadvantages which SMEs encounter merely because of their size

2. Contribute to regional economic development by promoting the use of information technology and by stimulating demand and supply on the local market

It is a well-known fact that some regions in West Germany do not appear to be participating in the growth of the information industry, while other regions are characterized by a high level of information technology use as well as dynamic development of the local market.

In slowly developing regions demand for and supply of systems and services remain on a low quantitative and qualitative level. The SMEs which usually focus their demand on local dealers, consultants and software houses, have only low budgets at their disposal and their demand is rather unpretentious. The small number of local suppliers has, therefore, no incentive to improve their products and services. For innovative suppliers and entrepreneurs the local market is not promising due to the low demand. As a result the local market is characterized by a certain stability on a low level of quality and innovation.

In highly developed local markets for products and services in the field of information technology, we can find ambitious users with individual and hard-to-please requirements, on the one hand, and a great number of rather innovative suppliers, on the other. Supply and demand stimulate each other and cause a reinforcing process of market development.

Market studies reveal that there is a very slow adoption of information technology in SMEs, which mainly is caused by a lack of competence, DP staff and financial resources. Most of them have no experience and no competence in this field, so they:

1. Are not able to recognize useful applications of information technology in their firm
2. Can estimate neither costs and efforts nor the possible benefits of using information technology
3. Can not specify their requirements of a DP system
4. Are not prepared to choose a suitable system

At the same time they are confronted with a market which is characterized by dynamic development and a great number of products. Thus, most SMEs feel insecure and disoriented. The lack of knowledge and orientation is often intensified by emotional thresholds. As a result of this situation SMEs are very reluctant to use information technology and tend to postpone decisions about its introduction.

What they urgently need is basic advice and orientation help. But this type of basic advice is not provided by commercial suppliers. SMEs are not an attractive target group for professional consultants and dealers because of their low budgets for DP systems and services. On the other hand, dealers are not willing to give free advice because of their declining prices and profit margins. Besides that it could never be impartial advice. Thus, there is a deficit in professional support for SMEs in choosing and using computer systems, the so-called service gap.

Additionally there are deficits in the qualifications of the personnel in SMEs and generally widespread "computer illiteracy" is still a problem in West Germany, constituting further barriers to innovation. Even the most recent studies show that the use of information technology in West Germany is far behind the level of Japan and the U.S.A.

Information technology centres are intended to provide professional and impartial advice to SMEs within a certain region. These centres are autonomous local institutions; they are not established or financed by the Gesellschaft für Mathematik und Datenverarbeitung (GMD), which is the German national research centre for computer sciences. But we promote and support the establishment of information technology centres by providing the concept, consultants and experience which result from running a centre of our own, called the Mikrocomputer-Zentrum.

Characteristics an Intended Effects of Information Technology Centres

Information technology centres can be defined by four characteristics:

1. They should be established and run by regional organizations and become permanent institutions for their target group within a small or defined region.

2. They are non-profit organizations committed to impartiality. They are independent from all manufacturers and suppliers and do not sell any hardware or software.

3. They demonstrate applications of information technology and offer impartial advice to all professional users.

4. They provide basic information and advice on how to use and choose information technology. Their primary aim is to enable potential users to analyse their requirements and to select the software and hardware which best suits their needs. Their aim is a knowledge transfer to potential users in order to make them "fit for the case". SMEs learn about how to buy products and services and then do so on their own responsibility.

Since information technology centres are permanent institutions, SMEs can consult them whenever they need impartial and professional advice. But as a second effect, their suppliers benefit from a rise in demand and of more qualified and pre-informed users. Local supply will be strengthened by this impulse on the demand side and in the long run be forced to improve their products and services.

Additionally, information technology centres should try to motivate SMEs to use information technology not only for in-house purposes but also for telecommunications. Using telecommunications services as a new media for the communication between firms mostly requires acting jointly. Such joint innovations often need a catalyst. An information technology centre could play this role by demonstrating the benefits and supporting the partners. In encouraging in-house applications as well as the use of telecommunications it might be possible to initiate a reinforcing process of interaction between qualified users and innovative suppliers (see Fig. 1).

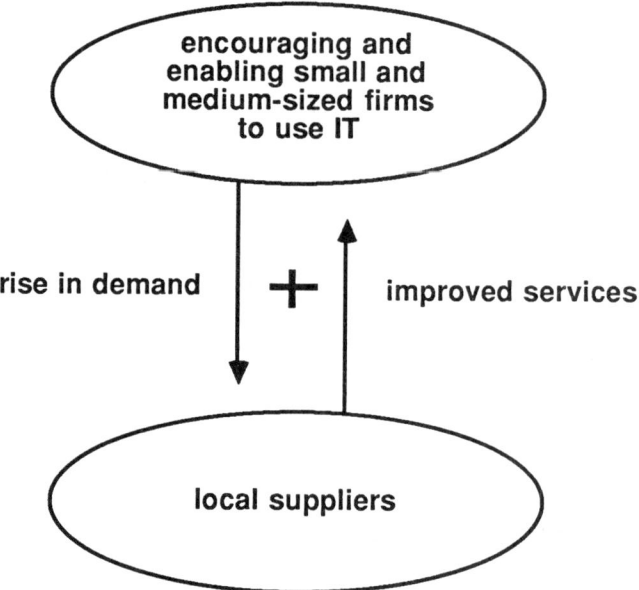

Figure 1:   How demand-side impulses stimulate market mechanisms

Strong regional development benefits may be achieved based on the result in stimulating the local market, including:

1. Increasing competitiveness of SMEs
2. Rise in demand for information technology related products and services
3. Increased number of jobs in the field of information technology

Aspects of Planning Information Technology Centres

Information technology centres can be described and have to be planned along three dimensions (see Fig. 2).

Information Technology Centres as Instruments of Regional Policy 259

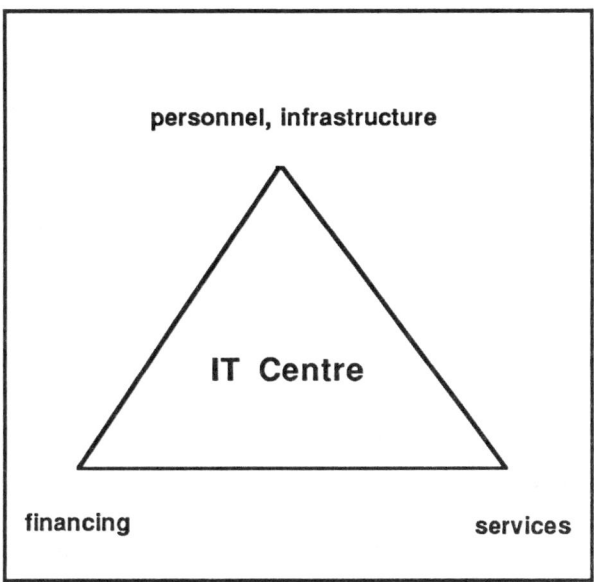

Figure 2: Dimensions of organizational design of information technology centres

In designing an information technology centre the local promoters have to consider local characteristics and specific restrictions, e.g. problems in the economic structure of the region, the existence of research institutions, the services of the chamber of commerce, a small budget, the chance of receiving public funding. They have to formulate a mission for the centre: What result concerning suppliers and potential users should be achieved? What is the intended contribution to the regional economic development?

Depending on these restrictions and aims the local planners have to decide about the services they will offer, e.g. which kind of consultants, which seminars and training courses, and their price. The consultants' services cover a broad range from brief advice (one or two hours) up to ten person-days (in the Beratungszentrum Informationstechnik). In some centres information and advice are free of charge, in other centres (like Cologne) clients have to pay a low price, e.g. up to 100 DM for one hour of consultation.

Most centres offer introductory lectures for managers of SMEs on how to choose and use information technology systems. Another type of seminar focuses on specific ways of applying information technology. In most cases, seminars in information technology centres are intended to transfer knowledge about the possible use of information technology and to lower the intransparency of market supply. Often short seminars are free of charge, others are offered at market prices. Training courses on software packages are explicitly excluded.

Further decisions are necessary about the personnel and the technical infrastructure. Information technology centres need at least a "critical mass" of employees with a broad range of know-how and experience and with a high capability of transferring knowledge to the clients. A typical staff could consist of three to five consultants / lecturers (including the manager), a secretary and a technician.

The most important technical component of an information technology centre is the demonstration area. In this permanent exhibition, which should cover the most important types of software, hardware and telecommunications services, visitors can explore the systems on their own without sales pressure. Also the exhibition is used by the staff to exemplify their explanations or criteria for selecting hardware and software as well as to demonstrate applications of software appropriate to SMEs.

Finally, one must consider the necessary budget and the deficit which results from the intended services and the planned resources. In many cases the unavoidable deficit can be reduced by public funding (e.g. in the first three years by a government and for a specific project) or by contributions of the manufacturers. An information technology centre may require a budget of about 1 to 1.5 million DM. In the early phase of an information technology centre perhaps 10% to 30% of this budget might be covered by fees.

Information technology centres are either a part of a host organization (BIT is a project at the Fraunhofer Institute IAO, MCZ is a project of the GMD, the personal computer laboratory in Bremen is a department of the university, the Zentrum für Informationstechnik Siegen is a part of the local authority) or an independent firm, like the Informationstechnik-Zentrum Köln GmbH or the Technologie Transfer Trier GmbH. Members of such independent companies can include institutions which feel committed to the regional economic development, especially local authorities, chambers of commerce and savings banks.

In supporting the establishment of information technology centres, it has been our experience that success depends on the following factors:

1. The concept must be based on the regional characteristics: Local authorities, chambers of commerce, suppliers and research institutions should participate in the planning process.
2. The necessity of promoting the use of information technology and the need for an information technology centre as a means of economic development should be approved by all important institutions.
3. The relevant institutions should be willing to co-operate and they should be accustomed to doing so.
4. The effort for planning an information technology centre must not be underestimated. It needs dedicated manpower and professional staff.
5. The planning process needs competent and powerful promoters.
6. Information technology centres need public funding.
7. If public funding by the government of the state is not sufficient, a host organization or local institutions should be prepared to finance the centre.

Some further critical success factors which have to be considered while a centre is operating include:

1. The knowledge base needs permanent renewal.
2. Every centre needs a "critical mass" of personnel, at least three or four professionals.
3. It is important to co-operate with scientific institutions in order to guarantee a permanent flow of information.
4. Building up a network of co-operation within a region facilitates addressing the target groups.

The Mikrocomputer-Zentrum of the GMD

The Mikrocomputer-Zentrum (MCZ) in Sankt Augustin near Bonn which may serve as an example of an information technology centre is part of the GMD. The GMD has an annual budget of about 100 million DM and has over 1300 employees. Its shareholders are the Federal Republic of Germany (90%), the state of North Rhine-Westphalia and the state of Hessen.

The scientific work is conducted in six institutes. One of them is the Institute for Technology Transfer where the transfer activities of the GMD are located. In the Education and Training Division of this institute we have launched the project TRANSIT which has the aim of spreading knowledge on information technology. Its activity consists of three components:

1. Running the Mikrocomputer-Zentrum
2. Supporting regional initiatives for information technology centres
3. Initiating an exchange of information and experience between such centres

The Mikrocomputer-Zentrum which is located near our headquarters at Schloß Birlinghoven is not only a local centre but also the central component of an ambitious project. It is intended to serve as a model where experience can be gained with new services. The primary target groups are managers and employees of SMEs. Additionally, we offer our services to the public administration which is a traditional clientele of the GMD. Since our opening in April 1986 we have had more than 4000 guests (see Fig. 3).

Our programme includes

1. Information and advice on using and choosing microcomputers which normally lasts one or two hours and is free of charge
2. Introductory lectures and seminars (e.g. on themes like how to choose software and hardware, comparison between operating systems, packaged software)

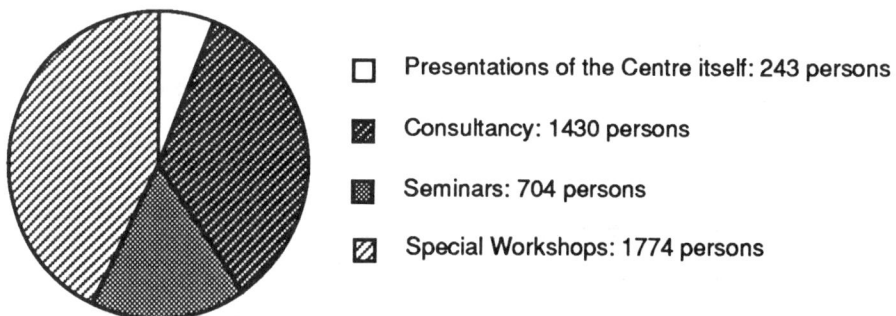

Figure 3:   4151 visitors in the Mikrocomputer-Zentrum from April 1986 to November 1987

3. Special presentations of application tools and application solutions:

   - Half-day presentations of certain classes of application tools (word processing, spreadsheets, business graphics, data-base management systems, integrated packages)

   - Presentations of new applications of information technology, like desk-top publishing, local area networks or on-line retrieval; new themes are adopted according to new market trends and strength of demand by our clients

   - Workshops for special target groups, e.g. craftsmen, in co-operation with chambers of commerce and unions, on the one hand, and software houses, on the other.

4. Presentations of the MCZ itself for visitors who are interested in the concept of information technology centres and its realization in our own centre

An analysis of the clientele supports our hypothesis that information technology centres have a restricted radius of influence because representatives of SMEs are not willing to travel long ways for information and advice on information technology. About 70% of our clients come from within a radius of 20 to 30 km, so that we serve as a centre for Bonn and the adjacent Rhein-Sieg areas.

An important component of our Mikrocomputer-Zentrum is the permanent exhibition which has been provided with hardware and software by hardware manufactures, dealers and software houses. The exhibition includes nearly 20 microcomputers (including several types of printers, plotter, scanner, a local area network, telecommunications services as interactive videotex, telex/teletex, Datex-P) and about 100 software packages (including systems software, application tools and application solutions) which are demonstrated exclusively by our staff. Within this demonstration area (about 100 m^2) we can demonstrate the characteristics of the different types of hardware and software or visualize technical selection criteria. Also visitors can explore microcomputer systems by themselves "without feeling the hot breath of a salesman on their neck". But only advanced users are able to take advantage of this opportunity.

The staff of the Mikrocomputer-Zentrum consists of four consultants, a technician, a secretary and a manager, all being employees of the GMD. In addition we employ some students and free-lance consultants.

Towards a Network of Regional Information Technology Centres

In early 1984 the initiative of the GMD for establishing a widespread network of information technology centres in the Federal Republic of Germany was started. At the same time two centres were planned independently but based on the same fundamental ideas: The Beratungszentrum Informationstechnik in Stuttgart and the predecessor of the Ostfriesisches Regionales Informationstechnik-Zentrum in Norden were both opened in 1985. In 1986 we launched our own Mikrocomputer-Zentrum near Bonn and in Cologne the Informationstechnik-Zentrum Köln was established. These centres constituted the nucleus of the intended network and since then the network has been continuously expanding.

At the moment six information technology centres are in operation, three will open soon, and another seven have definitely been planned. All centres except the Mikrocomputer-Zentrum are totally independent from the GMD. They all are committed to the characteristics of information technology centres but the outlined set of characteristics is only the common denominator. Most centres offer additional services and every centre has its own corporate identity and its own name.

We want to stimulate and facilitate the establishment of new centres and we try to prevent centres from making well-known mistakes, from "re-inventing the wheel". We want to act as a catalytic agent and so it is our task to:

1. Support local promoters of information technology centres

2. Stimulate co-operation between the information technology centres

3. Co-ordinate the exchange of information and experience between the centres

We have suggested that representatives of the existing and planned centres should meet regularly at so-called workshops which could provide a forum for the exchange of information and experience. The results of the two first workshops were very encouraging. We hope that the forthcoming third workshop will become a milestone on the way towards a national network of regional information technology centres in West Germany.

5.7 Contacts and Contracts Between Universities and Small and Medium-Sized Enterprises: Possibilities and Limitations

Pim Berculo

In comparison with the United States and Japan and also in comparison with newly emergent industrial countries, there exists in Europe a large gap between scientific research, on the one hand, and the commercial exploitation of the results of this research, on the other. Consequently the implementation of innovations and technological renewals takes much longer than we would like. It is a good thing that throughout Europe new instruments, which have been and will be discussed at length during this conference, are being introduced and used in an attempt to reduce this distance. Even more creativity will be required, however, especially if we wish to realize our aim of giving small and medium-sized enterprises (SMEs) access to the knowledge available at universities.

Whatever instruments are developed to stimulate activities in the area of research and development and technology transfer, their success ultimately depends on the efforts of those who must bring about a transfer of this knowledge into practice, that is to say success is dependent on individual researchers, entrepreneurs and employees. But these parties must be given the necessary opportunities and especially they must be able to come into contact with each other. This is the theme of the present paper, with special reference to the position of SMEs.

A decade ago the attitude of universities in The Netherlands and probably also elsewhere in Europe was more or less as follows: "We are institutions for scientific research and teaching. We are nationally and, to a considerable extent, internationally orientated. Our geographical position is of minor significance and we see no particular reason to develop special ties with the region and the companies established there."

The only exception at this time was, undoubtedly, the contacts of the technical universities with a limited number of large companies. Except for these large companies, the business world was virtually ignorant of the opportunities for the exchange of knowledge with the universities. Many entrepreneurs regarded universities as large, off-putting institutions, where very learned gentlemen conducted incomprehensible scientific investigations that had no bearing on industrial activities.

Indeed, this was not an attractive starting point for initiatives intended to bring about the transfer of knowledge between universities and private companies. At the same time, however, the neglect of so many potential opportunities presented a challenge to those with some understanding of both the university world and the private sector. I am pleased to be able to report here that a lot has changed in the last ten years. The willingness of universities and businesses - while not betraying their own identities - to collaborate has grown significantly and the new aids and means for bringing about such co-operation and knowledge transfer are being used imaginatively. Transfer points, open-house days for companies and entrepreneurs, industrial technological centres, science parks and industrial liaison commissions have been founded: in short, a considerable number of instruments are now available for the promotion of contacts between universities and companies.

But the ideal way of organizing the transfer of knowledge between universities and private companies has not, or so it appears to me, yet been discovered. In all probability it does not exist. In fact, all activities in this area have the air of a continuous experiment. All parties involved are looking for the most successful formula for the promotion of contacts between universities and industry and it seems to me a good idea on the part of the organizers of this conference to use these two days to draw up a mid-term balance.

I propose to go through the various forms which this transfer of knowledge takes with you and to discuss the bottlenecks which occur in this connection. I shall lead up to this by discussing eight focal points, and end my lecture with seven practical recommendations.

This report is based on experience gained as secretary of the Chamber of Commerce in Utrecht, The Netherlands, in long-term co-operation with the State University of Utrecht on the initiation and development of business contacts, and also on the related experience of my colleagues in other regions in The Netherlands.

My first point concerns the various forms of knowledge transfer between universities and private companies.

Let me start by saying that universities are educational institutions. They provide an academic training for their students and these graduates find employment in, for example, the industrial sector, as a result of this training. It is sometimes forgotten that this is the most widespread form of knowledge transfer and that, moreover, one of the primary duties of the university is to provide academic education. Graduation does not necessarily mean the end of the relationship between the graduate and his old department. In their new work situation graduates frequently maintain contacts with the departments from which they graduated. Moreover, scientific knowledge becomes out-dated more quickly these days. Postgraduate refresher courses will, therefore, become an increasingly routine matter in the future. The second main task of the university is to conduct research, and research which is not necessarily primarily directed to pressing social or industrial and commercial needs often ultimately - albeit in a very roundabout way - leads to commercially exploitable results. This, too, is a long-established, though indirect, form of knowledge transfer from universities to companies. The third primary task of the universities, providing services for the community, is also important in this connection. The efforts of, for example, medical and veterinary faculties and of dentistry departments in this area are very long-standing. More modern forms of service to the community, expressed, for instance, in "science shops" in which information and services in areas such as chemistry, physics and the law are provided, co-exist with these traditions. However, in my opinion, this form of social involvement has less direct significance for the transfer of knowledge to private companies.

The aim of this overview is to illustrate that the new forms of knowledge transfer which enjoy a lot of attention at the moment (and which will also be discussed today as transfer points, science parks and industrial-technological centres) will never be able to be more than a supplement to the broad mainstreams of knowledge transfer which spring from the primary tasks of the universities.

A sense of proportion is also warranted on another point. Successful contacts between academic research and business are entirely dependent on the willingness of researchers to co-operate, and it is not realistic to suppose that such a willingness is shared by all. Roughly speaking, there are three categories of academics. The first group focuses completely on scientific research and has no feeling for the open market and is not interested in industry or commerce. This is certainly not a disqualification, for there are brilliant individuals in this group. However, it would be unrealistic to expect them to participate to any great extent in the transfer of knowledge to businesses. Another group is genuinely interested in commercial activities and finds its own way to the private sector. It may be possible to praise the external contacts of this group on a number of points but efforts should really be concentrated on the third group, namely those researchers who are quite prepared to collaborate with private companies when the opportunity presents itself.

It should be emphasized that knowledge transfer is not equally advantageous to each and every company. Multinationals do much of their own research and development, and the local news agent will also not feel the need for contacts within the university.

I have shown that knowledge has, in fact, been transferred from universities to industry and commerce for a good number of years. Our present attention is focused on new initiatives to activate as yet unexploited possibilities for the transfer of knowledge between universities and business. The new forms of knowledge transfer with which we are concerned can not be more than a supplement to the long-established mainstreams of knowledge transfer from the universities. Nor will it even be possible to create a form of co-operation which will appeal to all academics.

It is essential that all parties involved take into account the fact that academic education and research and service to the community are the primary tasks of the universities and that, although interesting opportunities for contacts with industry and commerce must indeed be exploited, this sort of activity must never be allowed to take priority over the three main tasks of the universities. Incidentally it occurs to me that contacts between the universities, their institutions and government organizations which operate on a more or less commercial basis in fact follow the same pattern.

My second point is that there are interesting areas of knowledge for contacts between industry and commerce and the university. It can not be denied that technical universities have the longest tradition of contacts with private companies. This is, undoubtedly, partly a result of the fact that the distance between technical scientific research and industrial practice is relatively small. However, for both manufacturing industries as well as for new branches of commerce, such as business services, other disciplines are becoming increasingly important. Physics, chemistry, biology, medicine, pharmacy and veterinary science have interesting unexplored possibilities, but economics, psychology, geography, literature and the law can also supply companies with very relevant knowledge. Finally, at many universities there is now a broad understanding of information science and automation. This last attribute is sensed by companies.

Many transfer points report that, in addition to technical questions, information is increasingly requested on organizational matters, marketing and automation. If we wish to stimulate the interest of companies in these non-technical areas of expertise, then the knowledge and experience of universities in these areas must be presented and explained to companies in an attractive and comprehensible way. In this respect, particularly, it is true to say that the customary university divisions in faculties and departments which have proved convenient for their main occupations of teaching and research do not correspond with the demarcations of problems with which companies are confronted. A fresh approach to the presentation of the capabilities of the university is, therefore, desirable. To illustrate this, I would like to refer to the increasing amount of knowledge on information science and automation present within universities, outside the technical faculties. Here are clusters of information which could be of great value to companies but which override the traditional divisions in faculties and departments. For this reason, such knowledge often remains out of view for industry and commerce. Efforts to expand the contacts and contracts between researchers and entrepreneurs in such directions, therefore, must include a well-structured presentation of the non-technical know-how that universities have to offer.

My third point involves some remarks about the organizational differences between the university and companies. Companies, if you will forgive a sweeping statement, are placed under a central leadership with executive units subordinate to this central leadership. The groundwork for important decisions can, it is true, be done at a lower level, but the decisions themselves are taken at top level and have to be implemented at lower levels. The organization of universities is fundamentally different. Although the governing boards and the university councils have important decision-making powers regarding internal organization, decisions on matters concerning concrete arrangements about research, teaching, service to the community and contacts with the private companies are highly decentralized. The departments enjoy a great degree of autonomy. This must be taken into account in the organisation of the transfer of knowledge.

In the universities the transfer of knowledge cannot be imposed from the top but is absolutely dependent on the co-operation of departments or, rather, of individual scientists. Concrete co-operation on the part of the university governing bodies in activities promoting contacts with companies although being necessary, is by no means the only condition that must be met.

A transfer point, which is only rooted in the university organization at the centre and which cannot fall back on support from departments, will only be able to bring about contacts between researchers and entrepreneurs with difficulty, if at all. Entrepreneurs for their part will have to understand that questions and problems that can be incorporated in the current research or teaching programmes will be answered more readily and will cause less friction than problems that cannot be incorporated in current programmes despite the fact that they present no intrinsic problem. The only viable organization of knowledge transfer between industry and commerce and academics is one which takes into account both the strongly decentralized organization of the university and the more centralized organization of companies.

My fourth point concerns the interested parties in knowledge transfer. Knowledge transfer is only successful if both parties have a vested interest. Companies stand to gain from the transfer of knowledge because in this way knowledge, which they do not have in-house and which is too expensive to build up internally, can be hired or bought in. Moreover, the indirect, long-term result of knowledge transfer is that the research activities of companies and universities grow towards each other. The university top level is indeed interested in the possibility of generating a third money stream via commercial contacts. But it is equally important that the department or individual scientist who has to conduct the research has an interest in it himself. This interest may be, although often it is not, money. Other possibilities are the gaining of status or appreciation for the efforts made for companies or help with the purchase of equipment, the offer of facilities for attending congresses, new possibilities for traineeships for students and so forth. Without such stimuli there will be no great enthusiasm among researchers to tackle problems for companies. Partially for this reason, many contacts between entrepreneurs and researchers are not regulated by the university at the central level. An over-centralized approach to company contacts at the university or, worse still, the creaming off of possible income from these activities to the central university organs would seem to me to spell the death of the successful transfer of knowledge.

The similarities between marketing and knowledge transfer bring me to my fifth point. It occurs to me that the transfer of knowledge between universities and private companies exhibits many characteristics which reflect principles that apply to marketing a wide range of products. I shall describe a few.

A line of products only "sells" if it is clearly recognized by customers. Private companies can hardly display interest in areas of knowledge present at universities, if they are not familiar with these areas. One step in the right direction is the excellent booklets and brochures that have recently become available at Dutch universities in which the available knowledge and facilities are described. They are, unfortunately, not always presented in terms which can be understood by industry and commerce. One reason for this can be a too liberal use of scientific jargon but, here again, the divisions via the university departments often do not parallel market demands and do not reflect the problems with which companies are confronted. And finally, it must be remembered that the very best brochure is ineffective if not distributed to the right target groups.

The sales department (for example the transfer point) can only sell what the production departments (the departments) can and will supply. Herein lies an important recommendation to the transfer points, namely first ensure a thorough acquaintance with what the various departments have to offer which could be useful to companies and especially ensure a thorough familiarity with the degree of willingness present in the various departments to collaborate with the private sector. If the transfer points do not enjoy the full support of departments in making contacts within companies it is very probable that the enthusiasm and anticipation coming from the contacts between the transfer point and companies will lead to nothing at the departmental level.

In the transfer of knowledge, as in marketing, it is important to define product-market combinations. Direct sales of knowledge from a university to private companies will hardly ever work. The careful selection and association of certain knowledge clusters of the university with certain categories of company activities can have a better chance of success.

The definition of a market strategy is also important in making contacts with universities. Over-ambitious industrial liaison programmes seldom live up to expectations. It is better to build up a rapport gradually over a period of time per market combination, for example, and reinforce it by an effective publicity campaign specially tailored for specific branches of industry and commerce. A properly implemented, well-targeted programme is more effective than a broader campaign in which one can become stranded.

As is the case with marketing, after-sales is also a vital part of knowledge transfer. This applies equally to the organization that brought about the contact between the entrepreneur and the scientist (the transfer point, for instance) and to the research worker who supplied the knowledge. If there is no organization to regulate after-sales follow-up it is often completely forgotten even though it is true, also in this area, that after-sales contact results in satisfied customers and this is still the best advertisement.

Again as in marketing, in the area of knowledge transfer, investment precedes returns. University efforts to establish contacts with private companies will certainly not always lead to a well-stocked third stream of money for the university. Universities will first have to prove their worth before being able to charge a "fee" or expect other forms of remuneration.

As in commerce, general public relations, reputation and familiarity, and willingness on the part of the university to collaborate with business must be there for a successful transfer of knowledge. And this willingness will have to be propagated by a number of key figures from both academe and industry and commerce. In this respect, informal contacts are extremely important. A well-chosen industrial liaison commission consisting of, on the one hand, enthusiastic professors and, on the other, entrepreneurs who are interested in the transfer of knowledge can make a valuable contribution.

The sixth of my eight points, mentioned at the beginning, is concerned with the place of SMEs in the process of knowledge transfer. In order to examine this further it is worth describing more precisely what can be understood by "knowledge transfer". As I see it, this concept provides an umbrella for a broad range of activities which can be roughly divided into five categories.

1. First, there are straightforward queries from companies which, provided the right person in the university is approached, can be answered in a single telephone conversation.

2. The second category concerns questions from companies which cannot be answered immediately because something has to be looked up. However, these problems can also be solved quickly, again provided the right person is found to deal with them.

3. The third category is more complicated. In this case we are concerned with questions from companies which lead to a small investigation. It is

convenient if such an investigation can be incorporated into existing research and teaching programmes, but sometimes extra hours also have to be invested.

4. A fourth category of questions from companies requires more extensive research covering several weeks or months. Experience has shown that it is often possible to delegate such jobs to undergraduate research assistants.

5. The final category is extensive, long-term contract research.

Experience has shown that SMEs are mostly interested in the first three categories which are all concerned with relatively simple questions. This does not provide a third source of income. In fact, such activities will never earn back their costs. However, it is important to be of service to SMEs. First, because in this way the university makes an additional contribution to the community, second, because small companies can grow into big companies which will be candidates at a later stage for more extensive collaboration with the university and, finally, because small companies are sometimes the suppliers of larger companies and these contacts can be important for the university.

However, there are a number of bottlenecks in the relationship between the university and SMEs. It is more the case here than in other areas that what the university has to offer must be brought to the attention of the entrepreneur at the very moment at which he can use it. Entrepreneurs do not have the opportunity to keep themselves informed of developments at the university if there is no actual, immediate need. It is, therefore, important, especially for SMEs that possibilities for consultation and co-operation with the university should be indicated - continuously and repeatedly. SMEs often make habitual use of a number of established informative bodies such as the Chambers of Commerce, employers' organizations, sometimes but not always based on branch membership, and in some cases they refer matters to other businesses, accountants, banks and so forth. Universities would be well advised to make use of the information outlets of these intermediary organizations when bringing their store of knowledge to be attention of SMEs.

However, this is not the only role which intermediary organizations can play. There are fundamental differences between the academic atmosphere and the business culture, especially the culture of SMEs. Consequently, it requires time and patience to translate the problems with which SMEs wrestle into terms that research workers can understand and use as a basis for investigations. This task is not only time-consuming, it presupposes the ability to see things from the perspective of both cultures.

Many of the organizations mentioned above regularly undertake offensives in this area and I would like to recommend that such intermediary organizations also be engaged in establishing contacts between researchers and entrepreneurs.

There is another fact that applies to all businesses but which, to my knowledge, is most apparent in the case SMEs. Entrepreneurs often do not have the overview necessary to be able to distinguish what knowledge can better be gathered from the university and what from institutes for further occupational training. It occurs to me in this connection that a system of referral from universities to institutes for further occupational training and vice versa is of vital importance. A prerequisite is, of course, a good system of co-operation between the various institutes for further occupational training and the universities.

My seventh point deals with the necessity for a knowledge transfer network. It is, in my opinion, commendable that the universities and institutes for further occupational training try to answer questions coming from private companies first within their own ranks. However, this should not lead to a situation in which attempts are made to answer questions posed by companies internally when another university or institute for further occupational training can handle it more effectively. Referral to a more appropriate institute for further occupational training or university should certainly not be considered a sign of weakness.

Here, too, there is a market parallel. Companies cannot always supply what is asked of them. But a referral system only functions when the various universities and institutes for further occupational training are well acquainted and familiar with what is on offer and are prepared to co-operate with each other on this point. Such a form of co-operation between university transfer points, transfer facilities of institutes for further occupational training and the intermediary organizations mentioned is urgently needed.

Lastly, as point eight, I would like to focus attention on an exceptional category of SMEs, namely the "spin-offs", or companies with university origins. Spin-offs have the same initial problems as other start-ups and their founders also require sound information on all aspects of starting a company. The Chambers of Commerce are pleased to provide this information. But spin-offs also need support in maintaining good relations with the university. Business activities which have their roots in the university are often high-risk enterprises and are particularly vulnerable at the outset. Constructions of part-time university and part-time commercial activities are still rare. Furthermore, universities could offer facilities for this sort of company in the form of small, cheap, flexible working space on the university premises or outside with very short-term tenancy agreements. A co-operative attitude on the part of the universities to sharing things such as equipment and work space seems to me desirable. Another important factor influencing success is the possibility for spin-offs to continue functioning in the university atmosphere, especially in the initial phases. Suggestions from the university world satisfying these requirements would, in my opinion, be a major contribution. High-flying levels such as the science park, industrial-technological centre and academic-industrial centre are less relevant in this context. The provision of accommodation in combination with intensive contacts with university research workers seems to me essential. However, I do not think it would be right to limit such interchanges to the area of technology. There are also interesting opportunities, for example, in biology, medicine, pharmacy and in the information sector.

I shall close with some recommendations, seven in all, as promised.

1. It appears to me that attitudes are changing on two fronts and that such changes are necessary and should continue. More academic scientists must become business-minded and the university must be made more easily accessible to private companies. But the business sector must also make adjustments. It must increase its effort in defining what knowledge and facilities it expects from the universities and have more patience with university work habits and patterns of thought.

2. A system in which academics are eligible for promotion on the basis of their publications and not on the basis of research which is of value to the community or research for private companies does not encourage a healthy transfer of knowledge between the university and business. Fortunately this system is changing, but time is running out.

3. The product of the university must be described in terms its customers can understand. Although the division into faculties and departments is no doubt suitable for research and teaching, it does not encourage external contacts. The offer of interfaculty knowledge clusters which correspond better with the problems alive in the industrial and commercial sector would be an improvement. Fortunately there are, I understand, many such interfaculty organizations or knowledge blocks being constructed at universities.

4. Everything is dependent on enthusiastic individuals who can convince others of the value of the exchange of knowledge between universities and companies. It is vital that such individuals are picked out and involved in the expansion of knowledge transfer. There must be a portfolio for contacts with the private sector on the board of governors. Moreover, an industrial liaison commission has proved very useful in providing a platform for broad discussions between university and business, especially in those cases in which key figures from the academic world and from industry and commerce have been brought together. Moreover, transfer points must present their activities as a service to the university departments and be prepared to collaborate closely with them. Transfer points must not aim to bundle all knowledge transfer. We must avoid over-formalization of the process of knowledge transfer. The more official theinstitutions which are founded to regulate this process, the more cumbersome it will become. A generous acceptance of the fact that a very large proportion of knowledge transfer occurs at the base seems to me indispensable.

5. The rule that success can only be achieved step by step and after careful planning applies also to this area of activity. It is virtually impossible to sell the university lock, stock and barrel to the entire business community. The gradual growth of contacts between specific categories of academic scientists and specific categories of companies has a greater likelihood of success. It is also important that the private sector and the university organization should be informed via public information outlets and the media of the phases involved in knowledge transfer between the university and companies.

6. I would like to advise the government, especially the provincial and municipal authorities, not to involve themselves too much in the efforts of the university to form ties with private companies. The willingness of the authorities to contribute by creating a favourable climate is, of course, important but often expectations are exaggerated. No directly discernible improvement in employment figures should be expected from knowledge transfer. And, in my opinion, the excessive publicity at the start of knowledge transfer projects also often gives rise to unrealistic hopes.

7. And finally, to my mind, it can do no harm to include entrepreneurial skills as an optional subject in the university teaching curriculum.

I am aware that I have not presented a blueprint for a new regional economic policy on knowledge transfer: I have named a number of basic conditions which every knowledge transfer programme must satisfy in order to have a chance of success. Although the transfer of knowledge between universities and private companies is not itself new, the field does offer interesting new opportunities. Miracles do not happen but, if the present situation is thought through and the new instruments used to full advantage, the available chances can be exploited.

5.8 Research and Development of Projects: A New Service Offered by BIC

Claudine Guidat de Queiroz

In the face of a constantly changing environment, the increasing evolution of needs, exacerbated competition and the acceleration of technological changes, it becomes imperative to create the environmental conditions that will enable enterprises to withstand the momentum of this development. Despite the numerous discussions on the necessity of innovation and the technological undertakings, one finds out that there is still a lack of projects.

The necessary stimulation of technological innovation at the local level led us within the framework of the BIC Promotech to install a real project research and development service. BIC Promotech adopts a two-way procedure: (a) a constant search for new openings for development and (b) sufficient work on innovative projects, in order to limit wastes and save time.

Positioned within the framework of the BIC and based on the experience of Promotech, we are going to present here the relationship of this activity with the environment, the procedure adopted and the results obtained.

Integration of the BIC Within Its Environment

The BIC is composed of two complementary structures:

1. A school of industrial engineering whose mission within the framework of the BIC is to develop and diffuse methods and to train young engineers in the techniques of piloting innovation
2. Promotech, the animating structure of the centre, whose objectives include research and development of projects, management of innovation and provision of aid to business creation

This centre, situated in the heart of the Nancy-Brabois Technological Centre, interacts with the different economic partners (see Fig. 1).

Three phases characterize the animators of innovation (see Fig.2):

1. Research and development of projects aimed at mobilizing, within the environment (private or public laboratories, industries), projects and new concepts

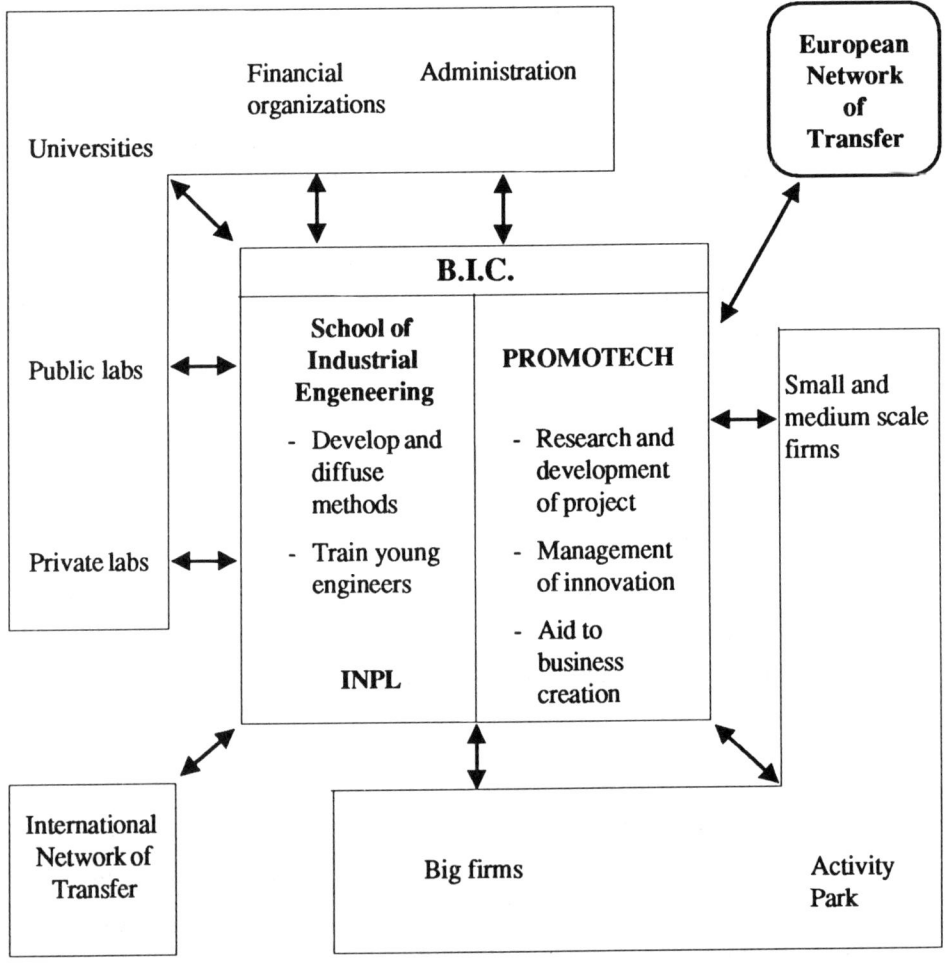

B.I.C. = Animation of Transfer

Figure 1:   Nancy Technopole

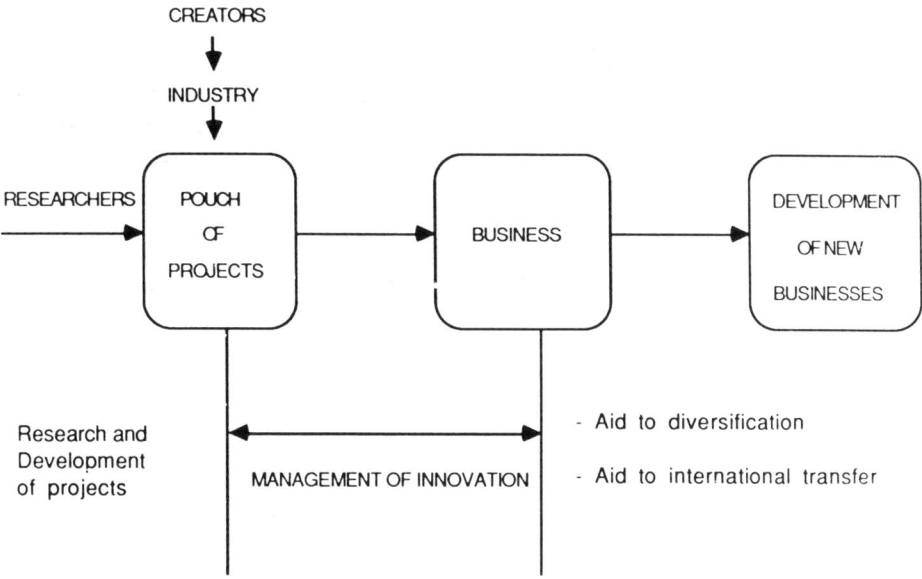

Figure 2:   The animation of innovation

2. Management of innovation, a new profession that includes all the techniques of project management with the aim of creating a business

3. Aid to diversification and development, which permits anchoring the activity to its environment, over a long period

The Nancy BIG provides services for companies, depending on their needs; Fig. 3 shows the six different services offered. We will discuss the first type of service which proposes a systematic procedure of mobilizing projects coming from laboratories.

Project Research and Development: a New Service of the Nancy BIC

The objective of this line of action is to find out what laboratories can offer and determine and install implementation procedures in view of organizing a veritable "technological marketing" programme. The success of such mobilization depends on the aptitude of the BIC to meet the expectations of laboratories.

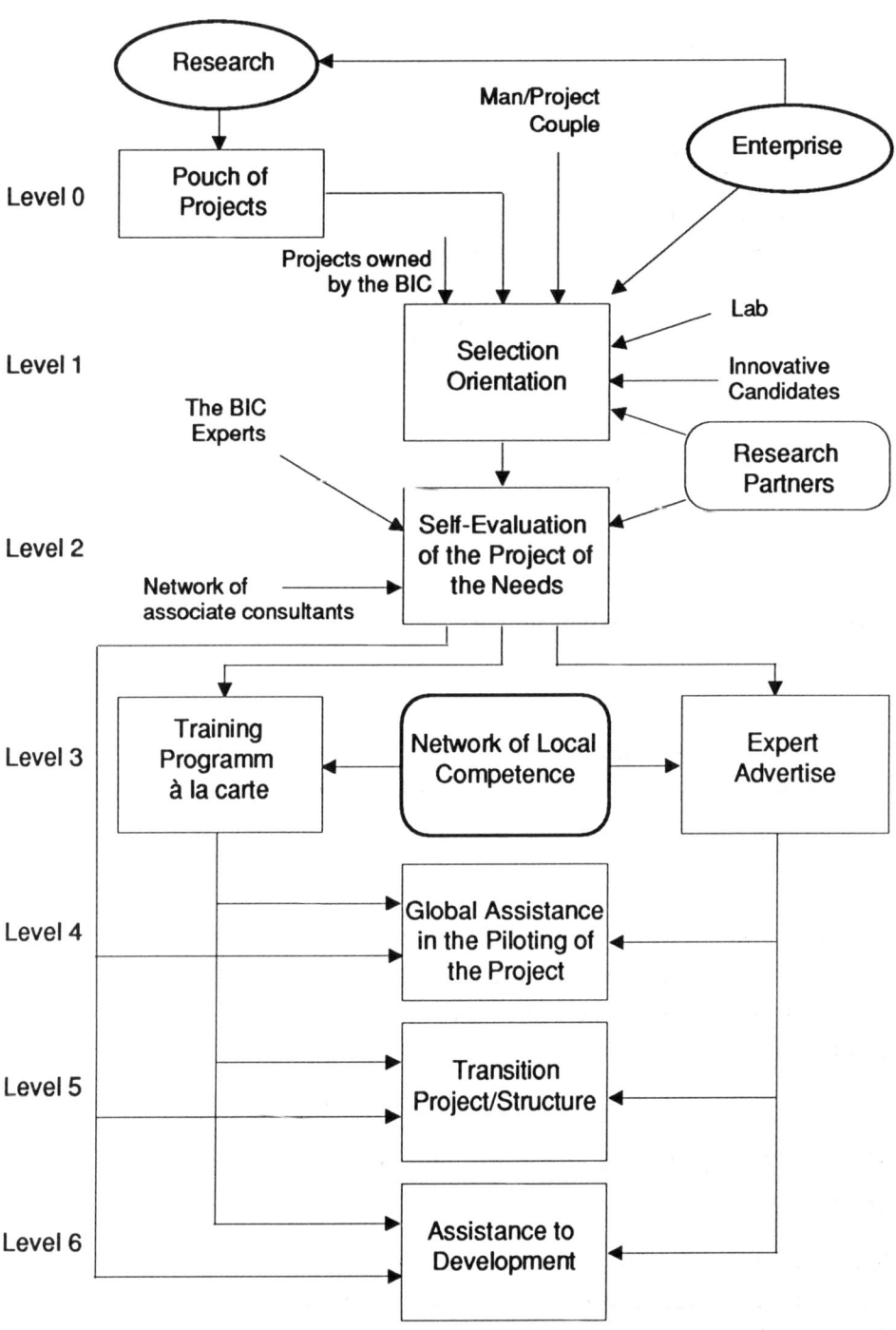

Figure 3: Services Rendered by Nancy B.I.C.

We have been able to identify four principal needs:

1. The search for technical and scientific popularity
2. The need for field verification of theories
3. The search for fields of practical application for the doctoral students
4. The funding of research

In the face of these expectations, the mobilization operations of the projects enable the BIC to propose the following aids:

- Reinforcement of research potentials
- Assistance in the search for industrialists as a step to industrialization
- Search for research partners
- Search for clients for the technical presentations
- Diagnosis of the advancement of the project
- Assistance in business creation
- Assistance in the construction of files

Fig. 4 shows the systematic approach of this procedure.

Two principal phases are identified:

1. Mobilization of projects: This action relies on the systematic collection of ideas or projects through investigations in different laboratories or firms which are involved in research.

2. Technological marketing: Projects mobilized in this manner form the subject of a first diagnosis in view of identifying the orientations of a possible implementation.

Results

Investigations carried out in 1986 in 100 laboratories resulted in six feasibility studies, seven projects being sold to industrialists, seven business creations and twelve contracts to sell know-how or technical presentation.

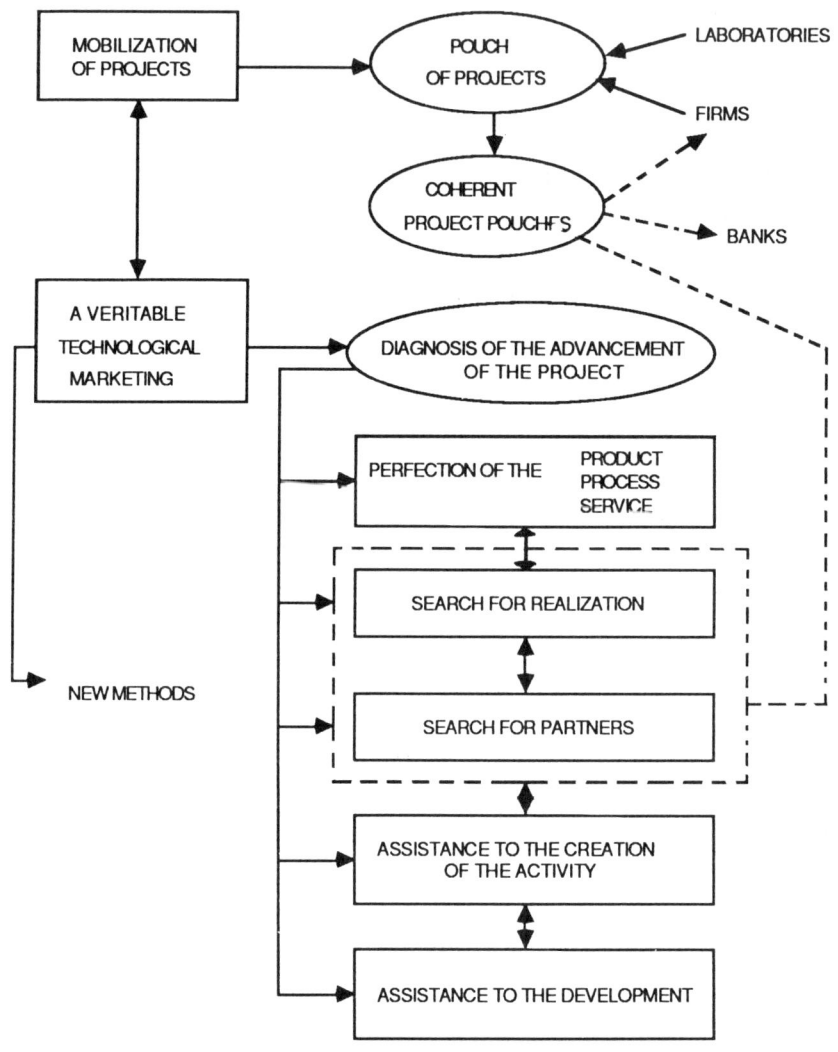

Figure 4: Global sketch of the procedure

Conclusion

Project research and development not only gives better knowledge of the potential of local research but also can:

1. Sweep out from laboratories projects that are often dormant
2. Propose to laboratories, which have the will to implement it, a technological marketing aid based on the diagnosis of the project and the

identification of lines of implementation

3. Diffuse a new language among researchers, thus enabling them to communicate better with businessmen

4. Save time in project research and development by working as early as possible on the market adaptation of the products or services

5.9 Lifelong Education and Training as Decisive Factors of Regional Development: "Training for innovation" - a Programme for Berlin's Industry

Dagmar Brodde

In the summer of 1986 the Technologie-Vermittlungs-Agentur (TVA, Technology Transfer Agency) was entrusted with a far-reaching training consultancy programme aimed at improving the technical and managerial qualifications in Berlin's small and medium-sized enterprises (SMEs). The objectives were to:

1. Help these firms to define, plan and realize essential innovation-oriented in-house training and qualification

2. Inform SMEs about the variety of financial facilities offered by the Berlin Senate and assist them with the adequate steps and forms of application

3. Foster structural, economic and technological change in most of Berlin's comparatively backward industrial fields to enable them to meet the long-term challenges of the future

On average the group of consultants consisted of six experts. During the pilot phase basic experience in the new consulting field was gathered. The first tailor-made training measures for enterprises were implemented. The instruments and means of support were tested and improved. During this diffusion phase - which is still going on - enterprises are contacted systematically to be informed about the new training promotion programme. The means are direct mail and personal calls or presentations in firms. Institutions like commercial associations are used as multiplyers or mediators. At the end of the consolidation phase the whole programme will be transferred to these institutions.

This particular innovation-oriented qualifications promotion programme for SMEs is based on the growing perception that investments in new technologies, new organizational structures organization or management techniques and instruments will only pay off when they are mastered by qualified manpower.

Since essential training measures in smaller firms tend to fall prey to rather limited capital resources, financial subsidies are being granted. Up to 80% of actually incurred costs (for trainers, rents, etc.) can be subsidized when - roughly - the programme is innovative, is carried out for the first time in this specific enterprise, amounts to at least 48 training hours, and includes at least six participants within this firm. The subject can be anything from marketing to technical knowledge which will help firms to foster their innovative and thus competitive capacity in order to secure economic prosperity, manpower qualifications, employment or even newly created jobs.

The Technology Transfer Agency as Programme-Managing Institution

The institution which was chosen to carry out the programme was Berlin's well-reputed TVA, an organization involved in many varieties of industrial relations. Under its auspices are various consulting services for modern technologies, innovations, advanced production methods, and worldwide marketing information. In this context additional integrated training advisory services are intended to produce fruitful synergistic effects.

Training consultancy is embedded in the institution's specific philosophy and culture. The leading idea is to offer complex modern production-related quality-oriented services to Berlin's industry to secure permanent structural change as the basis for economic survival.

The main target group for TVA's services are SMEs which are the backbone of Berlin's industry. They constitute a rather non-homogeneous clientele differing with regard to products, production methods, standards and levels of technology and openness towards innovation. A minority of innovation-minded firms are confronted by a wide range of more or less innovation-abstinent enterprises. The theory is (and experience tends to prove this assumption correct) that innovation and the diffusion of innovation start with those few firms on top, that is with the so-called probing elite, and - having produced a certain innovation-consciousness in the next group of firms - trickles down to the next layer of then open-minded firms and so on until the innovation has become the common standard. The process runs from top to bottom in determinable, but long-ranged periods. The secret of success for smaller firms lies in catching the train at the right moment, when for example technical innovation no longer bears too many risks and still offers market chances before it becomes more or less standard of the art.

For TVA's consulting services this means a top-down strategy starting with the innovation-minded elite, helping them to carry out their plans successfully, thus convincing the next group of firms to innovate and so on. A bottom-up strategy will blind all existing strength and soon erode it.

Education and Training - Difficult Consulting Fields

Consulting services regarding tailor-made innovation-oriented in-house education and training are products which are difficult to sell to SMEs. The field must already be cultivated:

1. There must be an understanding in firms that qualification bottlenecks do exist.

2. Concomitantly with other entrepreneurial tasks and investments, qualification and training are regarded as being of minor importance, even in bigger firms.

3. Above all in smaller firms training and education will not meet appropriate basic organizational structures. Thus, qualification and training happen more or less accidentally and often too late. Too often they are not considered essential elements in innovation.

Staff members are reluctant to take part in training measures or even reject them because, for example, they fear admitting to gaps in their knowledge, and training usually means extra input of both time and energy.

For consultants it is easier to start with firms which are already conscious of the importance of qualifications connected with innovation. It is a well-know fact, meanwhile, that in times of permanent technological change the need for permanent training grows:

1. Qualification is an essential systemic element of every technology.

2. New technologies bring about an actual and immediate demand for new qualifications which on a wider scale can only be met by continuing education and training (as production of the newly qualified at schools and universities takes too long).

3. Continuing education for individuals and enterprises also represents the most flexible way to fight imminent obsolence of qualifications and thus keep up with market demands.
4. The awareness of the importance of permanent education is spreading. The growing expenditures for training in industry indicate this clearly.

How the New Consulting Programme Works

A firm signals interest in training advice as qualifications problems have occurred lately. The procedure of the training consultants is thorough: In co-operation with this specific firm they try to define the problem as precisely and concretely as possible. A precise description is the basis for an adequate solution.

Then a solution is conceptualized. Are qualifications really the weak point or is it an organizational problem or a technological one? If qualifications are the bottleneck, can this be solved by recruiting manpower from outside or by training part of the current staff? The enterprises in this situation will profit from the complex consulting capacity within the TVA, because the special case will most probably be discussed with some experts from other fields. The appropriate trainers or training institution will be found on the market; market knowledge in the educational field is provided. The final decision about trainers, contents, and schedule will of course be left to the firm.

The development of a problem-oriented training concept comes first. Financial advice and actual help with financial schemes and forms, second. The TVA training consultants co-operate intensely with the respective partner at the Senate in order to avoid any difficulty or delay.

Survey on Results

Investment of Time

Each case of our training consulting service demands a considerable input of time, which can range from 2 to 35 (which is not unusual) or even more hours. It includes:

Concept development	20	hours
Assessment of the actual training demand	3	hours
Visits in enterprises	2	hours
Outline of financial schemes and support during the whole process of application,	7	hours
Repairs, etc.	3	hours

It will take much more time if a couple of enterprises are involved in one measure. The outcome of this process will be a problem-oriented training programme of at least 48 hours which meets the specific demand of the individual enterprise. Table 1 summarizes our results.

Table 1: Summary of TVA training consulting services, October 1986 to October 1987

Number of enterprises contacted	1000
Firms in need of consulting in personnel or training matters	339
Cases of consulting in this field	530
Among these:	
First consulting contacts	219
Programmes in preparation	154
Programmes in realization	157
Among these:	
In-house training	135
Pilot curicula	8
Personnel recruiting	14
Staff trained in programmes	1500

The TVA consultants give advice on special financial support instruments for personnel recruitment and training on the job as offered by the German Labour Administration. Statistics are kept and analysed there.

Volume of In-House Training

Within one year 110,000 hours of in-house training were initiated for staff in Berlin firms. A turnover of 2.3 million DM was reached, the average measure amounting to 17,000 DM.

Subjects of Training

Of the totals 10% were management programmes; 70% were programmes dealing with new office or production technologies; and 20% were programmes in marketing, motivation etc.

Other Data

Visited firms according to number of staff are shown in Table 2.

Table 2: Number of staff in the firms visited

Number of staff	number of firms	percentage
1 - 19	112	33
20 - 49	58	17
50 - 99	30	9
100 - 199	51	15
200 und mehr	88	26
	339	100

Visited firms according to branches are summarized in Table 3.

Table 3. Visited firms by industrial sector

	number	percentage
Machine construction	58	17
Technology-oriented services	54	16
Electrotechnics	30	9
Chemistry, plastics	27	8
Food, consumption	24	7
Papers, printing	20	6
Construction	20	6
Trade	14	4
Textiles, clothing	10	3
Optics, precision mechanics	7	2
rest	75	22
	339	100

Perspectives in 1988

The diffusion phase will be continued until the majority of Berlin's small and medium-sized production firms have been contacted (i.e. 2100). As incentives for change financial subsidies will remain important. Above all in the field of the most advanced key technologies, which have already proved to be secure in the applications but are innovative enough to open-market opportunities, public financial aid will be a must. Without subsidiary programmes smaller firms will not be able to realize these opportunities soon enough. As the qualifications' bottleneck in production firms grows even more acute in the course of Berlin's demographic development, permanent training and training consulting services will remain needed.

6 Programmes and Concepts in Promoting Industrial Innovations in Different European Regions (Working Group 4)

6.1 Piedmont and Aosta Valley, Italy: Technology Transfer Services for Entrepreneurs

Renzo Mosagna

The objective aim of our "Centro Estero" (Foreign Centre) is international promotion of industry in the Piedmont. The centre was created in 1976 on the initiative of the chambers of commerce, the industrials associations and the Instituti di Credito of Piedmont and Aosta Valley (located in the north of Italy). Its activities are organized along the following four lines: information, consultancy, training and promotion.

We promote and develop international relationships. Our activities are based on the following services:

- Fostering product and technology exchanges
- Researching agents and representatives
- Creating new sales channels
- Carrying out market research studies
- Providing specific conveyances, by means of experts
- Organizing collective participation in specialized exhibitions, where we can offer the best of Piedmontese production as well as increase contacts with the most selected and qualified Piedmontese enterprises

We are committed and diversified in information in several fields, to maintain a high technological level and improve its quality.

Training and consultancy are the essential conditions to maintain managerial specialization on advanced levels. Export managers or industrialists become more competitive than their Italian or foreign competitors.

Promotion is closely linked with the technology of the "Piedmont system".

The specialized exhibitions we promote provide the first contacts with world technology. When an enterprise presents its products among thousands of others, its proper value is disclosed and its future envisaged. The decorative fabrics we exhibit at Heimtextil are the outcome of machine and enterprise development. The foodstuffs we sell at I.S.M. are the outcome of the most competitive development processes. Or consider SITEV, where component manufacturers meet vendors and suppliers thus getting in touch with the world automotive industry. We can also mention Inter-hospital, Midest, Automan, etc.

There are many other initiatives in promoting the Piedmontese technology programme, such as the relationship with Algeria, industrial co-operation in Egypt, China, Malaysia, Quebec, as well as the granting of patents and know-how to Germany and the United States. The work performed abroad by our officials keeps us in touch with good trade operators, exporters, wholesalers, distributors and the like. We have likewise had the opportunity to meet technology purchasers, such as users, brokers or agents (a good example is the study of a piston for U.S. military vehicles carried out in an excellent way by Mondial Piston, after contact with a company had been provided by us). Our activity in external relations has introduced us to several research centres (private centres or universities) and technological sites such as Silicon Valley, ZIRST, MIT and others.

Table 1:   Participation in specialized exhibitions

CeBIT 1987:	World Exhibition of Office Telecommunications and Technology (Hannover Germany, 4-11 March 1987)
Electrotechnik:	Industriemesse Hannover, International Exhibition of Electronics and Electrotechnique (Hannover, Germany, 1-8 April 1987)
Canadian High-Technology Show	International Exhibition of Technologies (Toronto, 28-30 September 1987)
N.T.:	International Exhibition of New Technologies (Turin, 3-7 November 1987)
Salon des Composants:	Electroic Components Paris, (16-20 November 1987)

Table 2.   Activities connected with the foreign partners convention

Exhibit at Grenoble, (France, 13-14 January 1987)

Exhibit of Austrian operators in the Piedmont
(Turin, 19 February 1987)

Meeting of RECIT Convention Partners during
CET 87 (Stuttgart, 4 June 1987)

Meeting of Convention Partners at Chateau de Faverges
(France, 8-9 September 1987)

Presentation of N.T. Bulletin al Alessandria (Italy, 25 June 1987)

Participation in TECHNOVA (Graz, (Austria), 3-5 June 1987)

Meeting of RECIT Convention Partners (Turin, 6 November 1987)

Publication of the 1st N.T. Bulletin: New Technologies (October 1987)

Table 3.   Foreign section of the Piedmont Chambers of Commerce:

Technology Transfer Service for Firms in the Piedmont and Aosta

International promotion of Piedmontese industry:
Information - Consultancy - Training

Promotion (45 exhibitions/year, trade missions, etc.):
High-Technology Department; Technological Opportunities Centre;
Bureau for EEC Research Projects

Staff of 50
(of whom 25 are highly qualified in the field of
international trade and exchange)

Piedmontese industries need these types of contacts, and, on the other hand, foreign companies might draw real advantages by meeting Piedmontese, Italian or European purchasers. Our co-operation with ZIRST and the High-Tech Centre in Grenoble is thus particularly meaningful.

We have been warmly welcomed by many categories of associations, as the first Italian promotional organization (after the German, Belgian, Scottish, English and Japanese organizations; Tables 1-3)

High-Technology Exchange Centre

The High Technology Exchange Centre (HTC) was set up by the Foreign Section of the Piedmont Chambers of Commerce with the participation and support of the EEC in order to provide an adequate response to the new requirements of the Piedmontese production sector.

Over the past few years our region has witnessed the clear emergence of an increasing sophistication in production processes together with a tendency towards specialization aimed predominantly at new products, factors which have had a pronounced effect on the features and requirements of the manufacturing sector. This has led to an innovative response to the increasing competitiveness and rapid changes which currently characterize the international market and which have brought about significant updating in the processes employed in Piedmontese industry resulting in the substitution/diversification of its products.

The need to grow or even at times, simply to survive, stimulated creativity and innovation during a period of transformation which has involved not only the larger groups (Fiat, Olivetti), but has also brought to the fore countless small and medium-sized enterprises (SMEs).

It is the smaller firms that form the connective tissue of Piedmontese industry and although their innovative efforts have been remarkable, it is often the case that they lack those structures and that access to information which are necessary to deal with technology transfer in the most effective way.

Our HTC was set up to give support to these firms in particular, and has the following aims:

1. To promote innovation by making it as easy as possible to locate information, partners and sources of finance
2. To maximize the impact of those high-tech products that have already been developed by seeking out new market outlets for them
3. To back up companies undergoing diversification by supplying them with market research studies and sound products offers
4. To operate in such a way that innovation is timely and plays a significant role in a firm's success

The various services which have been implemented include: the setting up of a Technology Exchange for the sorting out of requests and offers; publication of a periodical bulletin, *Enquiries and Offers in the High-Tech World*; editing of an official catalogue of high-tech manufacturers; a special projects office; agreements with Italian and foreign science parks; and manager training.

Our undertaking fits into the framework of a European project aimed at rationalizing and developing technology transfer. Industrial transformation has been anything but linear and the European advanced-technology market is now in a decidedly fragmentary state, with the channels of exchange rendered difficult by bottlenecks and lack of continuity, which limit the flow of information and thus impede the technological growth of companies. Furthermore, in the context of Europe, it is often the case that there are difficulties in turning technological and scientific results into commercial successes. For this reason, a number of centres have been established in Europe with the aim of providing specific services to facilitate the process of finding partners, and to promote the transfer of patents, know-how and products, above all where SMEs are concerned.

Our HTC is an EEC-authorized service and its presence in Europe is already taking shape in the form of close collaboration with technology parks in Grenoble (France), Newcastle (Great Britain), and Graz (Austria).

Italy's Participation in the Mithra Project

Mithra is a project aimed at the development, construction and marketing of mobile robots for surveillance and protection purposes inside and on the grounds of civil buildings. These third-generation robots, designed to meet the ever-growing need for authorized services, will be capable of making intelligent connections between perception and action. The project is part of the Eureka programme and has brought together several Italo-Franco Swiss companies and organizations which are among the few European set-ups sufficiently advanced to be able to provide the required technological input.

The limited number of firms involved and the specific nature of the research topics has made it possible to break the work down into distinct but mutually complementing subprojects, thus eliminating from the start the problem of competition.

The Italian firms which are taking part in this project are situated in Piedmont, a region with a particularly well-developed industrial framework and a clearly defined sense of its role in the context of Europe. These include:

- SEPA. This member of the Fiat Group makes electronic products and systems with high technological content and considerable added value that have applications in industry, defence, energy and services. This company is particularly strong in the design and production of electronic materials for use in hostile and aggressive environments, for the processing of signals and images and for process monitoring. Within Mithra, SEPA takes part in defining the structure of the robot, developing and producing components and modules for mobile robotics and developing a monitoring system.

- ELKRON. This company manufactures security devices and systems which are highly innovative both technologically and conceptually and include high-security cordless command units and SMD technology. It is outstanding in the field of detectors (hyper-frequency, passive and active infrared, safes and vaults, ultrasonics, glass paste). In the context of the Mithra project Elkron carries out studies aimed at defining the surrounding environment, analysing foreseeable anomalies and their effect within this environment, and studying various possible courses of action.

- PIANELLI E TRAVERSA INDUSTRIES (Division of OLMAT) is a company committed to the improvement of standards regarding the electronic and mechanical aspects of industrial automation, robots, production and assembly lines and cable-command vehicles. Its role within the Mithra venture involves defining the structure of the robot, and building basic modules and assembly lines.

Italy's collaboration in this project can be attributed to the close ties that have long linked Piedmontese firms with the neighbouring regions on the far side of the Alps, ties which have been encouraged by ease of communications and by cultural similarities between the regions. In this case in particular, collaboration has been made easier by the close links that exist between the two regional bodies set up for the development of economic relations: the Grenoble Chamber of Commerce and the Centro Estero Camere Commercio Piemontesi. These two bodies were invited to enter into a partnership by both Grenoble's AID, a firm experienced in the production of small mobile robots, and from two Italian firms specialized in the field of sensors and alarms. The common need to expand and to develop an initial nucleus gave birth to this project. The group subsequently increased in size and complexity due to the efforts of the two regional bodies which continue to oversee its coordination, and thus it was that the operating programme was drawn up.

One of the most noteworthy features of this experience is the complete lack of distinction between the various nations. There is no "Italian force" within Mithra, there are only European firms committed to a joint applied research project.

These joint projects go far beyond the purely bureaucratic: they pave the way for technological achievements which would be unthinkable at a national level. Indeed, they are the expression of the interdependence which has existed for some time between the production systems of the different regions - and which has not waited until the official deadline of 1992 to make its presence felt.

6.2 Structural Changes in the Ruhr Area: Development Strategies in Promoting Innovations and Technology and Knowledge Transfer

Michael Morath

Characteristics of the Present Situation

First and foremost I would like to illustrate with the aid of graphs certain facts and data which reveal the nucleus of the problem and the necessity for structural change. These unfold the current picture of the Ruhr area which is in the grips of several sales crises which have particularly beset the coal and steel industries (see Fig. 1).

Through rationalization and specialisation in the steel industry competitiveness was retained, yet, the resultant fall in sales and the increase in productivity led to large job cuts which have not been compensated for (see Figs. 2 and 3).

The present unemployment rate in the Federal Republic of Germany stands at 8.3% on average as compared with 10.6% in North Rhine-Westphalia and 15% in the Ruhr area. It must be noted that approximately 30% of the national industrial turnover is produced in the region North Rhine-Westphalia. Of the 192,000 jobs in the steel industry, 35,000 are at risk; further job cuts are being prevented for the years 1988/1989 by subsidies from the EEC, the West German government and the local government in North Rhine-Westphalia.

Public attention is no longer concentrated on the large concerns but on small and medium-sized enterprises (SMEs) instead; the change in technical production objectives setting is expected to stem from the latter. The regeneration of the large companies such as Krupp, Thyssen, Hoesch, Mannesmann and Ruhrkohle AG has required more time for take-off. This has been achieved through diversification into new technology fields such as electronics, lasers, biotechnology and food, water and environmental technologies while keeping current manufacturing levels constant

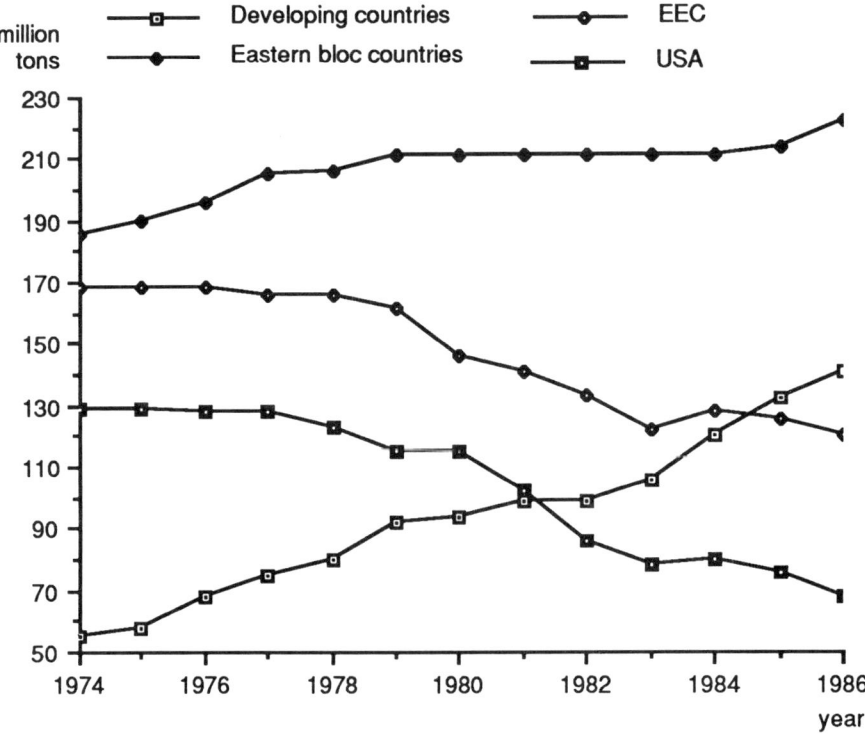

Figure 1:   30 % fall in steel production in the last 10 years (EEC countries)

through rationalization and innovation. One mammoth construction from the Ruhr area, to serve as an example here, is the curving roof of the International Congress Centre in Berlin which consists of 7800 tons of steel resting on 70 m wide supports.

Preconditions for a Change in Structure

Fortunately for the Ruhr area, or rather, out of political circumstances dating back 25 years, the area has the highest density of higher education establishments. The founding of five new universities in Bochum, Dortmund, Hagen, Essen and Duisburg, plus the existing colleges has not only created great intellectual potential for what was traditionally a labour market for blue- collar workers, but also a great

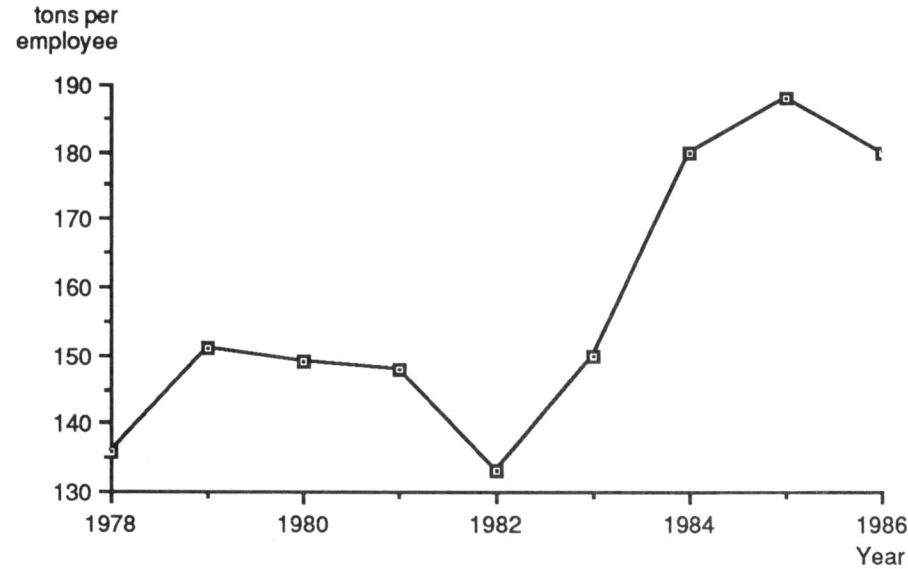

Figure 2: 30 % productivity increase in steel production over the last 10 years (FRG)

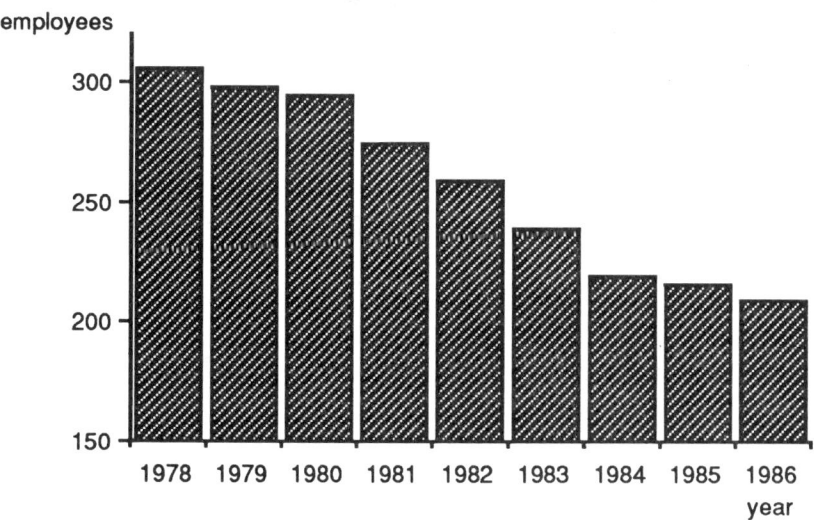

Figure 3: Reduction in the number of employees in the steel-industry (FRG)

source of specialized knowledge arising from the numerous different study subjects in the arts, social sciences, natural sciences and engineering fields. This has made it possible for many firms to move into new product areas, since the qualified personnel was readily available in the area and not elsewhere, although the high unemployment rate was not subsequently reduced. A total of approximately 3000 scientists are currently working in all areas of technological research in laboratories in the research establishments of the Ruhr area (Figs. 4 and 5).

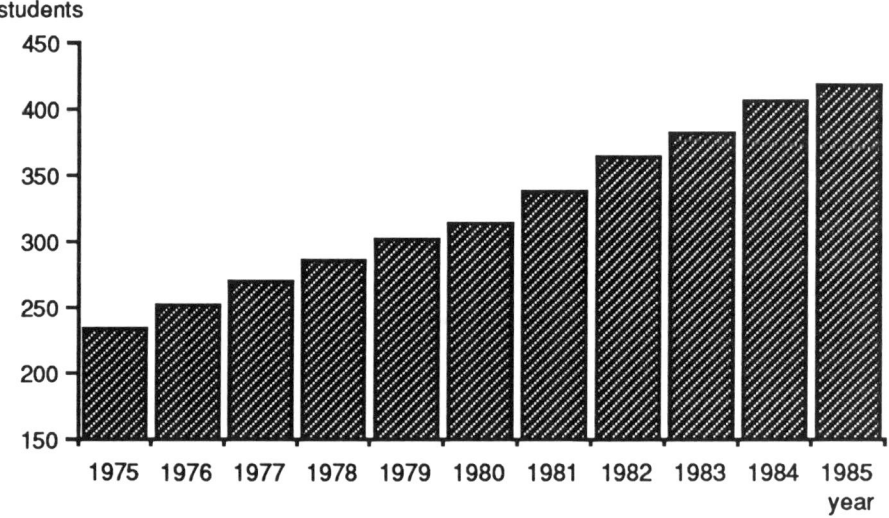

Figure 4:   Increase in the number of students over the last 10 years
            (Nordhein-Westfalen)

Measures for the Changes in Structure

A comprehensive set of measures was taken by the Trade and Industry and Science Ministries to exploit the impressive research infrastructure in the region. A good example is the "advanced technology" initiative in the North Rhine-Westphalia state government which aims to convert the acquisition of knowledge and new product developments into concrete jobs. The following schemes were set up by the Trade and Industry Ministry:

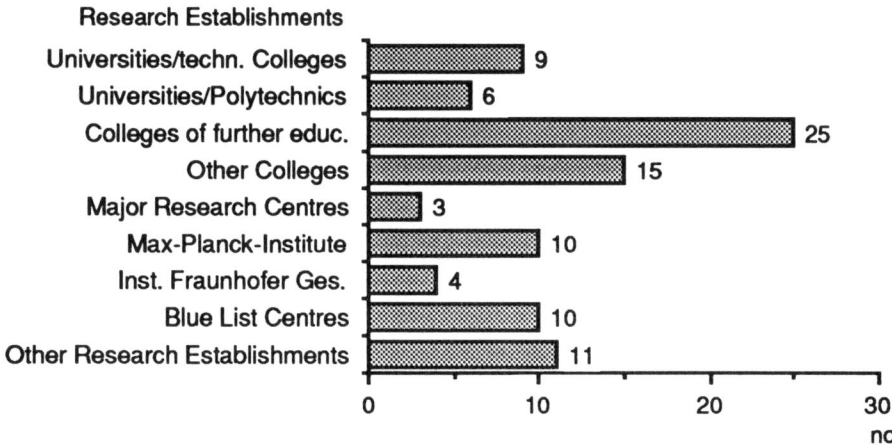

Figure 5: Research establishments in the state department Nordrhein-Westfalen (1987)

- Technologieberatung (Technology Consulting) North Rhine-Westphahlia (TBNW): Under this scheme teachers in higher education are paid for free consultancy (within limits) to SMEs. Approximately 5 million DM are allocated to this per year.

- Technologie Programm Wirtschaft (TPW, Technology Programme for Industry): This scheme supports innovation and new developments and has been running since 1987.

- Technologieprogramm Zukunftstechnologien (TPZ, Advanced Technology Programme): This initiative (begun in 1985) concerns those projects which are not quite ready to be launched on the market in the following eight fields of technology: environment technology, energy, microelectronics, measuring and control engineering, information and communications technology, biotechnology, work environment technology and tools and equipment technology. A total of 781 projects were set up by June 1987 at a cost of 464 million DM for investment and personnel.

- Zentrum für Innovation und Technik (ZENIT, Centre for Innovation and Engineering): ZENIT is a tool used by the Trade and Industry Ministry for supplying engineering assistance to medium-sized businesses. Through

ZENIT medium-sized businesses are provided with a grant for advice on how to integrate into their structures the following technologies: microelectronics, communications, flexible automation, laser and environment technology and artificial intelligence. Additionally, assistance is given by means of a personnel transfer scheme (50% of the first year's salary is financed by local government) and advice on EEC Technology Sponsorship Programmes.

Moreover, the state of North Rhine-Westphalia has the most technology parks in the country (14 to date), of which four are in the Ruhr area and all are situated close to universities. Subsidies for these technology parks in North Rhine-Westphalia have to date amounted to a total of 7.4 million DM; 200 new companies have been launched with approximately 1500 new jobs.

Structural change in the Ruhr area has further been advanced through the following:

- Funding of institutes other than universities (e.g. Fraunhofer Gesellschaft) with 50% investment.

- Setting-up of technology transfer departments at colleges of further education: These are closely co-ordinated with chambers of commerce and trade corporations and represent a service which may be used by scientists at the universities as an extra source of funding and by industry for contact initiation purposes for innovation and new product developments. The second task of these transfer departments, which is increasingly gaining importance, is their its role as a further education or training resource outside the scope of the university. Seminars, colloquiums and forums on special topics are organized for industry.

- Setting-up of new career-orientated courses at the colleges of higher education: Close contact to industry is conducive to transfer of personnel between the establishments involved.

To help attract this external source of funding which helps finance research in colleges of higher education, research is focussed on particular fields: 40 million DM thereby flow into the colleges through the Advanced Technology scheme.

Total external funding from EEC grant schemes, the Federal Ministry for R&D, from the state government North Rhine-Westphalia and from industry, which amounts to 482 million DM (of which approximately 150 million DM were allocated to colleges in the Ruhr area) is a proof of the capabilities of colleges of further education in the region.

A sum in the amount of 200,000 DM has been allocated for a high-tech-transfer scientist exchange with North Carolina in the United States.

From federal and EEC sources the heavy-industry regions (the Ruhr area representing a large section here) are to receive a total of 1 billion DM over five years in order to accelerate the change in infrastructure. New employment sectors are to be created and the traditional sectors are to be revived through innovative measures. Examples thereof are to be seen in Duisburg where the launch of a new space-communications institute (following the increase in European space activity) is under consideration, together with plans for the modernization of the docks and ports in the Duisburg Ruhrort, including the construction of a free port and a "teleport".

Results

According to a recent study 7000 new jobs have been created since 1980 and 40,000 of those at risk have been spared. Duisburg has become a major microelectronics centre in West Germany. Several technology parks now operate profitably. The environmental technology is well served by approximately 400 companies. North Rhine-Westphalia is now a major site for Japanese companies, having attracted 400 to date.

It may then be concluded that the importance to the economy of founding the colleges of higher education in the Ruhr area cannot be overestimated. They represent the most important factor in providing innovation and initiatives for economic restructuring.

6.3 Wales, Great Britain: Strategies of the Welsh Development Agency

Alun Daniel

In this paper I will describe the role of the Welsh Development Agency (WDA) in promoting innovation and technology in Wales; we have a remit to regenerate and restructure the economy of Wales.

In Wales we have been very heavily dependent on coal and steel and in the past twelve to fifteen years have lost over 100,000 jobs in those two industries. Previously there were about 150,000 working in those areas, now there are only 30,000-40,000. Thus we have a major job to restructure the country's economy.

During this fiscal year 1987/1988, we have total funds of £ 86.5 million sterling of which £ 40 million comes from the U.K. government by way of grant - the balance we generate ourselves. We have a staff of over 500 who are involved in all professional aspects from building factories, to advising small and medium-sized enterprises (SMEs), to making decisions on investments, and then we have the support services.

The development strategy will now be briefly identified. All the elements are important and they all contribute to the development of technology and new businesses.

First in ensuring the provision of venture capital funding we have a portfolio of a value of £ 28 million investments and we invest on average about £ 8 million sterling per annum. In Wales there is no alternative source of venture capital. There is a great problem because the City of London, where all the venture capital money rests, is reluctant to invest in an area which goes beyond one/two hours travelling from the City and Wales falls outside that area; thus, we have to substitute in Wales for the City.

We have been building factories since we were created ten to twelve years ago and we now have a total property portfolio of 18 milion sq ft and on average we lease 2 million sq ft per annum. We develop management capability for SMEs by provision of advisory and consultancy services. We give advice to over 70,000 businesses per annum. We provide business counselling to 10,000 companies and we handle over 20,000 enquiries from small firms.

We improve the environment through the reclamation of derelict land and environmental improvement. We devise special initiatives to reduce the economic and social problems of the rural areas, which in particular in Wales are very badly hit by the CAD changes which came through a couple of years ago, milk quotas in particular. We will be more heavily hit if there are changes in the structure for the sheep regime.

We are responsible for securing inward investment projects into Wales and in the past four years we have secured over 200 projects worth £ 600 million which represents 20% of all the inward investment projects coming into the U.K.

In the above, very briefly, with apologies for the brevity I have tried to identify all the powers and functions that we have that are essential to carrying out our statutory responsibility for restructuring the economy. They all contribute to the work of a particular department that we set up two years ago call "WINtech" which is shorthand for Wales Innovation and Technology.

WINtech was set up to promote commercial exploitation (and I stress "commercial" because we are in the commercial world) of technology and to improve the links between education and industry. WINtech services include aspects such as product development, technology acquisition, manufacturing systems, development, grant acquisition, market and technical appraisals, new company formation, collaborative research and development, and access to sources of finance and promotion of technology developed in Wales. What it is, essentially, is what we call in English "a one stop shop". A "one stop shop" ensures that a client or a customer coming to WINtech will get access to all the help and all the advice that he or she will require to set up a business and to obtain advice on technology. Again I will briefly run through different ways in which we provide this service.

First, to establish companies in Wales working with the University of Wales Institute of Science and Technology, we have a programme called "Aim for Wales" which is designed to ensure that Welsh companies make the best use of available advanced manufacturing technologies. Over the past year some 30 companies have been helped in the development of more efficient manufacturing production control systems. We have recently set up an AMT (an Advance Manufacturing Technology) centre where WINtech works with the private sector and with Welsh colleges to enhance the production capabilities of Welsh-based companies. We are involved very much with technology acquisition programmes and for the past two years we have been working with some 20 companies who are now involved in licensing technology from overseas and operating within Wales, and two or three new products are coming to the market as a result of this programme.

Biotechnology is another area where we have specialized. We have over 3000 people employed in companies where the companies have over £ 100 million turnover in biotechnology and we recently appointed a specialist in biotechnology to advise that sector.

We provide a whole range of information services, including major seminars, telecommunications, computer systems, engineering design, and data-base services on grant availability under government incentive schemes in the U.K. which are designed to help the small businesses in the world of technology. We have access to something that has been set up called BEST (British Expertise in Science and Technology) which is a data-base of research and expertise in the U.K.'s academic and government research establishments and it contains a vast store of knowledge on subjects such as biotechnology, computer-aided design, electronic devices, industrial design, lasers, market services, office organization, pharmaceuticals, robotics, statistics and tribology. What we say to the client is "Come to us, we find out what the latest state of research is, we can help you, we can advise you".

We have set up, with the Department of Education and Science, the Wales Technology Centre, which is to increase the training and consultancy links between Welsh companies and/or Welsh colleges.

One of the initiatives of interest perhaps is the AWACS Offset Agreement which the British government insisted that Boeing offers U.K. companies. As a result of the work that WINtech has been doing, 11 Welsh companies have received accreditization as potential Boeing suppliers and indeed this very day ten Welsh companies are in Seattle talking to Boeing about work which hopefully will come to Wales.

I mentioned earlier the "one stop shop". We can provide through our investment funds, through our property, through our advisory services, through our technological expertise, the whole range of advice needed by any potential businessman.

We have recently become involved in funding Centres of Excellence at Universities. We provided a grant of £ 400,000 sterling to Cardiff University for a semiconductor micro-electronics centre. That in turn has secured something like £ 3 million in other grants. We are involved now in an electronics material centre, the field of amorphous silicon, data communication centre, biotechnology centre, and plant biology centre.

Our concern and our obligation under the statute which created the WDA is to create long-term lasting employment for Welsh people. Now there is much talk about international and transnational co-operation - we are moving down that road - but our first obligation is to restructure the Welsh economy, to give it a much broader base than previously so that we are not overly dependent on traditional industries and we do not again suffer the very serious economic, social and community problems that we have suffered with the reduction in the coal and steel industries.

6.4 Regionalization in Niederösterreich (Lower Austria): Strategic Outlines and First Experiences with a New Instrument of Regional Policy

Richard Plitzka and Theodor Krendelsberger

The new Austrian instruments of regional policy, to be presented here, orient themselves very much towards the promotion of an independent regional development.

In 1921 Vienna was separated from Niederösterreich (Lower Austria) and declared a separate federal state (Bundesland). The seat of the state administration and government of Niederösterreich has remained, however, in Vienna. During the following decades again and again the question was raised whether Niederösterreich needs a state capital of its own. This question arose not only with respect to the necessity of a government and administration centre in the state itself, but also from the economic and regional necessity to support the development of a dynamic centre in Niederösterreich.

Due to a strong orientation for decades towards Vienna as a location of first-rate institutions of education and of a receptive labour market, Niederösterreich has suffered, at least in the regions which were particularly weakly developed, a considerable loss of real assets by migration. For instance, in the period 1971 to 1981 alone about 50,000 persons migrated from Niederösterreich to Vienna. This novum has been exacerbated in the 1980s by the increasingly acute labour market problems. In this connection the discussion of a state capital for Niederösterreich arose again.

After two years of intense public discussion and research, a referendum took place on 1 and 2 March 1986, as a basis for the decision on a state capital. Of a polling of 61.4% of the persons eligible to vote, 56% were in favour of a capital.

After this referendum the Landtag (parliament) of Niederösterreich passed a unanimous resolution on 10 July, 1986 for the establishment of a capital for Niederösterreich at St. Pölten, as well as the provision annually of 500 million ÖS (Österreichische Schilling) for the strengthening of the Niederösterreich regions during the next 20 years: 150 million ÖS are to be granted to the communities directly, 350 million ÖS will be contributed to the promotion of projects within the regions. The programme of regional policy for this promotion of projects is referred to as "regionalization".

The Problems of the State of Niederösterreich as a Starting Point for Regionalization

In Niederösterreich, the decelerated overall economic growth, rising unemployment, and general shortage of public funds aggravate economic and regional problems. Along with the measures at the capital of St. Pölten, regionalization is a strategy whereby these problems are to be tackled head on. Regionalization therefore is inseparably linked to the current and anticipated problems of the state. They are the starting point, the basis of reference and the standard of success for all efforts in regionalization.

A number of empirical studies reveal the basic conditions specific to Niederösterreich. Niederösterreich is part of an economic area which - in contrast to other areas and especially to the west of Austria - is constantly losing economic importance. Since the 1960s overall productivity in the eastern region (Vienna, Niederösterreich and Burgenland) has grown more slowly than in Austria as a whole: In the business periods 1961-1969, 1969-1973, 1973-1980 and 1980-1983 the average annual change in the (nominal) gross net output in the eastern region was 7.6% (Austria 8.1%), 9.6% (Austria 11.0%), 9.2% (Austria 9.5%), and 6.3% (Austria 6.7%) - all distinctly below the comparative figures for Austria (source: WIFO). Niederösterreich achieved above average economic growth in the boom years of 1969-1973 (11.5% p.a.), but was affected more severely than other federal states by the recessions of 1974/1975 and 1980/1981.

The decrease in economic importance of the eastern region goes hand in hand with the shift of emphasis of population from the east to the west of Austria. This is determined, above all, by disadvantages in the age structure and the general population trend (decline in the the birth rates). The proportional share of the resident population of the eastern region compared with the population of Austria as a whole in 1961 still reached 46.3%, in 1981 it was 42.7% and for the year 2011 it is estimated to be 39.5% (source: ÖSTZ, ÖIR).

Within the state of Niederösterreich there are especially marked differences in development. In examining the range of indicators relevant to regional policy at the district level (balance between highest and lowest district value), there are some substantial divergencies:

- Population trend 1971-1981 between +14.5% and -8.6%
- Job development 1971-1981 between +34.3% and -17.8%
- Rate of unemployment in 1986 between 8.2% and 3.2%
- Monthly wages in industry in June 1986 between 21,593 ÖS and 11,987 ÖS

(source: ÖSTZ, BMS, and BUKA)

The distinct differences in development come about because Niederösterreich includes regions with especially marked economic dynamics (above all the area of Mödling) and peripheral regions with weak development (for instance, the northern forest and vine area) as well as old industrial regions (for example, the southern Niederösterreich).

Exogenous Framework Conditions and Endogenous Structural Factors Require Regional and Economic Evaluation

Of course, the above-mentioned problems of Niederösterreich and the eastern region as a whole are not exclusively "homemade", but have to be seen in close connection with the national and international economic framework conditions and their changes. That Niederösterreich is particularly affected by these developments seems partly to be caused by its peripheral location in relation to European economic centres. Beyond that, other factors that are difficult to quantify are certainly of importance, for example, the deficiencies of information, a seriously low density of services from the point of view of functional value, and other, non-economic factors.

The problems stated have to be taken seriously, for they are increasing because of the growth in commuter traffic and migration. In 1981 50% more Austrian employees commuted beyond the state border than in 1971 (90,000 instead of

60,000). In the period 1971 to 1981 about 75,000 people from Niederösterreich migrated (of these about 50,000 to Vienna). Thus, there is the risk that, above all, people with the most initiative and highest qualifications are lost to Niederösterreich, unless enough jobs and additional attractions can be offered there.

Conclusions To Be Drawn from the Basic Conditions: Two Fundamental Requirements for Regionalization

The basic conditions in Niederösterreich make it evident that targeted attempts in different policy fields will be more urgently necessary in the future to positively influence the structures and trends pointed out above. Therefore, analysis of the basic economic situation is also the precondition for the formulation of two important requirements of regionalization.

Regionalization should not only have a compensatory dimension, but also a distinct dimension of economic growth. Together with measures at the capital of St. Pölten, something should be done to halt the weaknesses in the economic growth of Niederösterreich, in terms of the creation and safeguarding of jobs and the accompanying net output. Besides adjustment of regional development differences by an increased promotion of projects in structurally and economically weak regions, regionalization should make a contribution to economic growth. Each of the projects should have a clear economic effect for the region. For this reason, projects which only serve to solve community problems are excluded from the government assistance programme.

In practical politics these requirements mean that the regional and economic policy of Niederösterreich has to enter into an alliance in which objectives and measures are co-ordinated. This alliance can be seen to have come into existence already, when one considers the guidelines for the promotion of regionalization, the choice of members of "ECO PLUS" - the local company in charge of regionalization - and the real voting procedures between the regional planning and economic departments within the framework of project promotion. This represents, by the way, a situation, which, as far as I can see, is something quite new for Austria.

Regionalization should achieve something more than traditional economic and investment promotion. This additional effect is not to be understood as an addition to traditional instruments - more funds for projects in certain sectors - but as a qualitative supplement. It is also intended to influence deeper non-material reasons for the lack of economic pressure, e.g. by conveying an atmosphere of fundamental change, unconventional support of initiatives, networks of activities, reduction of impediments for activity, consultation, etc. This second requirement means that in view of the shortage of public funds, these have to be used more efficiently, not by achieving higher efficiency in certain sectors - it is not the goal of regional policy to take over sector competences - but by a special way of overlapping in the usage of funds, so that special synergy effects can be achieved, a working together of forces in the sense of augmenting the cumultative effect.

Criteria for the Evaluation of Regionalization Projects

In order to evaluate the contribution of projects from the perspective of regionalization three categories of criteria have been worked out.

The quality of a project in the sense of spatially far-reaching and effective basic and additional use for regional policy is the most important feature. Criteria are, for example, the number and net output value of the jobs created; the extent to which service and consumption opportunities are provided; or the character of innovation and creativity of the project. These criteria chosen as examples for evaluating projects orient themselves at the above-mentioned requirements in respect to the growth policy contribution of regionalization, the creation of attractiveness and the reduction of non-material causes for the lack of economic dynamism.

Furthermore, the regionalization projects should make a contribution to the realization of objectives of regional planning policy. In this way, regionalization is linked to the prerequisites of regional planning policy in Niederösterreich. The Niederösterreichische Raumordnungsgesetz (regional policy law) and the Niederösterreichische Raumordnungsprogramm (regional policy programme), therefore, become important for the evaluation of the individual projects. Future and existing spatial assignments of functions as well as the compensatory concerns of regional planning policy are taken into consideration.

Finally, regionalization projects should be supported to a high degree by the region, in order to enable a development as autonomous as possible and therefore a self-supporting development of the region in the long run. It would be desirable, for instance, that an initiative come from the region and use regional development potential.

These three categories of required characteristics of projects are described in more detail on the basis of a number of criteria in the Förderungsrichtlinien zur Regionalisierung (guidelines for the promotion of regionalization, ECO PLUS, 1987).

Special Strategic Features of Regionalization

Besides attention to and further development of the elements mentioned above, special strategies and directions have to be considered which offer, in our opinion, (good) regional policy prospects. These have, above all, three characteristics.

Regionalization Makes Regionally Adapted Individual Strategies Possible

It can be specifically determined for the regions which sector should be promoted, what project, to what extent and in what way. Thus, the regional synergy potential can be used better than in regionally uniform promotion, which refers in each situation to a certain field, as is the case with traditional instruments. Thus, projects in different fields can be supported which mutually influence and complement each other.

Regionalization Tries to Use the Advantages of Development Concepts Both "From Above" and "From Below"

An initiative coming from the region and guaranteeing the use of regional resourcs will be especially promoted to support independent regional development (third dimension). Regional policy priorities are also considered when evaluating projects (second dimension) whereby the deficiencies of voting and co-ordination of one-sided strategies of promotion, oriented at autonomous regional development, can be reduced. Thereby regionalization may also be characterized as regionalism of the middle course.

Regionalization Explicitly Takes into Consideration the Sociocultural Environment of Economic Development

The sociocultural environment gains increasing importance for the explanation of regional development differences. Successful entrepreneurialism in a wider sense not only requires easy terms of location, a sufficient capital basis and know-how in the field of production of material goods or services, but also originality, adaptability, creative will, risk, and the like. In a specific sociocultural environment the development and furtherance of these capabilities can either be favoured or hindered. I want to differenciate this idea even further in the following.

The Contribution of the ECO PLUS Within the Framework of Regionalization

The Landesgesellschaft ECO PLUS Betriebsansiedlung und Regionalisierung in Niederösterreich (regional corporation for plant siting and regionalization) has been given the task by the government of Niederösterreich of evaluating regionalization projects which deserve promotion. The organs of the ECO PLUS, the (regionalization) management, the advisory board, and supervisory board evaluate the projects handed in and work out the promotion recommendations as a basis for the final decision of the state government with respect to the allocation of funds.

One of the main functions of the ECO PLUS is the vetting of promotion applications and projects handed in and the working out of relevant promotion recommendations. The working out of suggestions for improvement, in respect to increasing the regional efficiency of projects as well as the initiation of projects, plays an especially important role.

What Can Be Expected from Regionalization in the Next Few Years?

The multitude of requirements demanded for regionalization projects gives rise to the questions, of whether it is generally possible to find enough of these projects and whether the formulation of such requirement profiles is not influenced too much by wishful thinking. These legitimate questions are answered by mentioning three aspects.

First, it is obvious that not all projects can meet all requirements. One can only claim that as many criteria as possible are fulfilled.

Second, regionalization in Niederösterreich as well as the development of the state capital St. Pölten has been planned on a long-term basis. Just as the measures have to be thoroughly planned in the capital to achieve the success desired, ideal regionalization projects cannot be presented overnight. For the promotion grantor as well as for the promotion grantee a process of learning will be necessary, to increase the efficiency of the instruments in the medium and long run.

Third, ECO PLUS has not only to check the projects handed in to see if they deserve promotion, but also to improve projects in the sense of the objectives of regionalization, as well as to initiate suitable projects. This is especially true for the field of plant siting; its promotion is still within the scope of activity of ECO PLUS and its duty of regionalization is carried out with the utmost application.

In future, promotion advice, the working out of improvement proposals, as well as the initiation of additional projects should play a special role within the scope of regionalization. Realistically, a certain start-up period will be necessary until this part of the enterprise can be established. Above all, pilot projects are to be initiated, which could demonstrate best where the peculiarities of regionalization projects lie and which allow a differentiation from the traditional sector's promotion of projects.

Summary

Regionalization, thus, does not ensue from a traditional sector-oriented concept of economic promotion, but from regionally adopted individual strategies.

Regionalization orients itself not only to regional planning models, but tries, starting from regional development potentials, to create the special conceptual and instrumental preconditions (e.g. use of regional know-how, consideration of labour, traditions, integration of regional initiatives and existing creative will, etc.) for a promising regional development.

Regionalization starts from the fact that economic dynamics are not independent from sociocultural dynamics. The promotion of regional, social and cultural dynamics, therefore, becomes an integrated part of a comprehensive regional and economic policy.

In this sense regionalization in the medium and long term has to present itself in clear outline as an overlapping additional instrument of promotion, apart from the existing sectoral policies and their promotional instruments. Its big opportunity lies in the mutual regional networks and in the additional development of projects in different sectors with regard to the achievement of utmost regional overall benefit. Its biggest risk lies in the local, regional and/or sectoral "egotisms", which could oppose this aim.

Thus, it becomes clear that regionalization is not offered as a regional and economic "miracle drug". It has in common with all future-oriented long-term programmes the fact that it depends to a high degree on the successful use of creative scope to achieve the objectives aimed at. For the project itself - and this is also true for the development of the capital of St. Pölten - one must already emphasize the utopian energy as a positive factor. A room without utopian energy is subjectively emptied, says Detlev Ipsen, and (thus), in our opinion, regional policy has to prevent this - both conceptionally and spatially.

Abbreviations used:

BMS,	Bundesministerium für Arbeit und Soziales (Federal Ministry of Labour and Social Affairs)
BUKA,	Bundeskammer der gewerblichen Wirtschaft (Federal Chamber of Industry and Trade)
ÖSTZ,	Österreichisches Statistisches Zentralamt (Austrian Central Statistical Office)
ÖIR,	Österreichisches Institut für Raumplanung (Austrian Institute for Regional Planning)
WIFO,	Österreichisches Institut für Wirtschaftsforschung (Austrian Institute for Economic Research)

Reference

ECO PLUS, Förderungsrichtlinien zur Regionalisiserung, Wien 1987

6.5 Technology Transfer Networks in Nord/Pas-de-Calais: Accomplishments, Limits and Questions

Martine Delpierre and Christian Mahieu

Technical change in small and medium-sized enterprises (SMEs) obviously involves actors both within and outside the enterprise who are increasingly diversified and interdependent, through complex links with the industrial system itself (links with management and major enterprises and interenterprise links) and also (and this is the most novel aspect) through links with the political and administrative sphere (in particular at the regional level) and training, research and know-how transfer structures. The closely meshed technology transfer networks correspond in this respect to a change in the public intervention process, in their practical procedures and in their criteria for intervention.

Within the framework of the new economic responsibilities granted to the French regions under the 1982 decentralization laws and in the context of major conversion problems, the Nord/Pas-de-Calais has introduced a particularly comprehensive programme of aid to promote the adoption of technological innovations by SMEs. For the most part involving co-operation with the central government through so-called planning contracts (contrats de plan), the programme involves financial aid on an individual basis (consultancy aid plan, regional process technology plan, aid for recruitment of young engineers and managers) or groups (collective action loans) and, since 1982, transfer networks.

The process technology "pole" is an amalgamating body combining the resources of universities and engineering schools in research, assistance, teaching and transfer in order to develop high-level applied research and to assist the introduction of new process technologies in SMEs, by contracted services.

The regional CAD-CAM network makes available to SMEs at preferential rates data-processing resources (hardware and human resources) of universities and engineering schools. The network consists of a set of "nodes" (e.g. computer centres, "light" units in a firm, "heavy" units shared by several companies).

The networks were not created from scratch by institutional will. The regional CAD-CAM network originated in the pooling and harmonization of higher educational institution data-processing resources. The process technology "pole" is linked to the prior mobilization efforts of university departments (experiments in laboratory-industry relations, the establishment of interfaces, relay structures and service workshops), regional financial flows towards research and transfer, certain major enterprises (failed experiment of the Robotized Production Research Institute initiated by Renault and the Société Française de Mécanique), socio-professional bodies (Social and Economic Interprofessional Committee, the Maison des Professions) organizing the electronic, data-processing and numerically controlled machine sector, and certain chambers of commerce and industry. The membership of the pole's scientific and technical guidance committee and that of the network pilot committee reflects these various types of actors.

Immediate Positive Consequences of Technology Transfer Networks in France

The network improved quality, achieving a "critical mass", i.e. a state of development giving the networks credibility in the face of existing or potential partners, by strengthening their material resources and introducing a sense of belonging, all of which is reflected in the increase in contractual activity of the firms. Fertilization occurred vis-à-vis peripheral structures (Nord/Pas-de-Calais Industrie 2000) participating in the dissemination of new technologies.

With regard to the question of introducing into the "pole" other resource centres (Centre de Formation et de Perfectionnement d'Haumont, Centre d'Etudes de Recherche et de Technologie de l'Artois in Béthune) and collective technical research, they served as a model.

A change could be perceived in the mentality and behaviour of universities and economic actors and the consequent new relationships. This was based on the informal relations which emerge through mutual exchange, as elements of a new industrial culture grounded on a joint assessment of what is at stake, and cemented by strong regional feeling taking root in a developing regional socio-technical community bringing together at varying levels people of different backgrounds. Such relationships are organized around a flexible grid of collective initiatives, agreements and actions directed towards SMEs.

The networks fostered the development of spatial structures which help to bring research and industry closer together, generating new externalities and favouring local development, either by specific projects (construction of the Maison de l'Entreprise et des Technologies Nouvelles by the Maison des Professions, or the Maison de l'Innovation and its branches by the département etc.) or on an overall urban level (Villeneuve d'Ascq Science Park), which generates new development (plan for Béthune) and urban networks.

Regional planning, was promoted by the networks. This applies both in substance (emergence of an "non-material economy" by opening up new areas of intervention for public financing, research, transfer, training, and utilization of human resources) and form (influencing the regional plan and planning contracts for highly diversified sectors to take account of a reality which is no longer modeled on intervention in a few major planning or financing sectors; replacement of an algorithm of simple causality in a well-defined period of time by an iterative procedure comprising negotiated, contract-based stages, and successive adjustments of strategies between several partners), requiring, moreover, assessments which are no longer only quantitative.

Technology Transfer Networks Have Greatly Differing and Limited Effects on Industry.

Only a minority of SMEs (those generally presented as "models", and for various reasons better equipped than others with regard to computerization) are positively concerned. A plausible hypothesis may be put forward that some of these enterprises can already claim to be innovating, that they know the networks and use them, that they avail themselves of aid and technological transfer possibilities. Their activity is based on highly personalized relationships, formed in recognition of their dynamism - and the regional actors naturally turn to them for co-operation. This situation shows that access to the network at any of its points is a determining factor. It also indicates certain risks: the risk of severed relationships between SMEs, which may lead to new distortions, risks of focussing on certain entrepreneurs or types of enterprise, on the home country or on certain regions given aid at the expense of other regions more remote from the transfer centres or less directly receptive regions; and the risk of fossilization of the regional socio-technical community.

On the other hand, transfer operations by the networks for SMEs involve few contracts outside the region or with medium to large enterprises. They are also of highly variable effectiveness (as regards the quality of input of the hardware, response time, etc.) in terms on the profitability and competitiveness of the firms.

In a wider context, where the company information technology is slackening, transfer network activities also begin to slow down and mark time. The question facing the networks, over and above that of their effectiveness, is that of their development and improvement.

The most easily detectable reason for this situation of limited, differing effects on the industrial fabric lies firstly in the regional specificity of the SME environment. Manufacturing SMEs, often acting as subcontractors for a single main contractor in prosperous years, exhibit (a) a considerable lag in investments and failure to develop certain, in particular, commercial functions; (b) their overall weak technical background at the managerial level (lack of strategic technically "receptive" structure) and in terms of personnel; (c) poor support from consultancy firms and services (affected by the demand from major enterprises and proximity to Paris).

The reasons lie, too, in the tangibility of the networks, i.e. in the way they are perceived and recognized. Their contacts with the managers generally operate in a traditional manner of interpersonal relations, sometimes based on relations external to networks, ("old boy" networks, etc.). They compete with the many pressures on information-saturated businessmen (hardware salesmen, private, public or semi-public structures).

The basic problem lies in the fit between innovation processes within the SMEs and the transfer models of the networks (and, more broadly, by all those acting on the firm from the outside).

For them to be mastered, the integrating character of the new technologies requires a strategic, overall approach, i.e. a new conception of the innovation project. The development of production computerization is not confined to the installation of an automated plant served by microelectronics equipment. The whole technical, organizational and human setting is overthrown from the outset, in particular by information flows.

For SMEs, whose strategy until recently has been based on stable markets and products, the new economic constraints centering on the issue of how to survive in changing markets confront the firm with an uncertain, unstable future, which in turn puts a premium on flexibility, either chosen or imposed by customers. Increased profitability and competitiveness can only be achieved by a forward-looking strategy.

The new innovation project requires more than just an "extended project management" in terms of interdependent problems of change in manufacturing processes, products, and the organization of training in the forward management of staffing, financial investment, etc.

Ill-Equipped Actors

First, the difficulty of strategic reflection and even more of co-ordination is reflected by the SME's failure to formulate and formalize an innovation project combining long-term technical, socio-organizational and cultural aspects. This difficulty is related to the very structure of the SME: the smaller the company or the older its structure, the more the problems are personalized and interconnected, the less they can be reduced to the functional and strategic differentiation possible in a major firm, and the less they correspond to dominant assistance or transfer models, which are predicated on the structure of the firm allowing for the formalization of a forward-looking strategy.

The difficulty is also due to the SME's incremental approach to technological innovation: change in the technical process generally calls for a reappraisal of the market and a redefinition of the product and product range; the "point of entry" of technological innovation may be modest and peripheral.

The difficulty may finally be put down to the SME's incapacity, in terms of its financial possibilities, to carry out combining functions, services and methods, production and maintenance surrounding the implementation of the new technology and to a lack of "strategic management" in terms of dealing simultaneously with large-scale investments and the resulting need to have recourse to investments which are fragmented and cumulative.

That is why, moreover - facing a multifaceted reality in an undifferentiated manner and ignoring formal distinctions of an organizational, structural and strategic kind which are generally characteristic of an innovation project - SME managers display varying, at times contradictory, attitudes corresponding to the network of their problems. They do not know who to turn to, or, on the contrary, after a long maturation process, too quickly choose "ready-made" solutions which draw them into a predetermined computerization process. They call on fragmented external skills, which generally do not allow them to reach an awareness of and master the organizational, social and product changes induced by the introduction of new technologies.

Second, for various reasons (e.g. a high technical level related to excellence in research, preferential contracts with best- equipped firms, their own evaluation and performance criteria) the networks are encouraged to put forward high-level technologies and transversal methodologies. Their "privileged" intervention tends to bring about a dual reduction of strategic management to project management and, within the latter, to technical issues as is reflected in the sophistication of the technical specifications. This also holds for decentralized technical structures dealing with the dissemination of automated production. While SMEs sometimes show an awareness at various levels, such as staff management or training, it is generally superficial, marginal, consequent to prior intervention and dependent on individual practice and existing interpersonal relations.

Third, the ways existing consulting agencies operate appears in the main poorly attuned to the innovation process specific to SMEs. One factor here is that the partner firms of consultancies are often those which have already entered into a formalization process, a decision of whatever sort. Consulting firms, thus, enter the process downstream of the innovation project, or more exactly, of a decision to innovate, which often has to be modified. Next, their areas of intervention are sectorized because they are influenced by their intervention in larger medium-sized enterprises, with their organizational and functional distinctions. Lastly, the profitability of consulting firms is generally ensured by intervention in larger medium-sized firms, and is hardly compatible with the longer, more complex intervention involving more modest cumulative, incremental financial investments characteristic of SMEs.

Fourth, the financial aids which supplement the transfer measures remain strongly linked to a type of large and medium-sized enterprise, which is capable of carrying out functional, strategic distinctions and making major investments, and to an earlier technical system - mechanization - consuming mainly unqualified labour, considering human work as a limit to production, attempting to surpass it by automation as highly developed as possible, and endeavouring to channel it and control what remains of it by restrictive forms of organization. From this viewpoint, financial aids tend to be allocated exclusively on the basis of a conception of "modernization" linked with technical achievement, material investment (financial auditing, technical auditing, preliminary and final) and on a conception of a "rupture" or a technologically limited, identifiable "shift" ("before" there was no modernization, "after" it has already taken place). They, thus, reinforce the reduction of strategic management to project management and, within the latter, to the technical process.

This maladjustment leads to a hiatus between the administrative or commercial models (in the case of service and engineering companies) which disseminate technological innovation and the process by which the SME integrates the latter, mainly characterized by the structural incapacity to devise a strategic plan and to ensure strategic management. Aid to modernize SMEs in their various facets remains to a large extent external and sectorized. There is no liaison between the action of the various networks nor is there any feedback between the latter and financial aid. While financial aids may be well co-ordinated through weekly meetings of the various institutional actors, such co-ordination follows a logic peculiar to them in the absence of a representative of the firm.

The firm's lack of understanding of the rules of the game is reflected, moreover at times by the fact that it encourages competition between providers of assistance in hopes to obtain more from them.

This situation also has the result that only those SMEs which have already done the work upstream of the innovation project and are ready to provide strategic management gain access to consulting advice (whatever form it takes) and have a chance of success, i.e. of a significant improvement in their profitability and competitiveness.

What Is the SME To Do?

How can one reconcile the external nature of, in particular, public aid and the need for assistance with strategic management which only the SME itself can provide?

Two phenomena appear vital today in order to improve the effectiveness of transfer and to increase the number of enterprises involved.

The first is the development of the content of the service to the enterprise, i.e. aid for devising the innovation project and for strategic management. The services must "fit" the internal structure of the SME, i.e. involve an approach which is both diversified and global; ensure constant feedback between the limited point of entry of innovation in the enterprise and the longer-term project; assess the needs for flexibility of the manufacturing process and the degree of irreversibility of investments and of the organizational and social structure; respect the balance between internalization (what can be achieved by the enterprise despite its small potential) and externalization, by checking that the external contribution is firmly rooted in the enterprise and is in accordance with its internal capabilities. All this must provide the SME with a greater sense of security as it discovers factors of uncertainty, while respecting the intervening party's specificity related to the "point of entry" of the innovation. This approach needs to give full weight to the human dimension of relations with the company manager, who at times may be unwilling to consider technological innovation from a global viewpoint.

The second is the fact that one must determine who in what "profession", with what skills and status can provide this type of aid to the innovation project and strategic management, given that the development of an all-round consultancy approach has to be a federative approach, calling on new skills and professions.

Most of the existing consulting firms are not at present the place where such new SME-oriented skills and professionalism can develop, owing to the sectorization of their fields of intervention, their being geared to dominant demand (large and medium-sized firms) and their fee structure. The first question they need to confront concerns the teaching of consultancy and the training of consultants. The second question, which also provides an opportunity for improvement, is the association of consulting firms with one another or with networks which do not have the same profitability criteria. A breaking down of such barriers may encourage a certain type of training by associating not only research and industry but also research and services.

They "service companies by default". The transfer networks, which have compensated for the shortcomings of the "market" system and contributed in a large way to the formalizing of the present situation, are not capable on their own of providing the comprehensive, integrated consultancy necessary for strategic management. But one may expect that a principle of such structures, given their performance criteria which do not depend directly on the market, is to acquire additional skills which will allow them to move towards this kind of comprehensive, integrated consultancy work.

In all cases, it appears that aid to SMEs for strategic management cannot be given at present by a single structure or type of structure. It implies a far-reaching change in consultancy work and in the actors involved in it. In particular, practice shows that it tends to depend on a network of public/private, commercial/non-commercial relationships which themselves depend on breaking down various barriers.

To work with SMEs consulting firms have to depend on public aid, while the publically initiated transfer networks must position themselves in the market and draw some of their revenue from it.

In a wider sense, one may legitimately wonder whether it would not be in the interest of public aid, in particular regional intervention, to in future undertake new sorts of activities instead of continuing to refine real estate and the other "hard" resources which have constituted the basic factors in structuring and improving the "regional innovative environment".

Such activities, aimed at mobilizing a greater number of SMEs and improving the effectiveness of transfer operations, would consist of polarizing the effort towards what currently appears to be a "missing link" in transfer aid and which involves non-material investment on the basis of existing structures: aid for the creation of a new sort of consulting firm, improvement in training of consultants, and for the development of new skills and "professions", a crystallizing of relationships between various actors or instruments external to the firm. A parallel must be drawn here with the basic question of non-material investment in the firm and in the structures which induce transfer to them.

Improvement of the efficiency of transfer networks and more widely of aid to strategic management within the SME thus seems to involve the integration of parameters, criteria and novel approaches which mark a new type of public intervention and accentuate the novelty already observed in relation to transfer networks and private/public relations. These developments relate to a wider problem. It is a problem - as against a notion of a perfectly identifiable enterprise, circumscribed and autonomous in its choices - which relates to the development of a composite reality of the firm whose contours are made blurred and more permeable by the public or private financial flows which go through it, and to the recomposition of the industrial system, and the various links which it has with the politico-administrative, research and knowledge-transfer spheres, under the pressure of change in the economic and technical environment. It is a problem of change in public intervention and of a transformation of the central government by associating actors peripheral to it - decentralized institutions, administrations and bodies with diversified public (chambers of commerce, etc.) and private (consulting firms, enterprises, etc.) actors for mastering a new stage of technological development.

6.6 The Loeben Technology Transfer Centre: A Contribution to Structural Change in the Problem Region of Upper Styria (Austria)

Peter Paschen

Styria is the second largest federal state in Austria (see Fig. 1). Its surface area is 16,000 sq kilometers and its population is 1.2 million. In central Europe, Styria is situated at the intersection of the traffic routes between southeastern Europe and northwestern Europe, and between northern Italy and eastern-central Europe. In terms of Western Europe, however, it is a peripheral situation. The seven political districts in northwestern Styria, comprise Upper Styria in contrast to Lower Styria with the capital Graz, a city with about 250,000 inhabitants.

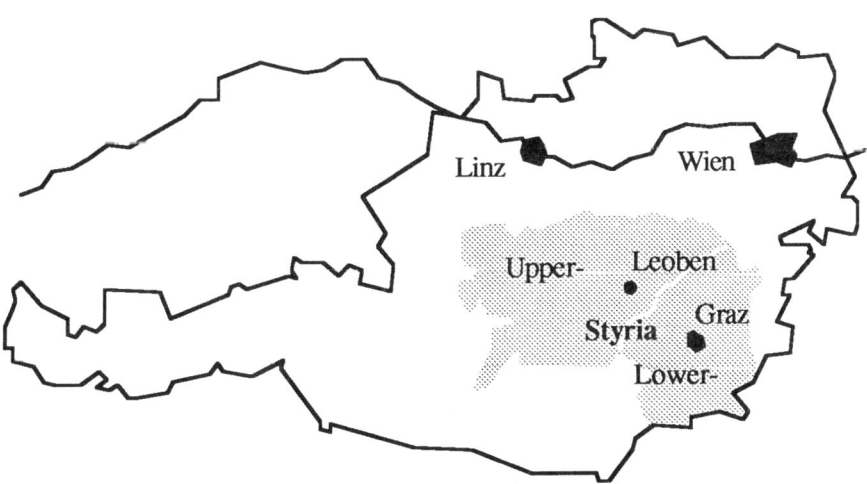

Figure 1:   The Region of Upper and Lower Styria

Styria was part of the Roman Empire (province Nordic). The production of iron originates already from that time, and from that time, then, iron and steel has determined the fate of Styria. Here the necessary resources were found: iron ore at the Erzberg, wood for charcoal, and skilled workers, who developed the know-how of iron- and steelmaking and passed it on from generation to generation. Due to the absence of other raw materials and the remoteness of the area (no access to the sea, no harbours, no navigable rivers) a highly developed branch of industry could arise - but from the very beginning it has been a monostructure.

In the middle of the last century a scientific-technical centre joined the industrial craftsmenlike structure; when in 1840, the predecessor of the present Mining University Leoben was founded. The second half of the nineteenth century, the major period of industrial growth, brought prosperity to Styria, too. Two decisive years for Austria were 1938, when it was joined to Germany, and 1945 when it regained its independent state; these events have a very strong effect on Austria's economy and industry even today. All big industrial enterprises were nationalized in 1945 as former German property. In addition to that, Austria's government in the post-war period was a coalition of the two major parties for decades, unifying conservatives and socialists in politically influencing the state-owned industry. The iron and steel industry, was pushed tremendously (Austria with 0.2% of the world's population produced 0.6% of its steel), while, wages and salaries soared to all-time highs - an irreversible process, as we all know.

A wrong socialist policy and a very strong trade-union position during the time of the absolute power of the socialist party in the government worsened the situation. The first oil price shock of 1973 was only the trigger for the crisis. Soon the specific unfavourable situation in Upper Styria became evident. Now it is characterized by its disadvantageous geographic-economic location for iron ore and coke transportation; high costs for environmental protection (Austria is looking for leadership in environmental legislation with a view to tourist traffic); high personnel costs per capita and lack of any rationalizing through staff reduction. The efficiency, in terms of tons produced per capita, is still considerably lower than in the EC - a result of the Austrian socialist philosophy: "Better debts than unemployment". Because of international competition it has been and is impossible to transfer these high costs to the consumer. So they were transferred to the economic loser, or in other words, to the tax-paying population. Figure 2 shows the "price-cost squeeze". The ratio steel price/steel costs is deteriorating continuously with losses of more than 2% yearly.

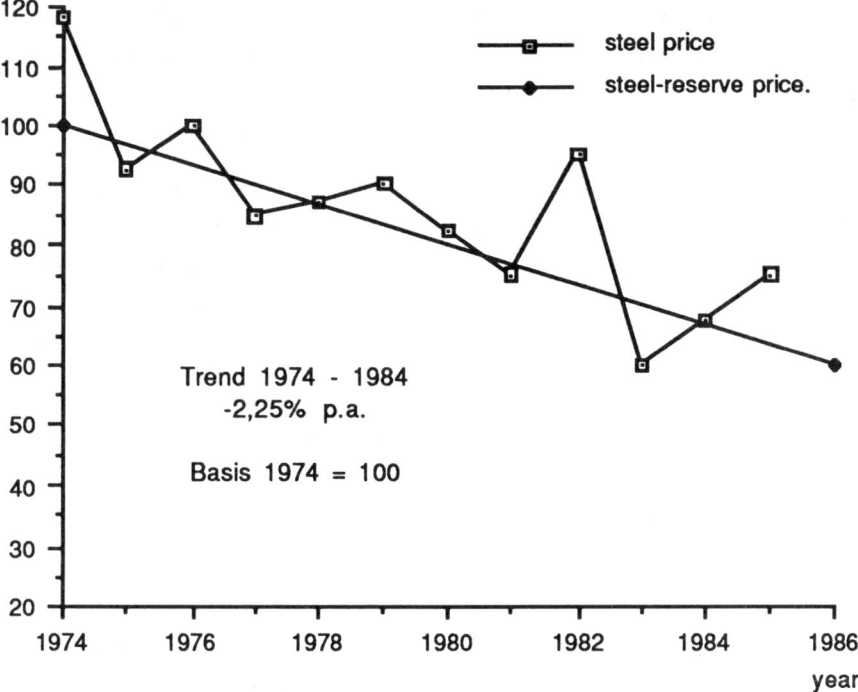

Figure 2:   Price-Cost-Squeeze (Source: McKinsey)

This is the economic situation of today. We are sitting on the ruins of a wrong government economic policy. Having given the diagnosis, we will now search for the therapy.

We have to change the behaviour and the attitudes of people. We have to get away from the immovable state-owned insurance company, called the public factory, and move to dynamic risk acceptance in small and medium-sized private enterprises (SMEs), together with geographical flexibility. To take on these risks, a financial stimulus must be given. We need social innovation to avoid and prevent a fear-oriented inhibitedness in our society. The state has to withdraw from investment and innovation subsidies. What we need is not "high-tech" at any price, but market leadership in carefully selected market segments. Official authorization procedures have to be shortened and simplified.

The employment structure has to be changed from the primary sector to the secondary and tertiary sectors, involving production-oriented services, e.g. tourism, conferences, etc.

The geographical disadvantage of Styria can partly be offset by modern communications techniques and improvement of the information structure, e.g. by data processing.

Consulting and advice to existing companies, especially for broadening their production programmes is necessary. The foundation of industry-oriented research centres must be undertaken. Styria is under-represented in research expenditures; it has 16% of the industrial jobs in Austria but spends only 12% of the R&D monies. Medium-level technical schools need to be founded, as well as technology transfer centres and technology parks in order to promote the establishment of new companies.

Structural change in Upper Styria is taking place too slowly. This again is caused mainly by politicians. Looking for re-election they drivel about "work-place guarantees" instead of animating the population to change jobs, to change location, to look for new opportunities. Perhaps it would be better to forbid totally the re-election possibility for parliamentarians after four or five years.

What is the situation in Upper Styria today and what has been achieved to date? Modernization is beginning, while the amount of production has been reduced. Specific costs need to be lowered by massive redundancies of workers and staff, by higher use of scrap and by extending the range of finished products.

What can be done outside of industry? Let me come back to the Mining University in Leoben. Earlier, and in a better way than politicians and heavy industry, this university induced a structural change that influenced the future. Besides the traditional studies in mining and metallurgy, new departments for mining, mechanical engineering and materials science and plastics engineering were established. These three new fields already account for one-half of the first-year students! This is a structural change, taking place in an area we are in a position to influence. Furthermore, for improving communication with the world outside the university, an Institute for External Relations was founded in 1986. In addition, the Ministry for Science and Research established a Leoben branch of the largest Austrian non-university research centre, the Österreiches Forschungszentrum Seibersdorf (ÖFZS). A third partner was a consulting agency for economics, established by the government, which had already existed for a long time.

With these three institutions, as equal partners, the Loeben Technology Transfer Centre was founded to contact, advise, help, and consult the industry in Upper Styria and to offer the manpower, the know-how and the facilities of the university and

ÖFZS and economic management to existing companies and to newcomers. The staff of this Technology Transfer Centre is 11 persons at present. The total costs will be in the order of 10 million Austrian Schilling per year - less than 1% of what has been and is still being pumped into the state-owned industry in Upper Styria.

The new Centre started work on 1 January, 1987. The three partners began to visit companies in the surrounding area, asking about problems and offering help in solving them. Only by these on-site visits can the well-known "threshold fear" of small and medium-sized companies in relation to universities and research centres be overcome. What the centre can do is to transfer a problem to the best-suited university institute or branch of ÖFZS, bring people together, and supervise progress. In addition, some sponsoring money is available, although real requests for problem solving have to be paid by the client.

We have been well accepted by the local industry. In the meantime we have visited more than 100 companies. In about half of all cases, at least one second contact for consulting took place and 20 co-operative contracts were carried out.

The Leoben Technology Transfer Centre is, of course, not the only institution to support structural change in Styria. There is a Technology Park in Graz and another one near Leoben is in the planning stage. Graz is also the base for the Research Centre Joanneum which also promotes industrial contacts.

Federal and regional activities and financing should be better co-ordinated, but this is difficult because the parliamentary majority in Vienna and in Styria is being held by different political parties.

Fortunately, we can conclude that our present politicians have finally recognized that something has to be done in Upper Styria. We gratefully acknowledge the establishment of the Leoben Technology Transfer Centre. We pledge to do our duty and to disburse the money, given into our hands in the best way we can. But - in view of the disastrous economic policy of the past - we urgently call upon the politically responsible with the following requests:

- Give up state majority ownership in industry
- Do not intervene with private enterprises
- Place more money at the disposal of Upper Styria for R&D, for a better infrastructure
- Take this money from state-subsidized organizations and institutions, which only hinder economic and social change

- Sponsor the individual efficient entrepreneur by better tax legislation
- Do not promote illusions (e.g. 35-hour work week!) but tell people the truth
- Let us make a profit - then jobs will come of themselves

With this in mind, we hope that we all can look forward to a better future for Upper Styria.

6.7 Technology-Based Economic Development in Northern Ireland

Thomas B. Copestake

Background

Northern Ireland is a community of about 1.5 million people, politically part of the U.K. but geographically separate. It thus has about 3% of the U.K. total population and accounts for about 2% of net output. Agriculture is a more important sector of the economy than for the rest of the U.K., employing about 10% of the total labour force, mostly on small farms specializing in dairy produce. It is, thus, significantly less rural than its southern neighbour, the Republic of Ireland (with 17% employed in agriculture) but more rural than the U.K. as a whole (with about 3% in agriculture, see Table 1).

Table 1: Workforce by sector in Nothern Ireland (000s)

Population (a)	1.58
Civil employment	542.40
Agriculture, etc.	54.50
Energy and water supply	9.00
Manufacturing	+103.30
Construction	31.20
Services (public and private)	344.30

(a) Millions, represents 2.8% of total U.K. population

Aircraft, shipbuilding, engineering and the garment and textile industries are major employers in manufacturing and the service sector has shown strong relative growth in recent years so that it now accounts for about two-thirds of total employment. But industry was badly hit by the recession of the 1970s and early

1980s and that, together with a growing population of working age, has produced the highest level of unemployment in the U.K. at around 20% of the availed labour force. (Table 2; Figs. 1 and 2).

Table 2: Economic trends in Northern Ireland (1960-1985)

Population increase:	Northern Ireland	11.2%
	Great Britain	7.5%
Declining employment	1960	1985
Textiles	58,320	11,200
Shipbuilding	24,100	5,100
Agriculture	97,700	53,380
Public sector employment		45% of total

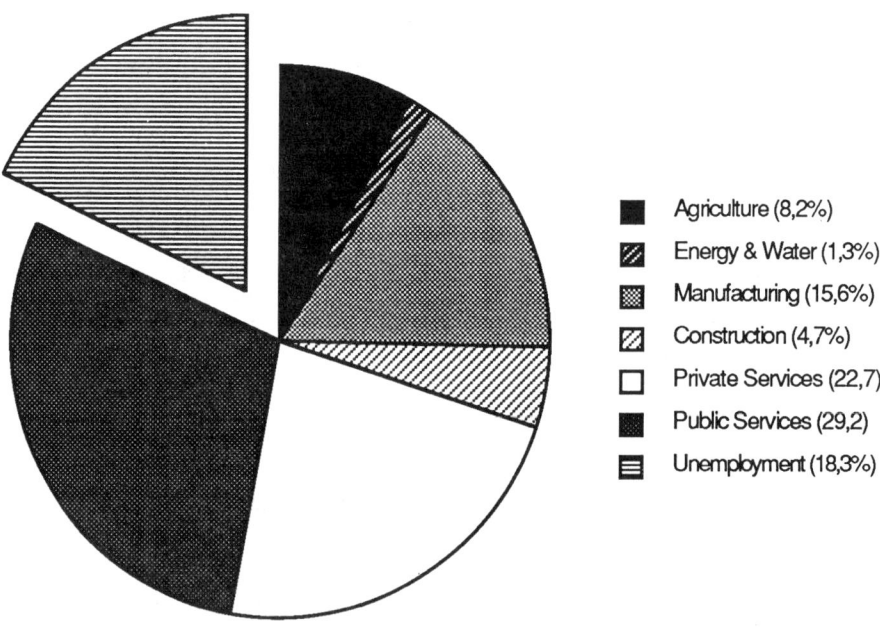

Figure 1: Northern Ireland working population (june 1985)

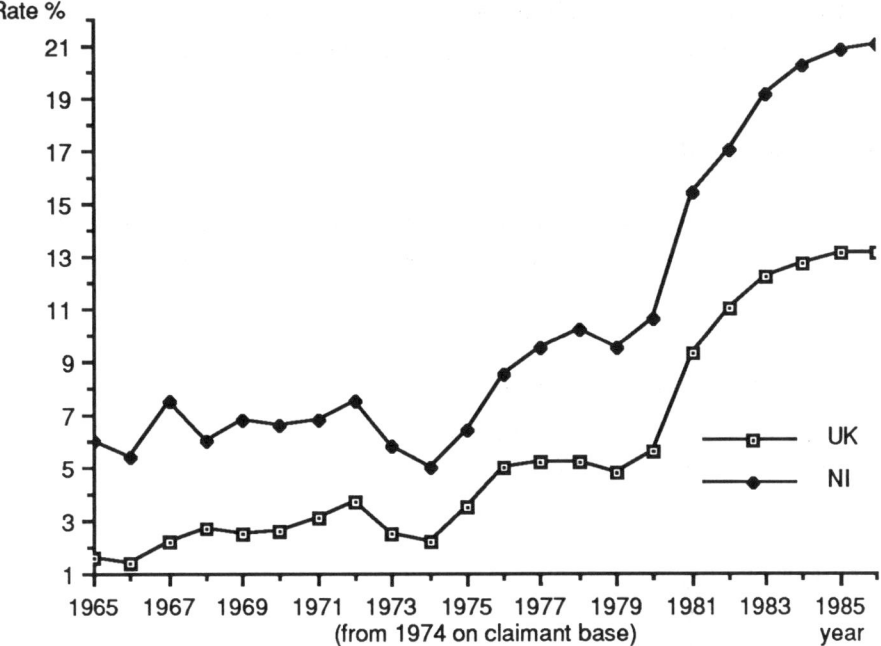

Figure 2: Unemployment rates 1965 - 1986 (as % of employees)

Northern Ireland (and the whole island of Ireland) has little in the way of natural mineral resources so that all oil and coal used for domestic and industrial purposes have to be imported. In consequence energy prices have been high even though they have enjoyed a government subsidy. Significant deposits of lignite have recently been discovered in the region around Lough Neagh and plans are being developed to mine this and burn it in a power station. Limited quantities of gold have also been discovered in the Sperrin Mountains but the economic potential is not yet certain.

These basic facts of a small domestic economy separated from its major markets, not richly endowed with natural resources and with an expanding labour force present major challenges to the authorities responsible for promoting economic growth - the Department of Economic Development and the two development agencies, the Industrial Development Board, serving the larger firms and promoting inward investment, and the Local Enterprises Development Agency encouraging new start-ups and supporting the smaller companies.

This paper deals with the efforts to harness research, development and the technological resources of the province towards economic growth.

Research and Development

The government spends about £ 14 million each year on research and development (Table 3) and industry probably spends a similar sum from its own resources.

Table 3. Recent initiatives in R&D in Northern Ireland

R&D grant schemes offering regional premium for R&D support
Advisory service to industry
Design advisory service
Quality initiatives
Teaching company scheme
Technology board
Antrim technology park
Increased support for technological infrastructure
International fund for science and technology programme

Agricultural R&D (about £ 7 million per annum; Table 4) is the largest component and the Department of Agriculture, Northern Ireland, operates 12 research laboratories providing technical support and advice to the agricultural and food sectors (Table 5).

Table 4: Research and development expenditures in Northern Ireland

Public Expenditure in Million £/year

Agriculture	7.26
Indusrtry	5.17
Other sector	1.32
	13.75

Private Expenditure

Non reliable estimate but unlikely to be more than £ 20 million/year

Table 5:   Research & Development infrastructure in Northern Ireland

Public sector (number of establishments)

Agriculture	12
Industry	1

Private sector

Lambeg Industrial Research Association	(65 staff)

Universities

Queens University Belfast
University of Ulster
(750 staff in science and engeneering)

Government support to R&D in the manufacturing sector is provided through an R&D grant scheme which encourages companies to undertake research and development, with subsequent exploitation in the Province, and this grant can meet between 40% and 50% of the cost of an R&D project. The rate is higher than on the British mainland and Northern Ireland is thus the only part of the U.K. that has a regional premium for R&D support. The scheme has been vigourously promoted recently and the number of applications for grants is rising rapidly. Grants are discretionary and projects are appraised by the staff of the government's own Industrial Science Laboratory (Table 6).

Table 6:   Research & Development grants in Northern Ireland

Maximum finance for any single project £ 250,000

Grant rate	Amount payable
50%	First £ 50,000
40%	Balance to £ 250,000

Special treatment may be given to SMEs

Corresponding measures to promote quality, design and to provide technological advice

Advisory and Technology Transfer Service

It is increasingly clear that financial incentives to promote R&D are in themselves not sufficient to stimulate economic development and a range of measures are now used to provide advice on technology, quality, design and marketing, to exploit university research more effectively for industrial and economic purposes, and to provide a good working environment with efficient transport and telecommunications infrastructures.

Northern Ireland is well provided with university research resources. The two universities have a total of 17,000 full-time equivalent students with more than 25% in science and engineering. The total number of staff in technological disciplines is about 750 so that the universities represent a major technological resource.

Both universities have promoted their links with industry. Ulster University has developed partly from a polytechnic tradition which provided a wide range of technician and graduate level courses and carried out applied, industrially relevant, research. Queens University, with its broad academic tradition has recently consolidated its services to industry by setting up an organization, Queens University Business and Industry Services (QUBIS) to forge stronger links to industry. The Department of Economic Development supports QUBIS in carrying out a series of evaluations of university research projects which might have exploitation potential. In recent years the university has established a number of small companies based on university research and these include:

- Kainos: a joint company with ICL developing electronic office filing systems
- Textflow: a company specializing in computer typesetting
- Bison: developing and marketing novel proteins

Grants are available to students for post-graduate research degrees and there are special arrangements for research which is conducted in collaboration with local industry. A mechanism which has proved to be particularly effective over the past few years in forming close links between industry and universities is the Teaching Company Scheme. Under this scheme, which operates in all parts of the U.K., good science or engineering graduates work in industry on projects chosen and managed by the individual companies, but the graduates have the support of academics from a participating university department. The name of the scheme derives from an analogy with the way in which doctors are trained by giving them practical, but carefully supervised, experience in "teaching hospitals". The Teaching Company

Associates, as the graduates are known, are normally appointed for two years although individual programmes run for three years. A group of graduates will join the programme in year 1, to be joined by a second group in year 2. At the end of year 2 the first group leaves the project, the second group completing the project in year 3. The scheme has six objectives:

1. To develop active partnership between academe and industry, principally in manufacturing
2. To raise industrial performance by effective use of academic knowledge and capacity
3. To improve manufacturing and industrial methods by effective implementation of advanced technology
4. To introduce and train able graduates for careers in industry
5. To develop and retrain existing company and academic staff
6. To give academic staff broad and direct associations with industry for research and as a background for teaching

The programmes have covered topics as diverse as the introduction of computer-aided design into a company, quality control in paint shops, the development of new textile machinery, the introduction of new technology into the food-processing industry and biotechnology. Nearly 200 such programmes are now in operation in the U.K. and the scheme is funded nationally. However, we have an arrangement that allows us to run an enhanced programme in Northern Ireland and expand faster than the national programme. We now have some 45 associate posts in the Province with the potential to expand to about 60 by the end of 1988. The scheme will thus be producing an output of about 30 associates per year in Northern Ireland, the size of a quite respectable university department. These associates should be able to make a significant input into the technological management of Northern Ireland's industry.

Funds for a Science and Technology programme in the whole of Ireland have recently been made available from an International Fund to which the U.K. and the Canadian governments contribute. In establishing the programme there has been emphasis on the role that universities can play in stimulating industrial innovation and economic development. About £ 1 million has already been allocated from a £ 6.5 million two-year programme. £ 250,000 has been allocated to the establishment of a university Chair in Information Technology at Magee College in the northwest of the Province and a further £ 100,000 to set up two industrial services at Queens University. One will provide chemical and analytical services to industry and the other will establish a materials testing centre for the construction industry. Financial aid will also be available to promote collaborative programmes between Northern Ireland and the Republic of Ireland, particularly where these will build up strong capabilities in areas of technology that can serve the industry of the whole island.

The Antrim Technology Park

To attract modern industry to locate in your area it is necessary increasingly to provide not just financial incentives but also an attractive industrial environment, good communications by road, and particularly by air, and a plentiful supply of well--qualified manpower. About two years ago work started to establish Northern Ireland's first Technology Park at Antrim. Four miles from the international airport the site is pleasantly wooded and landscaped. Thirty-five hectares of land will provide accommodation for up to 14 buildings. The site was formally opened just one year ago. Three 700-sq metre buildings are already occupied and a fourth is under construction and allocated to a tenant. A 1500-sq metre advanced factory was handed over from the builders last month. The International Fund has provided £600.000 for an additional building suitable for a software company.

When the park was conceived it was decided that the planning regime should be a liberal one with accommodation being let to any activity that was environmentally acceptable. In practice the site has proved to be particularly attractive to software companies and three of the first four firms already on the park are in that sector. A mutually supportive information technology community is therefore developing. A reception facility, exhibition space and conference room is now being fitted out.

The park has no formal links to the universities and is some 15 miles distant from each, but both are represented on a steering committee that determines the development policies of the park. Companies can establish their own appropriate liaison with universities through research contracts and by other means.

The setting up of the park has been a considerable success. It has attracted high quality industry and the companies locating there anticipate that their work-forces will grow steadily over the next year or two. The buildings have won praise for architectural merit and the whole development has been commended for the unobtrusive way in which it fits into the environment.

Conclusions

The promotion of new technology based economic development needs many inputs. It is not sufficient to provide only financial incentives for research and development. Companies require a supportive infrastructure with a good educational system providing technically and managerially qualified manpower. They need a good research base that can not only generate industrially relevant technology itself but can also draw on new technology being developed worldwide. They need mechanisms to transfer that technology into industry and they need ready access to advice and expertise on technology, quality, design and marketing. The ultimate aim of all government assistance is to strengthen the individual firms and the economy to the point where it can generate much of its own resources for further growth.

6.8 Research as an Economic Factor: Initiatives in the Region of Aachen, F.R.G.

Wolfgang Heidrich

Perspectives and Point of Departure

The Development Plan presented by the chamber of commerce for this region includes the following statement:

> The region of Aachen is faced with serious problems causing concern as regards its outlook in the labour market, the economy and development of the whole region in general. Following the latest announcement in particular of the Eschweiler Bergwerk-Verein to close down its plants in the region, immediate measures are necessary. (1)

The economic region of Aachen which embraces not only the City of Aachen but also its neighbouring towns, Düren, Euskirchen and Heinsberg, has a population of approximately one million. The region is classed as one of the so-called traditional industrial zones together with the Saarland and the Ruhr areas. The region's geographical situation has played a major role in shaping its character: the Dutch and Belgian borders to the west, its rural sectors and nearness to the major development areas of West Germany.

The 310,000 strong workforce is employed primarily in the following sectors: building and construction (27,000 approximately), mining (18,000 approximately) and mechanical engineering (11,000 approximately). Other important sectors include electrical engineering, luxury and paper goods and the glass industry each employing approximately 6,000 to 9,000 persons.

---

1) Development Scheme for the Economic Region of Aachen("Regionalprogramm Aachen") submitted by the Aachen Chamber of Commerce in June 1987.

The range of products offered by firms in the area is highly inadequate. For the area covered by the Chamber of Commerce in Aachen, industry structure is primarily composed of medium-sized firms This is due, on the one hand, to an over-concentration on "traditional products for traditional markets" such as textiles, clothing, foods, luxury goods, and paper. Meanwhile, technology-intensive industries such as mechanical and electrical engineering continue to aim at the old markets, neglecting the new.

The manufacturing industries and mining intend to considerably reduce their workforce quotas over the next few years. Company structure weaknesses and a lack of rationalisation are the major contributory factors to this loss of jobs. At present the rate of cut-backs lies above the national norm and it may be expected that the unemployment rate will also remain above average at least until the 1990s.

The economic region of Aachen is faced with the following perspectives:

- Loss of up to 30,000 jobs before the year 2000 (expert forecast 1983)

- As a direct result of the Eschweiler-Bergwerk-Verein (EBV) closures in the region:

    - Loss of an immediate additional 8,000 jobs and, indirectly, 4,000 jobs externally which are dependent on the company: the regional unemployment forecast for 1990 of between 14.5% and 15.5% has consequently been updated to well over 20%

    - Loss of wages/salaries in the region of several hundred million DM

    - Loss of EVB orders and subcontracts for other firms in the area amounting to more than 100 million DM

The Region's Scientific and Technical Potential

The situation described above is contrasted by a dense technical and scientific infrastructure which has few equals in the world. Within the Aachen region there are three important research centres, numerous universities, polytechnics and other colleges of further education, as well as the Max-Planck-Institute and several institutes belonging to the Fraunhofer Gesellschaft. Moreover, across the border in Belgium and The Netherlands further international research sites and international markets are also within reach.

The large research centres in the region, including the Rheinisch-Westfälischen Technischen Hochschule (RWTH; Technical University) in Aachen, the nuclear research station at Jülich and the Fachhochschule Aachen (College of Further Education) employ approximately 800 professors and several thousand other staff. In total, 17,000 highly qualified people work in these research centres. More than 43,000 students, most of whom read technical subjects, represent a well-educated, easily deployed workforce of enormous potential. This scientific and technical potential together with the scope of research activity are thus conducive to intensive technology transfer.

Initiatives

The research facilities available and the following two establishments provide the basis for regional economic initiatives:

- The Rheinische Gesellschaft zu Förderung innovativer Existenzgründungen und des Technologietransfers e.V. (Rhine society for the promotion of innovative business launches and technology transfer)

- The Aachener Gesellschaft für Innovation und Technologietransfer mbH (Aachen Innovation and Technology Transfer Company)

Initiatives and efforts focus on the following areas:

1. Improved information flow between research facilities and industry

2. Greater effort towards the strengthening of co-operation between research facilities and industry

3. Greater effort to encourage industry settlement in the region with emphasis on the research potential available

4. Special concentration of activity in training and further education to meet the technical and innovation requirements

Improved Communication and Information Channels

With the aim of improving the information flow to and from small and medium-sized businesses, in particular, a research handbook giving details of available research facilities and a business handbook with details of industry structures were drafted. These handbooks describe particular strong points of the individual organizations, thereby increasing the possibility of contacts and co-operation.

To further improve communication links between research and industry, discussion groups were arranged for specific industrial branches. These meetings set the scene for interested parties on both sides to discover the possibilities and problems of the respective partners. These meetings gave rise on several occasions to the establishment of important contacts. The advantage of these discussion groups was, however, set back by the fact that several competitors all sat at the same table, thus preventing any open debate. Individual requirements could not plausibly be aired without revealing the direction of future R&D activities or plans.

These efforts were complemented by various exhibitions and industrial days, such as the Jülich Industrial Conference, which aimed to provide information for industry in a limited specialized field. The Jülich Industrial Conferences for "high temperature resistant materials", "biotechnology", and "supercomputers and mainframe computers" held at the nuclear research centre at Jülich in 1987/1988 are good examples thereof and were well attended. Furthermore, regional conferences and exhibitions held by the Aachen Polytechnic and other research centres on similar topics complete the initiatives taken.

The latest project at the Jülich nuclear research centre hinges around an information concept which lays out the possibilities for industrial firms to monitor trends and latest developments in the scientific and technical fields in which they are interested, in order that they may make strategic decisions for future R&D and production projects based on up-to-date technical information. In this context the capacity of the KFA (nuclear research centre) to conduct literature studies was extended to include access to international data banks. This increased information potential was then made available to medium-sized businesses in the Aachen region. It is also planned to complement the studies carried out with expert advice from research personnel. This project was initiated in early 1988. The KFA has defined a pilot project which is due to run for the next two years, at the end of which an analysis of experiences made is to be carried out.

The Transfer Office and Agency as Active Mediators

The setting-up of Technology Transfer Offices and similar consultancies in the chamber of commerce and the trade corporation reflect a move towards increased technology transfer activity. One major objective here is improved co-operation between research and industry. Existing co-operative relationships have found written expression in a general agreement which should lead to improved utilization of research know-how by regional industry. To strengthen this co-operation, consultancy periods were organized at the chamber of commerce for which KFA staff were present to provide necessary information. This measure made it possible for personnel at the chamber of commerce to receive a detailed understanding of the functions and activities of the KFA, thereby equipping them with the knowledge necessary to advise and instruct relevant industrial firms in their particular fields on concrete possibilities for the utilization of KFA services. A similar agreement was formed between the chamber of commerce and the RWTH in Aachen.

Start-Up and Location of New Companies

To encourage the founding of new technology-based companies special sponsorship programmes were elaborated. Aims include extensive support of new founders by making the research facilities available to them and by reducing start-up risks through the granting of a stated period of leave for necessary set-up preparations. The focal point for new technology-based company set-ups is the Technology Centre in Aachen which in 1987 housed approximately 25 firms. To date, following successful launch, six companies have already moved premises.

In the growth stages of a new business, scientific and technical support and co-operation from research institutions plays a vital role in the development of the product range. For this reason it is important to strive for a high level of co-operation (experience exchange) between sampling firms and research centres.

On an international scale, activity centres around emphasizing incentives to attract foreign companies to the area. The available scientific and technical resources which offer co-operation and development possibilities represent the most important factor in the attempt. One important feature here consists in advertising to invite U.S. companies to create sister companies in the Aachen region.

Initiatives in Training and Further Education

The efforts described above to improve innovation potential are further complemented by special training and further education schemes in the research centres and the regional economic promotion organizations. Within this framework, employees at these centres are given the opportunity to familiarize themselves with the latest practical technical developments. This helps to build a basis for further development and innovation activity.

Research: a Factor in the Economy

Research centres in the Aachener region are indeed an important factor in the economy. Numerous orders granted primarily to small and medium-sized enterprises (SMEs) provide a welcome incentive for the research centres to comply with the latest scientific and technical demands and requirements of industry. This mutual relationship results in an overall improvement in the level of personnel qualification and the quality of products manufactured. From individual case studies it has already been shown that close co-operation between research centres and medium-sized businesses has led to better and newer products and the acquisition of new markets.

Conclusions and Perspectives

In the Aachen region an apparatus for regional development has evolved which flexibly combines the following precepts: information, co-operation, new business launch, attraction of industry to the area, training and further education. The two leading participants who have initiated these measures for regional development are the Aachener Gesellschaft für Innovation und Technologietransfer mbH (Aachen Innovation and Technology Transfer Company) and the Rheinische Gesellschaft zur Förderung innovativer Existenzgründungen und des Technologietransfers e.V. (Rhine society for the promotion of innovative business launches and technology transfer). The latter composes several sub-participants including the chamber of commerce in Aachen, the Rheinisch-Westfälisch Technical College in Aachen, the town and district of Aachen itself, municipal authorities and the Trade Corporation in Aachen, the nuclear research centre at Jülich, the polytechnic, credit institutes, insurance brokers and various other companies. An extensive interacting network has thus emerged in this field between research centres, regional organizations and industrial bodies. However, the diversity and duplication of activities performed by the research centres, development organisations and banks for the allocation of credits for innovative new business launches together with sponsorship regulations and conditions laid out by the regional and national governments represent such an "innovation jungle" in the bureaucracy for any potentially interested parties that it becomes a mammoth obstacle to a clear and well-defined regional structure. In my opinion, it is thus essential to better co-ordinate the "egoistical nature" of the different transfer and innovation organizations, in order to replace the fragmentary activities which exist with a solid and harmonious set of procedures. The scattered areas of jurisdiction, the extent of autonomy of individual bodies and their self-interest call for great caution to be exercised during the lengthy manoeuvres necessary to breach this problem. In the light of the difficulties facing the region of Aachen, greater coordination and harmony are vital to the success of the various initiatives.

6.9 Selected Qualification-Oriented Measures in the Saarland: Initial and Continuing Training for Small and Medium-Sized Enterprises

Bernd Bach

The Basic Situation in the Saarland

The economic situation in the Saarland is characterized by the coal and steel industry and its development in recent years: The labour market there has greatly been determined by the reductions in the number of workers in the coal and steel industry.[1] The development of new qualifications measures in this region must always be seen against the background of the high unemployment there.

Table 1: The unemployment figures for the Saarland at October 1987

Number of unemployed persons

Men	30,075
Women	20,131
Total	50,206
Unemployment rate (October 1987)	12.2 %
Unemployment rate (September 1987)	12.3 %

---

[1] According to Fritz Linneweber, President of the regional employment office of Rhineland-Palatinate/Saar in a speech given 3 November, 1987. In his opinion, about 5000 jobs have been lost in recent years due to the negative development within the iron and steel producing industry as well as in the mining industry. Positive trends in the automobile and electronics industries, however, have only led to the creation of a total of 1000 new jobs.

Future efforts must be directed especially towards new enterprises or branch establishments of existing firms. Here above all, the small and medium-sized enterprises (SMEs) are to be considered. In addition to the creation of jobs for unemployed persons or persons threatened by unemployment, initiatives have to be created which prevent the migration of qualified employees.

Particularly for college and university graduates of the Saarland there is a strong orientation towards the agglomerations in the south of the Federal Republic of Germany, with their new technologies and developments.

Objectives of Regional Development Policy

Improvement of the Basic Conditions

The change and improvement of general conditions should lead to extensions and to the setting up of industrial plants. An example for these improved general conditions is the Saarbrücker Innovations- und Technologie-Zentrum (SITZ). In the last three years several innovative enterprises have been able to establish themselves there. The job creation potential of these enterprises must be seen in the medium and long term. Newly founded enterprises cannot to be expected to hire a great number of persons in the first years after their foundation. But in the medium and long run, important labour-market effects could arise from the multitude of SMEs.

Creation of Highly Qualified Jobs

New activities also aim at stopping the human capital outflows from the Saarland to other regions of the Federal Republic. Highly qualified university graduates of the Saarland are often confronted with an inadequate supply of vacancies. Through the creation of new, additional jobs with corresponding requirements also in SMEs, the migration of human capital potential can be prevented.

Integration of Displaced Labour

The opportunities for re-employment of unemployed workers from the coal and steel industry lie in a strengthening of those economic sectors which have not been affected by the crisis of the iron and steel sector. The occupational requirements of new firms providing re-employment presuppose an up-dating of qualifications in many cases. The measures in the Saarland, therefore, aim especially at initial and continuing training in newly created occupations, which are demanded by the new economic branches of the energy and environmental technologies, as well as by the automobile and electrics industries.

Selected Qualification-Oriented Measures

The considerations about how to qualify employees and employers better for the requirements of the future mean that plans have to be drawn up with which the objective "new jobs for the region" can be achieved. I want to describe two initiatives taken by the Saarland government, which try to improve the basic conditions for the assignment of qualified workers.

The Research and Technology Programme of the Saarland

This programme aims at risk minimization in the development and introduction of technologically new products and processes. Medium-sized industrial enterprises of the Saarland and self-employed persons whose businesses have a turnover of up to 200 million DM can obtain subsidies of up to 350,000 DM for the development and introduction of new products and processes. The programme is designed, above all, for the transfer of know-how and thus for the commitment of qualified staff.

Sales Promotion

The trade fairs of the Saarland offer young enterprises with innovative products and processes their first important contacts with the markets. Participation in these fairs is assisted both financially and organizationally.

In the following I would like to describe three measures representative of the improvement of qualifications of employers and employees.

a) Zukunftsqualifizierungsprogramm Saar (Qualifications programme for the future of the Saarland region)
   This programme is financed by the Saarland Ministry of Economics, and aims at qualifying people for work in the Saarland. Measures are promoted which qualify people for the requirements of the future. Target groups are employed young persons and adults, self-employed persons in SMEs, as well as unemployed persons. The programme especially promotes those projects which contribute to the imparting of occupational knowledge and skills in new techniques.

b) Measures for Qualifying Employers

In the Saarland several institutions offer programmes of initial and continuing training for employers. In this context I would like to give you an illustration of two special initiatives of the Institut zur Förderung von Existenzgründungen an der Fachhochschule des Saarlandes (INEX, Institute for the Promotion of the Setting Up of New Business Enterprises at Saarland College). INEX offers young entrepreneurs and people interested in setting up new enterprises a three-day basic seminar for setting up new enterprises and qualifications programmes for setting up and managing enterprises, with 260 hours in all. The qualifications programme imparts basic knowledge in business economics for the setting up and know-how for the managing of enterprises. The qualifications programme is carried out in collaboration with the Zentrale für Produktivität und Technologie (ZPT, Centre for Productivity and Technology). In addition to this, the ZPT offers several seminars and courses, especially in EDP.

c) Qualifications Measures for Vocational Training

Besides the possibilities for entrepreneurs and managers to take part in seminars of the ZPT and the INEX there are new initiatives for vocational training. The Gesellschaft für Innovation und Unternehmensförderung (GIU, Company for Innovation and Promotion of Firms), which runs the SITZ, is responsible for the Ausbildungszentrum Burbach (AZB, Burbach Training Centre). In the AZB young people are trained in co-operation with private firms as information electronics experts and mathematical-technical assistants. This training is oriented to the new requirements of information technologies within the firms.

Contributors

Jürgen Allesch	Technologie-Vermittlungs-Agentur Berlin e.V. (TVA), Berlin
Dr. Eberhard Auchter	Ostbayerisches Technologie Transfer Institut (OTTI), Regensburg
Bernd Bach	INEX - Institut zur Förderung von Existenzgründungen an der Fachhochschule des Saarlandes, Saarbrücken
Pim Berculo	Chamber of Commerce and Industry, Utrecht, Netherlands
Dr. Stefano Boffo	FORMEZ Centro di Formazione e Studi per il Mezzogiorno, Roma
Umberto Bozzo	Tecnopolis Novus Ortus, Valenzano (Bari), Italy
Dagmar Brodde	Technologie-Vermittlungs-Agentur Berlin e.V. (TVA), Berlin
Dr. Gerhard Burian	Department of General Economic Policy Affairs in the Federal Ministry of Economic Affairs, Wien
Dr. Thomas Barry Copestake	Department of Economic Development, Belfast
Alun Daniel	Welsh Development Agency Treforest Industrial Estate, Pontybridd, Mid Glamorgan
Giovanni de Felice	SPI - Promozione e Sviluppo Industriale S.p.A., Roma

Prof. Jean-Paul de Gaudemar	Université d'Aix-Marseille, Les Milles, OECD Working Group on Regional Policies, Paris
Véronique Debisshop	Délégation à l'Aménagement du Territoire et à l'Action Regional (DATAR), Paris
Dirk Jan Dekker	European Business and Innovation Centre Network asbl (EBN), Bruxelles
Martine Delpierre	U.F.R. Sciences Economiques et Sociales - Université des Sciences et Techniques de Lille, Villeneuve, France
Willem E. During	University of Twente, Centre for Innovation and Entrepreneurship, Enschede, Netherlands
Prof. Dr. Hans-Jürgen Ewers	Technische Universität Berlin, Institut für Volkswirtschaftslehre, Berlin
Claudio Fornari	SPI - Promozione e Sviluppo Industriale, Roma
Dr. Francesco Gagliardi	Centro di Formazione e Studi per il Mezzogiorno, Roma
Dr. Hans-Dieter Ganter	Forschungsinstitut für Arbeit und Bildung, Gemeinnützige GmbH, FAB, Heidelberg
Dr. Alexander Gerybadze	Arthur D. Little International, Wiesbaden
Andrew Gould	Segal, Quince & Wicksteed, Economic and Management Consultants, Cambridge, U.K.
Claudine Guidat de Queiroz	Institut National Polytechnique de Lorraine, Nancy
Prof. Dr. Holger Haldenwang	Fachhochschule Regensburg
Dr. Wolfgang Heidrich	Kernforschungsanlage Jülich GmbH, FRG

Contributors

Dr. Hans Heuer	Deutsches Institut für Urbanistik (difu), Berlin
Theodor Krendelsberger	ECO PLUS Betriebsansiedelungs-Rationalisierungsgesellschaft des Landes Niederösterreich, Wien
Sénateur Pierre Laffitte	Sophia Antipolis Foundation, Valbonne, France
David Lightbody	Scottish Developement Agency (SDA), Glasgow
Christian Mahieu	3 I E, Innovation, Intervention, Institution, Entreprise, Villeneuve d' Ascq, France
Marilia Rosa Millan	Ministry of Science and Technology FINEP / MCT - Financing Studies and Project Agency, Rio de Janeiro
Dr. Michael Morath	Transferstelle Hochschule - Praxis, Universität Duisburg
Renzo Mosagna	Camere di Commercio Piemontesi, Centro Scambi Tecnologie, Torino
T. Joseph Mulcahy	Commission of the European Communities, Directorate-General XVI (Regional Policy), Bruxelles
Harry Nicholls	Birmingham Technology Ltd., Aston Science Park, Birmingham, U.K.
Dr. Nino Novacco	IASM - Istituto per l'Assistenza allo Sviluppo del Mezzogiorno, Roma
Dr.-Ing. Klaus-Dieter Otto	ExperTeam, Gründungs-, Beteiligungs- und Innovationsberatungs GmbH, Dortmund

Prof. Dr. Peter Paschen	Außeninstitut der Montanuniversität Leoben, Austria
Dr. Antonio Pedinelli	European Association for the Transfer of Technologies, Innovation and Industrial Information (TII), Luxembourg
Marie Pierret	European Centre for the Development of Vocational Training CEDEFOP, Berlin
Dr. Richard Plitzka	ECO PLUS Betriebsansiedelungs-Rationalisierungsgesellschaft des Landes Niederösterreich, Wien
Albert Strub	Commission of the European Communities, Directorate General XIII, Luxembourg
Pierre Yves Tesse	Association pour le développement économique de la Région Lyonnaise, Aderly Technopolis, Lyon
Norbert Tüschen	Gesellschaft für Mathematik und Datenverarbeitung mbH GMD, St. Augustin, FRG
Dirk van Barneveld	Transferpoint, University of Twente, Enschede, Netherlands
Dr. Wolfgang Watter	Staatsekretär beim Senator für Wirtschaft und Arbeit, Berlin
Karl-Heinz Wodtke	Arbeitskreis deutscher Technologiezentren, Technologiepark Syke GmbH, FRG

Dieter Frick (Editor)
The Quality of Urban Life
Social, Psychological and Physical Conditions

1986. 17 x 24 cm. X, 262 pages. With 35 illustrations. Cloth. ISBN 3 11 010577 2

Hans-Jürgen Ewers/John B. Goddard/Horst Matzerath (Editors)
The Future of the Metropolis
Berlin – London – Paris – New York
Economic Aspects

1986. 17 x 24 cm. XII, 484 pages. Cloth. ISBN 3 11 010498 9

J. Friedrichs/A. C. Goodman et al.
The Changing Downtown
A Comparative Study of Baltimore and Hamburg

1987. 17 x 24 cm. X, 256 pages. Cloth. ISBN 3 11 011113 6

Jürgen Friedrichs (Editor)
Affordable Housing and the Homeless

1988. 17 x 24 cm. IV, 191 pages. With 15 figures. Cloth. ISBN 3 11 011611 1

Richard P. Schaedel/Jorge E. Hardoy/Nora Scott-Kinzer
(Editors)
Urbanization in the Americas from its Beginnings to the Present

1978. XII, 676 pages. Cloth. ISBN 90 279 7530 2 (World Anthropology)
Mouton de Gruyter

Poul Ove Pedersen
Urban-regional Development in South America
The Process of Diffusion and Integration

1974. XVI, 294 pages. With figures, maps and tables, summary in Danish. Cloth. ISBN 90 279 7753 4

Walter de Gruyter · Berlin · New York

Rolf Wolff (Editor)
Organizing Industrial Development
1986. 15.5 x 23 cm. XI, 391 pages. Cloth. ISBN 3 11 010669 8
(de Gruyter Studies in Organization, Vol. 7)

Peter A. Clark
Anglo-American Innovation
1987. 15.5 x 23 cm. X, 404 pages. Cloth. ISBN 3 11 010572 1
(de Gruyter Studies in Organization, Vol. 9)

John Child/Paul Bate (Editors)
Organization of Innovation
East-West-Perspectives
1987. 15.5 x 23 cm. X, 238 pages. Cloth. ISBN 3 11 010700 7
(de Gruyter Studies in Organization, Vol. 11)

Kuniyoshi Urabe/John Child/Tadao Kagono (Editors)
Innovation and Management
International Comparisons
1988. 15.5 x 23 cm. XX, 372 pages. Cloth. ISBN 3 11 011007 5
(de Gruyter Studies in Organization, Vol. 13)

Urs E. Gattiker/Laurie G. Larwood (Editors)
Managing Technological Development: Strategic and Human Resources Issues
1988. 15.5 x 23 cm. VIII, 232 pages. Cloth. ISBN 3 11 011084 9
(Technological Innovation and Human Resources, Vol. 1)

Günter Dlugos/Wolfgang Dorow/Klaus Weiermair (Editors)
Management Under Differing Labour Market and Employment Systems
1988. 17 x 24 cm. XXVI, 488 pages. Cloth. ISBN 3 11 010947 6

Walter de Gruyter · Berlin · New York

MAR 3 0 1990